THE NGV STORY

A celebration of 150 years

ngv
National Gallery of Victoria

The publication of *The NGV Story* has been generously supported by The Vizard Foundation.

*

THE NGV STORY

A celebration of 150 years

Phip Murray

*

*

CONTENTS

*

*

FOREWORD

In 1967 I came to live in Melbourne from Tasmania, and my family lived close to the NGV's St Kilda Road site. After school I would wander up and watch the Roy Grounds building being constructed. Like everyone, I shared a sense of anticipation for the big moment when the building would open. I remember that it was enormously exciting. After the launch I got into the habit of dropping in nearly every day after school. I would often see Eric Westbrook, the director at the time, in the gallery spaces and I used to think to myself, 'he has the best job in the world'. It was very definitely a privilege, then, to have the opportunity to become Director in 1999. I think many Victorians share this fondness for the NGV. They have adopted it as their own, and this is symbolised perhaps by the rituals observed within the building – many visitors feeling that their visit is not complete unless they have laid flat on their backs gazing up at the Leonard French ceiling in the Great Hall, or run their hands through the water wall as they arrive – and by the high rate of local attendance that the NGV enjoys. 'The people's collection' is visited by its local population at far greater levels than at most other museums worldwide.

The National Gallery of Victoria has a rich and complex history. My colleagues and I thought that an interesting way to celebrate the NGV's 150th birthday would be to commission a publication that explores 'The NGV Story', a project that would enable us to share with a wide readership some of the great moments from the history of the NGV. *The NGV Story* is not intended as a comprehensive history; rather, it aims to survey some of the highs – and a few of the lows – of the past 150 years. It is also intended as a good read: the text is broken into a series of short stories around particular historical moments and includes many anecdotes and observations by directors, trustees, curators, artists and visitors. In this book you will find discussion of notable occasions, such as the founding of the NGV in 1861; the acquisition

(p. IV)
Bruce Armstrong
Guardians 1987 (detail)
Blakely's Red Gum
(Eucalyptus blakelyi)
171.0 x 307.5 x 137.4 cm (overall)
(parts f–j)
Presented by the Bardas Family as the winner of the Bardas Family Sculpture Commission, 1987

of William Blake's watercolours in 1918; the story behind buying Tiepolo's *The Banquet of Cleopatra* from the Russian government in 1933; the theft (and rapid return) of the Picasso in 1986; and the building of Australia's first dedicated museum of Australian art, which opened in 2002. Some of these stories are very familiar, but the book also gives an opportunity to discover some of the behind-the-scenes stories, less known by the general public. The book also collects together much archival material, which adds a fascinating sense of historical texture.

The author, Phip Murray, is an independent writer and she brings a fresh voice and different insights to *The NGV Story.* We have greatly enjoyed working with her. While researching she consulted and interviewed many people who have been closely involved with our Gallery. Not all are quoted within these pages, but their insights contributed to building a multifaceted portrait of our Gallery, and we thank them wholeheartedly for their contributions. Frances Lindsay, our Deputy Director, also deserves special thanks as one who has worked closely on the development of the manuscript, and thanks are due also to Jasmin Chua, Publications Manager; Eugenie Baulch, Publications Editor; Megan Patty, Publications Coordinator; Dirk Hiscock, Designer; and the Graphic Design and Photography departments for their careful work on the project.

The NGV has adapted over the past 150 years in response to changing ideas about the role of art and the function of a public art gallery like ours. *The NGV Story* offers a fascinating overview of these transformations, which also reflect how society has changed in Melbourne. My colleagues and I hope you enjoy *The NGV Story* and the special insights it will give you into life at the NGV.

Gerard Vaughan
Director

*

(opposite)
Interior,
The Ian Potter Centre:
NGV Australia

THE DESIRE FOR A GALLERY

(pp. 2-3)
Bertram Mackennal
Circe 1893 (detail)
bronze
240.0 x 79.5 x 934 cm
Felton Bequest, 1910

(above)
Nicholas Chevalier
Public Library, Melbourne 1860
watercolour
59.4 x 119.3 cm
Architectural drawings collection,
State Library of Victoria
Gift of Mr McEwan, 1965

ART AND THE NEW COLONY. Archibald Michie, the Library and Gallery Trustee, recollected that Melbourne in 1852 was 'a very inferior English town'.[1] Just a few years on, in 1860, it had transformed as he wrote, into, 'a great city, as comfortable, as elegant, as luxurious as any place'. By the mid nineteenth century grand projects were being realised by ambitious and energetic Melbournians: the University of Melbourne was founded in 1853; the first Town Hall and the Melbourne Terminus (later to become Flinders Street Station) were both opened in 1854; the first football match was held in 1858; the original Trades Hall and Spencer Street train station both opened in 1859; city streets were lit up with gas in 1857; inter-city telegraph services were established in 1858; and Melbourne's population hit around 125,000 in 1860, the same year that Burke and Wills set off from Royal Park on their ill-fated expedition. The year 1861 was a big one for both sport and art (those eternal rivals): the first Melbourne Cup was run and Australia's first 'Museum of Art' was founded.

Chevalier's watercolour of the Public Library, also home to the Museum of Art, embodies this sense of ambition. The front section of the Library had been completed by the time it was painted in 1860, but the full complex as drawn here was never achieved. Chevalier's image is an idealised one, which embodies the determination felt by the new settlers to build great cultural institutions worthy of a great city. The Public Library appears grandly, dwarfing the people around it with its imposing size - even the clouds overhead seem to assemble with lofty purpose.

Remarkably, by 1870 four of the six Australian colonies had created institutions similar to Melbourne's Public Library. This desire to build public institutions was part of a distinctly nineteenth-century ethos, which had developed out of Enlightenment ideas around progress, education and self-improvement. While in the past the museums of Europe had been the domain of the aristocratic and the wealthy, by the nineteenth century the focus had shifted. As art historian Ann Galbally writes: 'From being an expression of the personal tastes and interests of the educated and the dilettante, [the museum] was re-formed into a central focus of nineteenth-century urban idealism. No longer was it held acceptable that knowledge was the exclusive prerogative of the wealthy and ruling classes'.[2] This 'public spirit' led to the development of a series of civic institutions across Europe as well as in the young colonies of Australia. At the launch of the Victorian Institute for the Advancement of Science in 1854, Sir Redmond Barry stated: 'Men are no longer content that the search for knowledge should be delegated to the exclusive charge of any particular body'.[3]

Many colonists also believed that the fine arts played a crucial role in a civilised society: they cultivated morality, developed 'good' taste and instilled noble aspirations. Many of them saw art, as art historian Bernard Smith wrote, 'through the stained-glass windows of religion, morality and history'.[4] They were eager to invoke the power of the arts in a young colony. They were optimistic and ambitious and they cared deeply about the town of Melbourne: Melbourne's prospects were their prospects, after all.

SIR REDMOND BARRY AND THE PUBLIC LIBRARY.

A great city could not be complete unless it possessed noble and useful institutions such as a university, museum, art gallery and library. Back in the 1850s, when the Colony of Victoria had only just been established, plans had been set in motion to create a government-funded university and a public library, out of which the National Gallery of Victoria and the Melbourne Museum were to grow. On 2 July 1853, the Board of Trustees of the new Public Library of Victoria was announced.

The entrepreneurial spirit that had motivated each of the Trustees to leave their homelands to seek adventure and advancement elsewhere was harnessed for the development of new institutions for the colony. They were presided over by the spirited Irishman His Honour (later Sir) Justice Redmond Barry. He was a driving force behind the establishment of the Public Library, as well as a host of other institutions. Barry had trained as a lawyer but found limited prospects in his homeland of Ireland and so, like many other adventurous spirits, he threw in his lot with the new Colony of Victoria.

Thomas Foster Chuck
Sir Redmond Barry in Chancellor's robes 1878
albumen silver photograph
17.0 x 11.0 cm
State Library of Victoria, Melbourne

Barry loved books. He was also a great advocate for public education. From 1840, the year after his arrival in Victoria, he opened the library in his house – a little room off his kitchen – to any member of the public who wished to peruse his collection of (what he considered) the best books and journals. His contemporary Alexander Sutherland recounted how Barry liked to 'go out and meet the readers, who recognised his unaffected kindness even if they sometimes had to listen to a ponderous, though improvised, lecture on some subject that they did not yearn to master'.[5]

The colonial architect Sir Joseph Reed designed the Public Library. It was to be a grand complex, loosely modelled on the British Museum. The Colony of Victoria, buoyed by income from gold and imagining itself as a cosmopolitan city, sought to develop cultural institutions like those in Europe, especially London. In 1854, Reed's plans were accepted. At noon on 3 July 1854, the foundation stone was laid for the University of Melbourne and by 3 p.m., having travelled a little further down the road, the group laid the foundation stone for the Public Library. Barry's speech on the day displays the Trustees' sense of achievement: 'Seventeen years had scarcely elapsed since the foundation of the colony ... Probably in the world's history no country had attempted to found both a University and a Public Library within a score of years of its first settlement'.[6] In 1856, the Public Library first opened its doors. It held 3846 volumes, the most treasured of which was Gould's *Birds of Australia*, bought for £140. The Library was forever dear to Barry: he visited it every day to write his letters and was dedicated to its development.

THE GOLD RUSH: 'WHOREMONGERS, FLASH JACKS AND THREE-PEA MEN'. The Colony of Victoria was still in its infancy when Chevalier painted his image in 1860. It had been a mere ten years since the ship *Lysander* had brought with her the news that the Queen had assented to the separation of the Port Phillip District from New South Wales, sparking four days of enthusiastic celebration among Melbourne's 29,000 residents. The following year, on 1 July 1851, the Port Phillip District had officially become the Colony of Victoria. Around the same time, Victoria's fortunes were irrevocably changed when rich gold deposits were discovered at sites throughout the colony.

The gold rush transformed Melbourne from a little frontier community into a thriving, cosmopolitan metropolis. In 1840, when the town was five years old, the population was around 10,000 people. However, after the discovery of gold in 1851, hundreds of thousands of people flowed into Victoria to try their luck on the goldfields. 'People are swarming to the diggings like folks go to a fair', wrote the artist Thomas Woolner.[7] By 1861, the population of Victoria had climbed to more than half a million people. In a very short space of time, Victoria had metamorphosed from a stable and settled pastoral community into a large, fluid population that, under the spell of gold fever, had journeyed there from Europe, America, Asia and Africa in hope of a quick fortune. The huge and sudden influx of people caused strife for Governor La Trobe's beleaguered administration. Robert Hughes later wrote of this time in the colony: 'Adventurers, cranks, foreigners, whoremongers, Flash Jacks and three-pea men crashed through it', creating intense social upheaval.[8] Many gold-diggers bore no real allegiance to the new colony – they had come with plans to get rich, and then get out. The artist Frederick McCubbin also later observed that many were chiefly concerned with 'material success, everybody wanting to get back to the old land with long purses'.[9]

Nevertheless, the riches of the gold rush bankrolled the development of Victoria, and the Museum of Art was also the beneficiary of this flush of riches pulled from the ground. Henry Burn's scenic picture of Swanston Street gives charming insight into Melbourne in 1861, the year the Gallery was founded. Here is a city on the rise.

*

'In Melbourne, the NGV is a source of inspiration. It refreshes and educates me, and I return to my work with new enthusiasm. It allows me to marvel at the struggles and solutions of other artists'

– Geoffrey Bartlett, artist

Henry Burn
Swanston Street from the Bridge 1861
oil on canvas
71.8 x 92.2 cm
Gift of John H. Connell, 1914

The hotel on the corner will later become Young & Jackson's; St Paul's Church will be transformed into St Paul's Cathedral; tombstones on the site of the Coroner's office are spaced across the area that we now know as Federation Square that, at the time, also backed onto the Registry of Births, Deaths and Marriages, from where the bride and groom in the carriage have presumably just come; and the wide expanse of Swanston Street bustles with a burgeoning population of Melbournians – and their little dogs.

THE FIRST COLLECTION: 'OBJECTS OF MISCELLANEOUS VERTUE'. In May 1859, the government had responded to calls for the establishment of a public art collection by allocating £2000 for the purchase of works of art. How this was to be spent was a matter of great discussion among the Library Trustees. Somewhat surprisingly, the Trustees decided that no original works of art should be bought. Rather, they specified that casts, photographs, medals, coins, gems and other 'objects of miscellaneous vertue' were to be acquired, and they carefully allocated a portion of the £2000 to each category.[10]

Their reluctance to invest in original works of painting and sculpture can perhaps be attributed to a sense of anxiety that Melbournians may be uninterested in 'the Fine Arts'. There had been earlier exhibitions of painting in the colony and these had not generated much enthusiasm in audiences. The Trustees, as Barry put it, 'are sensitively alive to the danger of a failure, and are apprehensive lest the first impression produced upon our visitors may be apathy or dissatisfaction'.[11] A collection of other objects, then, seemed a better bet to the Trustees. Former Gallery Director Eric Westbrook (1956–73) wrote that Barry was also 'probably motivated by a desire to plant a sound classical taste in a raw young civilisation'.[12] A letter was dispatched to Hugh Childers, a former Library trustee who had returned to England, requesting him to make the acquisitions. Thus, the first collection was initiated.

THE MUSEUM OF ART. The first acquisitions arrived by the end of 1860, although very damaged by seawater. Barry wrote in exasperation, 'Our museum looks at present like a field of battle, such is the mutilation'.[13] The Melbourne sculptor, Charles Summers, was brought in to repair the works. Despite this setback, Victoria's first Museum of Art opened to the public on 24 May 1861, Queen Victoria's birthday. Australia's first museum of art was founded.

The Museum of Art was situated in a room in the south wing of the ground floor. Visitors could peruse casts of the Elgin Marbles; seventy casts of famous antique statues; sixty-three busts; medals, coins, seals and other gems; photographs of architectural monuments; and replicas of other fine and applied arts. The exhibition was a great success, with 62,000 visitors attending the Museum in its first two months. The wood engraving (overleaf) from 1863 gives a sense of visitors' experiences at the first art gallery: dressed in their Sunday best, they wander among replicas of classical antiquity and two formidable bronze lions that Barry had purchased in London in 1862.

The experience of mounting the exhibition had made it clear that the Museum of Art must be housed more appropriately: in its current form it was only 'a rudimentary Museum of Art', as Barry described it.[14] The Governor of Victoria, Sir Henry Barkly, agreed. He thought it churlish to constrain the Museum: 'To cramp such a noble Institution by withholding the few thousands necessary for its completion, whilst tens of thousands are appropriated to less important or less worthy objects, must, I am confident, strike all who have the welfare of the people at heart as poor economy'.[15]

The first collection was an exercise in importing culture from Europe, and its aims were didactic. As Governor Barkly observed, it was designed to develop 'the foundation of a correct taste'.[16] It is astonishing to think that a replica of the Parthenon frieze made its way 12,000 miles – and in a leaky boat – to the young city of Melbourne. A copy of the apotheosis of classical Greek art, made about 447–438 BC and acquired by the British Museum in London in 1816, was proudly displayed in a gallery in a western city founded

VESTIBULE OF THE PUBLIC LIBRARY, MELBOURNE.—(See Page 6.)

(above)
Charles Nettleton
Sculpture Gallery, National Gallery of Victoria c.1872
albumen silver
12.0 x 17.0 cm (each)
The Pictures Collection,
State Library of Victoria

(below)
Ebenezer and David Syme, Melbourne
Vestibule of The Public Library, Melbourne. 21 October 1863
print, wood engraving
The Pictures Collection,
State Library of Victoria

only sixteen years before. Reviewing the NGV's new sculpture gallery in 1865, James Smith wrote in the *Argus* that it was 'enough that we can contemplate the creations of Phideas as fresh and real as if actually chiselled in the marble by his own hand. We may indeed be well satisfied with the beginning we have made of such excellent and beautiful casts'.[17]

'THE PROMOTION OF THE FINE ARTS IN OUR SAID COLONY.' In 1863, matters were formalised when the Commission on the Fine Arts was appointed with the objective to: 'Inquire into the subject of the promotion of the Fine Arts in this our said Colony, and to propound and submit unto us a scheme for the formation, conduct and management of a Public Museum or Museums, Gallery or Galleries, and Schools of Art for our said Colony.'[18] Eleven commissioners were appointed to think about the subject of Fine Arts in our said Colony. Three came from the legislature and three from the public service and government. They were joined by William Parkinson Wilson, Professor of Mathematics at the University of Melbourne; Augustus Tulk, Chief Librarian at the Public Library; James Smith, journalist and Editor of *Melbourne Punch*; and Charles Summers, sculptor. The redoubtable Barry continued to preside over matters as chairman.

One of the commissioners' first projects was to decide how to spend the £1000 pledged by the Government of Victoria for works of art. Much vigorous discussion ensued that gives wonderful insights into the commissioners' ideas of the role of art. There was great debate, for instance, about the merits of buying copies of Old Masters versus original works of art. Professor Wilson put forward that the sum was best spent on original works of art by contemporary artists whose work would ultimately 'rise in eminence' ('even though', he quipped, they currently 'labour under the disadvantage of being alive'). 'Who ever heard of a celebrated collection of copies?' he asked.[19] William Wilkinson Wardell put forward a different view, believing that the new colony was best served by obtaining '*good* copies of the best pictures' in European collections, his argument supported by quotations from Royal Academicians. He thought copies were indispensable, maintaining that it was 'essential ... to have the example present' and that 'in England there is hardly a collection, including that of the Sovereign, without them'.[20] James Smith put a vote in for the local artists, urging that £200 be earmarked for buying the work of an Australian artist. A compromise was reached: original works of art would form the bulk of the collection but some copies would also be acquired. Smith's proposal was also accepted.

SIR CHARLES EASTLAKE: 'EXAMPLES IN VARIOUS CLASSES OF ART'. Sir Charles Eastlake was identified as an appropriate authority in England. Eastlake was not only a distinguished artist but also the Director of the National Gallery in London and President of the Royal Academy. Barry wrote to him emphasising that he sought a collection by which 'the mind of this community should be instructed, its taste directed, and upon which its judgement should be advised'. He spoke of 'the standard of excellence assumed by the Trustees', and was adamant that there must be 'a resolute exclusion ... [of] the false, or that merely showy and superficial' in art.[21]

Eastlake's job would have been difficult: the Trustees' expectations were high but Eastlake's budget was low. The £2000 allotted him would scarcely cover one good work of art, but the Trustees expected several to be shipped back. In 1864, he wrote of this dilemma to Barry: 'In consequence of the increasing prosperity of the country, the demand for good works of Art is now so great, and the prices paid are so enormous, that I am by no means sanguine'.[22]

*

The Trustees' taste for art was undeniably conservative

Nevertheless, Eastlake fulfilled his role, steadfastly aiming, as he said, to acquire 'good works of Art' and to provide 'examples in various classes of Art' that would 'assist the practice of young artists in Australia, as well as to form the taste of the public'.[23] Eastlake's choices included Robert Herdman's atmospheric *A fern gatherer – West Highlands*, 1864, and John Bedford's English rose *La Belle Yseult*, 1863, described to readers of *The Australasian* in 1865 as 'a fair lady of noble lineage, with luxuriant wavy hair of the golden colour which painters admire'. John Frederick Herring's elegant *Horses and pigs,* c.1864, was appreciated ('the horses look so plump and sleek that you feel inclined to pat them' continued *The Australasian*'s writer), as was the historical set piece *Bunyan in prison*, 1864, by G. F. Folingsby, who will soon figure large in this narrative as director of the NGV.[24] Other trustees also recommended works as the occasion arose: Augustus Tulk, for instance, was enamoured with William Beechey's winsome *Portrait of a lady*, created in the early nineteenth century, and recommended it for the Gallery in 1865.

The Trustees' taste for art was undeniably conservative. Leonard Cox, an early historian of the Gallery, summarised it nicely: 'Taste was for genre, the historical or religious motif, the fine moral act, the newly discovered landscape; for detail, and a high technical achievement'.[25] While works by Turner and Constable could have been relatively inexpensively acquired, the Trustees and Eastlake looked instead to the establishment, preferring classic works by contemporary Royal Academicians and their European counterparts. Eastlake prescribed a conservative approach for the new colony and its new artists. 'Original minds', he said, 'may be left free to follow their impulses, but in works intended as examples, the method of execution should, I conceive, be sound and efficient, and the style unaffected'.[26]

THE NATIONAL PICTURE GALLERY: 'GREAT SATISFACTION EXPRESSED'. On Christmas Eve 1864, an exhibition opened in the newly completed picture gallery in the north wing of the Public Library. The thirteen

(above)
William Beechey
Portrait of a lady
early 19th century
oil on canvas
125.7 x 95.3 cm
Purchased by the Commissioners of Fine Arts for Victoria, 1865

(opposite)
Ebenezer and David Syme, Melbourne
The National Picture Gallery at the Public Library, Melbourne 25 January 1865
print, wood engraving
The Pictures Collection, State Library of Victoria

THE NATIONAL PICTURE GALLERY AT THE PUBLIC LIBRARY, MELBOURNE.—See Page 7.

pictures purchased in London were presented, as well as forty-three Australian paintings. The exhibition was a great success. On the opening day, 'nearly 500 people inspected the paintings', wrote Barry. 'A goodly number considering that it was a mail day and wet.' He continued, in a letter to Augustus Tulk of January 1865: 'During the last month we have had a large number of visitors to see the Paintings; great satisfaction expressed on all hands at the excellent judgement displayed by Sir Charles Eastlake'. And a few weeks later to Tulk: 'Our five weeks' exhibition of paintings was a complete success, more than 26,000 people visiting the Gallery, and tho' the crowd was great particularly during the first week, and we were so very short handed in the very height of our catalogue work, everything went off harmoniously; not a stick, umbrella or parasol was lost; not a rudeness or unpleasant occurrence took place; and "*mirabile dictu*" there was not a single complaint in the newspapers'.[27]

The exhibition also presented an opportunity to spend the £200 earmarked, as per James Smith's proposal, for the purchase of work by an Australian artist. The works submitted to the competition were mostly unfavourably reviewed in *The Age*; many works were, the writer opined, 'below mediocrity, and a few might justly be banished to a chamber of horrors'.[28] The judging panel was also disparaging of the overall selection

*

Chevalier's painting had the honour of being the first Australian work of art purchased for the collection

Nicholas Chevalier
The Buffalo Ranges 1864
oil on canvas
132.4 x 183.7 cm
Purchased, 1864

but settled on Nicholas Chevalier's *The Buffalo Ranges*, 1864. Barry wrote: 'The Fine Arts Commission selected a landscape by Chevalier, a bold mountain scene on the edge of Gipp's Land, in the Buffalo Ranges. It was the best of a very poor lot indeed, and in itself capable of much improvement which he has undertaken to make. Von Guérard did not compete'.[29] Chevalier's painting had the honour of being the first Australian work of art purchased for the collection, although the first Australian work to enter the collection was Henry Short's *Fish, fruit and flowers*, 1860, which was presented by the artist in 1861.

The first Australian works acquired by the Gallery evidence the Trustees' taste for artists working in the landscape tradition. Soon after Chevalier's work was acquired in 1864, the Gallery also acquired works by Eugene von Guérard. In 1866, the barrister and writer Sir Archibald Michie presented von Guérard's *Spring in the Valley of the Mitta Mitta with the Bogong Ranges*, 1866, and in 1870

the Trustees acquired his *Mount Kosciusko, seen from the Victorian border (Mount Hope Ranges)*, 1866. The great esteem with which the Trustees held von Guérard is evidenced by their decision in 1870 to appoint him Painting Master at the Gallery School and, in an honorary capacity, the Curator of Pictures, Works of Art, Prints and Photographs at the Gallery. The Trustees were also supportive of von Guérard's colleague Louis Buvelot. They purchased Buvelot's *Winter morning near Heidelberg*, 1866, and *Summer afternoon, Templestowe*, 1866, in 1869 and *Waterpool near Coleraine (sunset)*, 1869, in 1870. Buvelot was also the first artist to be honoured with a retrospective exhibition, which was held in 1888, after the artist's death.

'ADVANCING THE GROWTH OF FINE ARTS IN THIS DISTANT QUARTER OF THE WORLD.' When the Gallery's advisor, Sir Charles Eastlake, died in 1865, Barry wrote to London-based Alfred T. Thomson to invite him to take on the role. Thomson had made a fortune as a squatter in Victoria and had returned to Europe to settle there in relative comfort. Barry's letter to him remarked upon Thomson's 'familiarity with Art' and his 'Extensive acquaintance with artists'. The Gallery no doubt thought him well placed to acquire art – to 'put the matter to these Gentlemen', as Barry wrote – but also to understand the unique needs and culture of the new Colony of Victoria.[30] Thomson took up the role, and remained in it for twenty-eight years.

His first task was very specifically outlined in a letter Barry wrote to him in 1866. The Commission on the Fine Arts, Barry stated, had a budget of £1500, from which they intended to invite five members of the Royal Academy to each paint a picture for a fee of £300 each. That the Commission understood that this was a small fee for such work is evidenced by the fact that Barry enclosed nine separately addressed letters. He evidently assumed a high number of rejections. Not entirely persuasively, Barry wrote: 'The sum fixed is small in comparison with that usually offered ... It is probable that if the gentlemen addressed will undertake to work they will do so ... with the worthy purpose of advancing the growth of Fine Arts in this distant quarter of the World, furnishing means of elevating public taste [and] encouraging feelings of social refinement. To men of liberal views it may be agreeable that their names should be associated with the early endeavours to form a Picture Gallery in Victoria'.[31]

Thomson diligently delivered each letter in person. He did not enjoy great success: of the nine letters distributed, only three artists accepted the commission, one of whom would only agree to make a copy for the allotted sum. The response by artist Frederic Leighton Esq. to Barry's sentiment that he might lower his fee to advance 'the growth of Fine Arts in this distant quarter of the World' is somewhat amusing. Writing to Barry, Thomson reported: 'I then called upon Leighton, who had laid the papers aside under the impression that they were circulars from the South Kenzington Museum. He could not paint anything whatsoever for a public gallery on the terms offered; he certainly was inclined to make a sacrifice to promote the growth of fine arts in any portion of Her Majesty's dominions, but when he considered the energy and wealth of the Australian colonies, he could not perceive why the sacrifice should be always on one side. I replied that, although vigorous and energetic, the population of Victoria was a small one, and that in such a young community a taste for the fine arts must be fostered and encouraged by care and economy until a love and appreciation of them was so generally diffused as to justify its Legislature in voting large sums of public money for such a purpose'.[32] The NGV still has no work by Leighton, although he remains high on the desiderata list.

THE COLLECTING POLICY: SOWING 'THE MORAL HARVEST OF THE FUTURE'. In the development of an art collection for the Colony of Victoria, the Gallery Trustees and their advisors looked to Europe. Fine art, they firmly believed, was generated from Europe's academies, and it was their job to import it. There was little support for local artists. The Trustees were also much influenced by Victorian morality. Art was often, as a writer in 1848 described, 'subservient to the cause of virtue'. Its role was to 'propagate noble thoughts and sow the moral harvest of the future'.[33] *Anguish*, c.1878, by Danish artist August Friedrich Albrecht Schenck, is representative of their tastes, a style of painting memorably summed up by the twenitieth-century critic Robert Hughes as 'dominated by the thick voice of evangelism' and 'soggy with moral uplift'.[34]

Taste changes over time and works of art are continually reappraised, of course. Lindsay Bernard Hall, who became director in 1892, for instance, lamented what he thought were funds lost: 'It is catering to popularity, & making a kind of scrapbook of the Gallery, that such pictures as *La Derniere Étape de Coco* come to be bought … not the stuff worthy of a collection made by the State. [It is] a mass of purely commercial work – untrue to itself, & untrue to its period – that confuses the public'.[35] Later, in the early 1940s, newly appointed Director Daryl Lindsay, who regarded most Victorian work as lacking in good taste and of low artistic value, de-accessioned many works of art bought by the NGV in the mid to late nineteenth century. Today, however, as current Director Gerard Vaughan states, 'we regard much of that de-accessioning as a significant loss and a cause for real regret'.[36]

THE 'NATIONAL' GALLERY OF ART. The second half of the 1860s saw the Gallery Trustees host two ambitious exhibitions. The *Intercolonial Exhibition of Australasia*, an antipodean version of the world's fairs popular in Europe and America during the nineteenth century, opened in October 1866 in the new Great Hall designed by Joseph Reed and annexed to the Public Library. The exhibition featured a 'Fine Arts Gallery' in the south wing, as well as a dazzling array of other colonial products classed in subject areas such as 'Manufactures and the Useful Arts' and 'Machinery and Implements'. In 1869, the Trustees held the extravagant loan exhibition, the *Exhibition of Works of Art:*

(previous above)
August Friedrich
Albrecht Schenck
Anguish (*Angoisse*) c.1878
oil on canvas
151.0 x 251.2 cm
Purchased, 1880

(previous below)
Pierre-Marie Beyle
The last resting place of Coco
(La Deniere Étape de Coco) 1878
oil on canvas
93.0 x 117.5 cm
Purchased, 1881

Charles Nettleton (and other)
Views of the Exhibition of Works of Art, Ornamental and Decorative Art July 1869
State Library of Victoria, Melbourne

Ornamental and Decorative Art. The exhibition brought together over 2000 items loaned by more than 1400 private lenders or, as Barry commented at the opening, 'a large number of pictures of undoubted worth, and of objects rare and curious'.[37] It became a major event, with around 70,000 paying visitors, and ended with a 'Grand Closing Concert in aid of a fund to endow a Scholarship for the best pupil of the year in the School of Design'. The Trustees generated sufficient profit to set aside £450 for a travelling scholarship for an artist, and to give £50 to the adjacent Melbourne Hospital (despite later complaining that their paintings were 'suffering perceptible injury' because of the smoke generated by the hospital).[38]

At the end of 1869, the 'Museum of Art' was renamed by an Act of Parliament the 'National Gallery of Victoria', thus initiating an historical quirk that has continued both to bemuse and amuse people. The use of 'National' was a direct homage to the National Gallery in London, which the Trustees deeply desired to emulate, and it was also historically appropriate: until Federation in 1901, Victoria was a self-governing colony. The other major state galleries all once carried the word 'national' in their titles but one by one dropped the word in the decades after Federation. Only Victoria, buoyed by a confidence that its collection was preeminent in Australia, declined to drop the 'national' from its name, a custom that is occasionally challenged and never more so than at the time of the opening of the National Gallery of Australia in Canberra.

THE SCHOOL OF ART: 'DEPLORABLE DAUBS'. In 1870, the National Gallery School opened its doors with the objective of initiating an Australian tradition of fine art. Eugene von Guérard was appointed Painting Master at the Gallery School and, in an honorary capacity, the first curator of the NGV. Thomas Clark was appointed Master of the School of Design, which students entered to learn drawing before they progressed to painting. The school was modelled on European academies, reflecting von Guérard's and Clark's own experiences. In those early days, the students were largely left to their own devices. Von Guérard let them loose in the art gallery with an instruction to copy the paintings. The idea of 'the copy' was crucial to classical training – by dutifully copying older masters students could be inducted into the canonical styles deemed appropriate for serious art.

There was fondness for von Guérard – in a letter to the Trustees the students stated that, 'as far as we are capable of judging', von Guérard was 'a thoroughly efficient Teacher, & a most kind and considerate Master'.[39] However, his lack of attention drew criticism. Von Guérard replied indignantly that he was already working far beyond his meagre salary and devoting much time for free 'purely out of love for the advancement of art in others'.[40] Clark was apparently more attentive, but as Frederick McCubbin stated, the elderly painter was 'partly paralysed, he could only speak in the faintest whisper and he was that feeble he could hardly hold a crayon – so we youngsters did what we pretty well pleased'.[41] Trustee and *Argus* art critic James Smith was derisive of the teaching at the Gallery School. He wrote in 1883: 'Numerous more or less clever, more or less indifferent, copies of certain favourite works were produced from year to year, but this sort of Chinese industry did nothing whatever to promote the artistic education of those who devoted themselves to it. What they did was purely mechanical … the deplorable daubs which have been exhibited from time to time on the walls of the Victorian Academy of Arts were melancholy illustrations of the evils of a system which was diametrically opposed to all the ordinarily conceived canons of instruction'.[42]

THE RISE OF THE ROYAL FAMILY – AND THE BUNYIP. The year 1875 was an important one for the NGV: the first substantial custom-built exhibition hall, later named the McArthur Gallery, opened to great fanfare and the Trustees published their first catalogue, an album of photographs of works in the collection accompanied by lively commentaries from the Deputy Librarian Marcus Clarke. Clarke was a colourful man of letters, well known for writing the ripping yarn about convict experience *For the Term of His Natural Life*. The following text was written for Nicholas Chevalier's *The Buffalo Ranges.* Perhaps surprisingly, this art criticism commissioned by the NGV resulted in a fantastic treatise on the bunyip: 'The natives aver that when night comes, from out of the

bottomless depth of one of the huge lagoons the Bunyip rises, and in form like a monstrous sea-calf, drags his loathsome length from out the ooze. From some corner of the silent forest arises a dismal chant, and around a fire, dance natives, painted like skeletons. All is fear inspiring and gloomy'.[43]

In 1876, the pastoralist and philanthropist Sir William Clarke of Rupertswood commissioned Charles Summers to create marble statues of Queen Victoria, Prince Albert and the Prince and Princess of Wales, which were presented to the NGV in 1878. The Trustees thanked Clarke for his act of 'well-directed liberality', which would 'inspire and sustain in the hearts of the people of Victoria the highest feelings of loyalty to the Crown'.[44] They were proudly displayed at the entrance to the building, symbolic of a culture that was determined to maintain its connection to the British Empire. As Gerard Vaughan, Director of the NGV, states: 'It was formidable. When you came into the NGV they were the first things you saw, you walked *through* the royal family. There could be no doubt about the Anglo-colonial establishment's patriotic position'.[45]

Sculpture presented to the National Gallery by the Hon. W.J. Clarke 1879
Illustration in the *Illustrated Australian News* 21 February 1879
wood, engraving
The Pictures Collection, State Library of Victoria

Times have, of course, changed and with them so has the – literal and symbolic – position of the royal family. 'In the 1870s', says Terence Lane, former Senior Curator of Australian Art, 'they were a prized acquisition, but they ended up on a kind of slippery slide and were eventually de-accessioned'. Many of the prized acquisitions of colonial Victoria suffered a similar fall from grace. 'Hundreds of works were gotten rid of in the 1940s and '50s,' says Lane. 'Some of the casts were given to institutions like RMIT or to private citizens, others were bulldozed. It's a pretty terrible story – those casts and antique statues would be wonderful to have now.'[46]

THE NGV GETS NUDE. Over time a group of Gallery School students began to protest about the style of tuition and lack of studio facilities. The situation worsened when Thomas Clark retired in 1876 and Oswald Rose Campbell became Master of the School of Design. 'Well, under the new regime', lamented McCubbin, 'began the most dreary and hopeless period of our student days ... Not an idea, not a hint that could help us in any way'.[47] The students banded together to support each other to explore more innovative art practices. They painted together en plein air, visited the University of Melbourne to study anatomy and took turns modelling for one another: 'Tom Roberts was the model one day, but the act of gazing at a blank wall for an hour so overcame his feelings that he fainted'.[48]

Things came to a head over the life-drawing class imbroglio. Social mores of the time prohibited the use of a life model, yet some students – and their Painting Master, von Guérard – believed that life drawing was essential to developing an understanding of the figure. Campbell did not share this outlook and stated definitively to the Trustees: 'life study unnecessary to figure drawing'.[49] In 1878, a group of students led by Roberts, McCubbin and Charles Richardson provocatively started their own life-drawing class. Fellow student Alexander Colquhoun recalled, 'They drew from the nude in a somewhat furtive and conscious fashion, for the public mind had not then been educated up to the point of nice discrimination in such matters'.[50] Campbell was most displeased and threatened them with dismissal. The blacklisted students appealed to the Trustees and, no doubt to Campbell's extreme vexation, the rebel students were victorious: a life-drawing class was initiated.

*

'Tom Roberts was the model one day, but the act of gazing at a blank wall for an hour so overcame his feelings that he fainted'

A strong student culture emerged at the Gallery School. Reminiscing about his days there, McCubbin said: 'There used to be a sort of legend about that time that Australia would do great things in Art. Where it sprang from or how goodness only knows'.[51] This strong culture was to pay dividends within a few years.

THE NGV GETS A BIT TOO NUDE. The boom decade of the 1880s started with a magnificent display of art and technology. The Melbourne International Exhibition of 1880–81, attended by more than a million people, featured exhibits from thirty-three countries. The British represented themselves with carriages, carpets, chemicals and paper-hangings; the Americans with lawnmowers, electric lights and barbed wire. Victoria exhibited locomotives from Ballarat and a huge sculpture symbolising the amount of gold mined in Victoria since 1851. The exhibition was housed in the new and very grand Royal Exhibition Building, designed by Joseph Reed. Its tall dome was reminiscent of Florence's *duomo* and it was the highest structure in Melbourne, symbolic of the great aspirations of a city enjoying astonishing wealth and prosperity.

This flourishing city was a vastly different place from that which Sir Redmond Barry had encountered on his arrival in 1839. In late 1880, Barry passed away, an event that could be said to mark the end of the first era of the National Gallery. The Trustees noted his extensive contribution over twenty-seven years, and their minutes acknowledge his 'zeal, urbanity, and distinguished ability', his 'public spirit' and his 'ardent sympathy with the cause of public education, and refined enjoyment'.[52] Barry contributed very meaningfully to the public life of Victoria. His contemporary, the writer Garryowen, said of him: 'He was the most remarkable personage in the annals of Port Phillip, for he threw in his lot with the destiny of the Province when it was a weak, struggling settlement in 1839, and identified himself with every stage of its wonderful progress until he left it a bright and brilliant colony in 1880'.[53]

The International Exhibition also featured a display of international art. The Trustees had asked their London advisor to hold off buying in order to save their money for it; however, a government funding delay meant that they missed out on purchasing the sure-fire hit, Jules Lefebvre's representation of the nude ingénue, *Chloe*, 1875. Her new owner, Melbourne surgeon Thomas Fitzgerald, generously offered to lend her to the NGV, an offer taken up despite the reservations of the more conservative trustees. *Chloe* caused mischief at the NGV, and she was at least partly to blame for the Gallery being charged with frank indecency and for desecrating the Sabbath. The NGV had been experimenting with opening on a Sunday, aiming to enable men who worked a six-day week to attend. Sir Redmond Barry had previously lobbied for Sunday opening in 1878. It was an idea put forward again by Professor Strong, the Chair of Classics at the University of Melbourne, but not one unanimously supported by the Trustees. The Sunday opening had proven to be quite successful; by 1883 it also became something of a lark for gallery goers to go

CHLOE—A QUESTION OF PROPRIETY.

*

***Chloe* caused mischief at the NGV, and she was at least partly to blame for the Gallery being charged with frank indecency and for desecrating the Sabbath**

and peruse the unclothed *Chloe* on the Sabbath. A furore ensued. The *Argus* had to inaugurate an ongoing column called '"Chloe" at the Picture Gallery' to deal with the large volume of correspondence. Fitzgerald, perturbed at the upset caused by his painting, withdrew *Chloe* from the NGV. She was hung in his house in Collins Street, where she still managed to cause offence - apparently upsetting people on the street who could see in his window - until he moved her to a more discrete back room.

With *Chloe* gone, the Trustees bravely decided to continue opening on a Sunday and let parliament make a decision about it when it next sat. Their decision was supported by an enthusiastic lobby group banded together under the marvellous title 'The Sunday Liberation Society', and condemned by an equally enthusiastic lobby group equally marvellously titled 'The Sunday Observance League'. Parliament sat a few weeks later, and parliament was not impressed. The Legislative Assembly roundly

David Syme and Co Melbourne
'Chloe - a question of propriety'
print wood engraving and article
The Illustrated Australasian News
13 June 1883
State Library of Victoria,
Melbourne

Jules Lefebvre
The grasshopper (La Cigale) 1872
oil on canvas
186.7 x 123.8 cm
Felton Bequest, 2005

condemned the Trustees by an incontrovertible thirty-seven votes to twelve. Sunday opening was to cease *immediately*. Furthermore, parliament reprimanded the Trustees for getting above their station; the assembly decreed that the Trustees' actions 'in declining to postpone the opening til Parliament met, was regarded as a slight upon the Government and an infringement of the rights of Parliament'.[54] For twenty years the NGV was forbidden to open its doors on a Sunday. *Chloe* now resides at Young & Jackson's pub, and the NGV, having conceded that *Chloe* could never be acquired, purchased its own work by Lefebvre in 2005, *The grasshopper* of 1872. 'Chloe's little sister' – as some curators have nicknamed her – has not caused as much of an upset.

THE SCHOOL OF ART: 'NO ROYAL PALACE EVER CONTAINED A BIGGER PERCENTAGE OF HOPE, FEAR, PRIDE, ENVY AND AMBITION'. Despite the progress made with the establishment of a life-drawing class, the Gallery School students were still on the verge of mutiny. A letter handed to the Trustees and to the *Argus* in 1880 set out their ongoing complaints: 'The fact is that out of the numerous pupils who for years have benefited by the classes in the galleries – none have distinguished themselves as original painters or professional artists, although many have become very proficient as copyists. We believe that this arises from neither indifference nor lack of ability on the part of the pupils, but that it is caused ... by the want of earnest and careful teaching of the higher practice of painting'.[55]

When von Guérard retired in 1881, George Frederick Folingsby took on the role and restructured the school. His 1882 report to the Trustees detailed an entirely different approach from that of his predecessor: 'Copying pictures in the Gallery,' he said, 'unless in exceptional cases, has ceased, the practice being in no way beneficial to art students, and one that can only have a pernicious and lowering effect on the public taste'. Folingsby also supported life drawing, writing to the Trustees that he would 'attend personally the posing of each new model, as nothing can be done in painting or sculpture without good drawing'.[56] The students seemed to admire him greatly. Alexander Colquhoun wrote that 'the coming of Folingsby had a magical effect on the students ... the number of students at this time was small, and the accommodation limited, yet surely no royal palace ever contained a bigger percentage of hope, fear, pride, envy and ambition'. Folingsby evidently had gravitas, as this lovely passage, again from Colquhoun, suggests: 'No sooner was "The Boss" uttered, than Longstaff and Gibbs ceased their wrestling; Fox quietly dropped his cigarette in someone's else's siccatif; and McCubbin, who had been warbling *My Pretty Jane*, began setting his palette'.[57]

While most students readily adopted Folingsby's disciplined approach to painting, some were less inclined to be as faithful to his techniques. Folingsby taught a classical European painting technique that gave an effect described later by art historian Bernard Smith as similar to holding an 'old, dark mirror up to nature'.[58] Many of his students, however, preferred a higher-keyed palette, which they thought better suited to bright Australian light. Furthermore, while Folingsby supported sketching from nature, he was contemptuous of the desire of some of the students to paint outdoors. 'The man who paints landscape in open air is a fool', he stated.[59]

Throughout the 1880s, many talented young artists aspired to be such 'fools'. When Tom Roberts returned from a study trip overseas, he brought with him many innovative ideas about outdoor painting. Roberts exerted a formidable influence and, before long, some students drifted away from Folingsby and took their canvases outdoors to accompany Roberts on his outdoor painting expeditions. As Arthur Streeton wrote: 'The impressions brought out by Roberts had the fresh air, true-tone-in-values idea, which was in conflict with the academic training at the art school under Folingsby. I was painting a head after the manner of Roberts when F. told me not to paint like that, but to put in the subject first with bitumen and vermillion. I didn't argue with him, but left the school and worked again with Roberts'.[60]

*

'Copying pictures in the Gallery, unless in exceptional cases, has ceased, the practice being in no way beneficial to art students'

MARVELLOUS MELBOURNE. Between 1885 and 1890, Melbourne was a boomtown, building upon the great prosperity brought by the gold rush. Money was dug up, but money also poured into the property boom from investors from the old and new worlds. The city was absolutely transformed: little wooden houses were cleared to make space for grand buildings. In 1885, the visiting English journalist George Sala gave the city its enduring nickname 'Marvellous Melbourne'. The NGV was also the beneficiary of this good fortune: Verdon Hall was completed in 1883 and the Buvelot Gallery in 1887.

The year 1888 was the occasion for great celebrations marking the centenary of Australia. Patriotism among the white settler community ran at fever pitch. To mark the milestone a grand – and very imperially focused – exhibition was held at the Exhibition Building. Two million people attended the various exhibits, which included a Fine Art Court displaying in excess of an astonishing 3000 paintings from which the NGV acquired a handsome group of works. 'The International Exhibition of 1888 was a significant moment', states Director Gerard Vaughan, 'because the Trustees went shopping with government funding. We spent quite a few thousand pounds buying a group of major and quite expensive contemporary British pictures. Until then, we were only spending hundreds a year, not thousands'.[61] The NGV also acquired its first work by J. M. W. Turner when *Dunstanborough Castle, north-east coast of Northumberland, sunrise after a squally night*, 1798, was presented by the Duke of Westminster. The Governor of Victoria, Sir Henry Loch, was a close friend of the Duke and encouraged him to be generous to the colony.

***THE 9 BY 5 IMPRESSION EXHIBITION:* 'A PAIN TO THE EYE'.** *The 9 by 5 Impression Exhibition* held at Buxton's Rooms in Swanston Street was intended as a direct provocation to the art establishment in Melbourne, especially the NGV. Tired of being overlooked by the Gallery, a group of artists including Roberts, Streeton, McCubbin and Charles Conder organised their own independent exhibition. Nothing was conventional about *The 9 by 5 Impression Exhibition*, and deliberately so. The exhibition comprised swiftly executed oil sketches painted on cigar box lids that, through their 9 by 5 inch scale, gave the exhibition its name. These 'impressions' were provocatively unfinished compared with the precisely executed style of painting customary at the time. The exhibition completely failed to impress James Smith. He thought them completely unfit for public presentation and thundered in the *Argus* of August 1889: 'Of the 180 exhibits catalogued on the present occasion, something like four-fifths are a pain to the eye. Some of them look like faded pictures seen through several mediums of thick gauze; others suggest that a paint-pot has been accidentally upset over a panel nine inches by five; others resemble the first essays of a small boy, who has just been apprenticed to a house-painter'.[62] The artists were relatively untroubled by Smith's diatribe. The brouhaha only raised the profile of the exhibition; Streeton wrote that 'the people thronged ... to view the dreadful paintings'.[63]

Nevertheless, artistically there was much at stake. Terence Lane, curator of the *Australian Impressionism* exhibition, 2007, described how 'Tom Roberts and his mates were trying to gain for plein air painting the acceptability it already had in Europe. There were wild aspects to *The 9 by 5 Impression Exhibition*, but it did have a very serious intent. The artists were setting out

(opposite)
J. M. W. Turner
Dunstanborough Castle, north-east coast of Northumberland, sunrise after a squally night 1798
oil on canvas
92.2 x 123.2 cm
Gift by The Duke of Westminster in 1889

(below)
Tom Roberts
By the Treasury 1889
oil on wood panel
23.6 x 14.2 cm
Purchased through the NGV Foundation by The Hugh D. T. Williamson Foundation, Founder Benefactor, 2002

La Trobe Gallery,
National Gallery of Victoria c.1893
gelatin silver photograph
16.5 x 21.7 cm
The Pictures Collection,
State Library of Victoria

to educate the public, to bring the Australian public up to date with what was happening overseas. Melbourne was a great cosmopolitan city - it was one of the great cities of the world - but it was isolated and it depended greatly upon entrepreneurs and activists like Roberts to bring in cultural ideas. At the time, however, the NGV was not prepared to cut through all the hype and get to the message of it. Today, the *9 by 5s* are among the most sought-after Australian pictures'.[64]

THE 1890S: BOOM AND BUST. In the 1890s, the economic bubble burst, ushering in a decade of severe economic depression. Construction ground to a halt, and retrenchments rose dramatically. The colony went from an age of glittering plenty to a time of grinding poverty. When the money dried up, the unfinished construction projects at the Public Library were stopped; the remaining £35,000 promised by the government for capital works was simply no longer available. Although two new custom-built exhibition spaces - the Stawell Gallery and the La Trobe Gallery - were built in 1893, it was largely a time of fiscal austerity.

HUBERT HERKOMER: AN ETCHER OF NOTE. The NGV experienced a changing of the guard when the London-based advisor Alfred T. Thomson retired in 1890, and a few months later, at the start of 1891, the Master of the Art School, George Folingsby, passed away. The Trustees noted in their report: 'The death of Mr Folingsby ... caused the Trustees deep regret. His administration was very successful and marked a new departure in the progress alike of the National Gallery and of the Art Classes. He first took the students away from copying the pictures in the Gallery to original work, and laid the foundation of what may become a school of art of which the subjects are purely Australian'.[65] These two key positions at the NGV needed to be filled.

The Trustees were much influenced by the advice of Louis Alexander Fagan, an employee of the British Museum who travelled in Australia around the years

1890–91. With regard to the selection of an advisor in London, Fagan was direct: 'Trust to one individual to make your purchases, and dismiss him if he does not suit. Do no business with an art dealer. I have no faith in them ... He will sell you what he cannot get rid of at home. I have been struck by the fine pictures I have seen in every city of America I visited; you can follow the same course'.[66]

Hubert Herkomer, a German-born artist and respected etcher who had settled in London, was invited to take on the role of advisor. The year 1891 proved to be an important one for the Prints and Drawings collection, as Cathy Leahy, Senior Curator of Prints and Drawings, explains: 'The Gallery had been buying works on paper since 1861, but the first really significant acquisition was in 1891, when there was a famous sale in London of Sir Francis Seymour Haden's collection. He was an artist and a surgeon and also a great collector of Rembrandt. Herkomer selected sixty-four works, which included eleven Rembrandt etchings, Dürer's three great engravings and a selection of Van Dyck works – three great masters in the history of the graphic arts. He also bought some nineteenth-century Charles Meryon etchings and works by Max Klinger, James McNeill Whistler and Seymour Haden. Those acquisitions still stand as benchmarks, establishing the principle that we would collect at the top end, we would collect Old Masters right through to contemporary and we would collect really supreme quality'.[67]

Rembrandt Harmensz van Rijn
The three trees 1643
etching with drypoint and burin
21.3 x 28.0 cm (plate)
21.6 x 28.4 m (sheet)
Purchased, 1891

The Trustees enlisted Fagan to assist them in finding suitable candidates for Folingsby's role. Back in London, Fagan sent word in late 1891 that, of the suitable applicants, his recommendation was Lindsay Bernard Hall, a thirty-three-year-old artist who had trained in London, Antwerp and Munich. The Trustees did not unanimously agree with the idea but ultimately there was enough support for Hall, and he was soon aboard a ship making the long journey from England to Australia.

LINDSAY BERNARD HALL: 'UPRIGHT IN CARRIAGE'. On 21 March 1892, Hall contacted the Chief Librarian, Dr T. F. Bride, to let him know that he had arrived in Melbourne. He requested that a studio be made available to him – one that was available at all hours and in which he could smoke. Smoking was apparently fine, but the Trustees would not allow access to the building outside normal opening hours. Once settled in, Hall began a tenure that was to last forty-three years.

Hall was a very conscientious man who ushered in an age of increased professionalism at the Gallery and its school. He prepared detailed reports, made strong recommendations to the Trustees, and put much energy into formulating policies. Many accounts describe him as a reserved man, though one of strong opinions who was not retiring when buoyed by the courage of his convictions. He was clearly respected by his peers, even if they seemed to find him an aloof figure. The artist Arnold Shaw described him as 'upright in carriage, straight-laced, eagle-eyed, with hair cut *en brosse*' (that is, trimmed so short that it stood up like brush bristles), who 'literally terrified nervous students'.[68] Bernard Smith described him as 'an earnest, meticulous and methodical man, respected rather than loved by his pupils'.[69]

THE GALLERY SCHOOL: 'WE UPHOLD THE IDEA OF *SCHOLARSHIP*'. Drawing was central to Hall's art practice and his teaching; he believed 'drawing to be the basis of all sound Art Education'. His curriculum for art students was not innovative; it was a sturdy, traditional system aimed at developing solid technical skills. 'There is nothing new in the system,' he wrote to the Trustees in a report in November 1892, it 'is based in the first instance on *drawing*, with good *outline*, *anatomy*, and therefore *form*'. The NGV holds many lovely pencil sketches by Hall. Studies of legs, sandals, chairs, tables, portraits, monograms, angels, nudes, tiles; all are carefully drafted in his methodical way. He hoped to instil a similarly measured approach in his students: 'We uphold the idea of *scholarship*, or thoroughness, rather than *brilliance*, & look for *performance*, as opposed to *promise*. The school needs, & to their credit I may say desires, a strong hand to impose this discipline'. Hall does not seem to have had to use his 'strong hand' in too dictatorial a manner. He found the pupils studious and seemed well pleased after his first few months. 'I am well content with the progress made, all things considered', he said, '& congratulate myself, as well as the students, on the *enthusiasm* & *industry* they have given proof of'.[70]

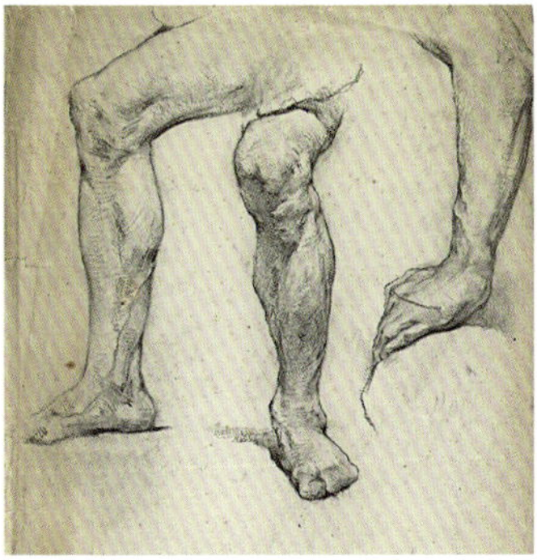

(opposite)
Bernard Hall
Sleep c.1906
oil on canvas
64.0 x 141.1 cm
Felton Bequest, 1919

(clockwise from top left)
Pegg Clarke
Portrait of Bernard Hall, the Director of the National Gallery in Melbourne 1915–1935
black and white sepia print
20.0 x 15.0 cm
University of Melbourne Archives
Courtesy of the University of Melbourne

Bernard Hall
Studies of limbs c.1880
charcoal
29.6 x 30.4cm irreg. (image)
Gift of Mrs Beardsley, 1984

Bernard Hall
Sketch of sandals for sleep c.1905
pencil
9.2 x 7.6cm irreg. (image)
Gift of Mrs Beardsley, 1984

Bernard Hall
Bust of a man 1889
pencil
17.2 x 11.2cm irreg. (image)
Gift of Mrs Beardsley, 1984

THE COLLECTION: 'BAD WORKMANSHIP IS THE ONLY IMMORALITY'. Hall brought a similarly studious approach to the development of the collection. His recommendations moved away from popular, anecdotal paintings towards a more sophisticated, art-historical approach. This change in acquisition style was immediately evident; within two weeks of arriving Hall recommended a group of works, including Henri Fantin-Latour's *Marigolds*, 1891, that, although still relatively conservative recommendations, heralded a definite change in direction.

Within a few years, Hall had meticulously reviewed each work in the collection. He was not pleased: he thought the collection a jumble of works of art, many of which were popularist and unsuitable for a public collection. He believed that the NGV lacked 'a scientific method' underpinning its collections policy. In a report sent to the Trustees, Hall put forward his misgivings – and plainly: 'The trait of the Amateur & the irresponsible artist is plainly visible through our collection, & it is a serious thing ... I can assure you, Sir, I am not making lamentations idly. The decrement incurred by such a system is enormous. I am sensible that in calling your attention to it I must wound many long-cherished prejudices, but I must speak frankly, if at all ... although £60,000 has been expended upon pictures & statuary, we as yet have hardly commenced to collect in the proper sense of the word'.[71]

Henri Fantin-Latour
Marigolds (Oeillets d'inde) 1891
oil on canvas on wood panel
51.4 x 38.8 cm
Purchased, 1892

Hall's complaints about the 'amateur' and the 'irresponsible artist' were essentially complaints against acquisitions that were predicated on the taste of an individual. In his definition, 'irresponsible' did not mean reckless but rather that the purchaser acted independently and was not attached to an institution or a committee. This type of advisor may have meant well – he may have been, as Hall said, 'a gentleman zealous & punctilious in the discharge of his responsibilities' – but he nevertheless lacked a professional art-historical overview. 'It is the *amateur* & the *irresponsible artist* that I am afraid of', Hall said. He continued to be forthright in his opinions: the Monticelli, he griped, 'looks for all the world like a bit of old carpet' and the drawings by Swan were 'depressing and ugly'.[72] The advisors were mostly dismissed as 'amateur' or 'irresponsible': J. R. Herbert's selections, for instance, 'further depressed' and were so dire they had been 'happily dispatched to the provinces'.[73] He must have offended the Trustees, yet their minutes are resoundingly silent. The Trustees also, however, regularly made life difficult for him.

Hall was always anti-populist. He warned the Trustees not to acquire 'the more popular form' that 'fulfils no artistic or educational function' and would 'corrupt the public taste'.[74] He believed the advisor must be a professional who could make scientific recommendations and who would buy something, even if not to their taste, because they understood its art-historical value and its significance within the collection. Hall believed in art for art's sake; art enables us 'to see *variously* and *beautifully*', he said. 'Art illustrates nothing but its own particular point of view ... [its] aim is "its own excellence". Art has nothing to do with the ethics of the Sunday-school – bad workmanship is the only immorality known to it'.[75]

This contrasted greatly with some of the Trustees' perceptions of the role of art. James Smith was sufficiently provoked by Hall's critical report to write a long letter in response. Smith believed that art should have a moral purpose and that it was the responsibility of the Trustees to harness the educational powers of art. The chief objective of a national gallery, he wrote, was the 'ministration of national delight [and] stimulating the moral and spiritual facilities, [while at the same time] developing, educating and refining the sense of beauty ... The special field of the operation of painting is the expression of spiritual ideas'. He defended the earlier acquisitions and lamented Hall's 'art for art's sake' position. Smith thought that a painting such as *The mitherless bairn*, 1855, may be sentimental but at least it had some elevated purpose. Referring to a McCubbin painting bought on Hall's recommendation, he asked incredulously: 'Are we to replace them with Mr McCubbin's lively family of ducks and ducklings?'[76]

*

'Are we to replace them with Mr McCubbin's lively family of ducks and ducklings?'

FINALLY, AN AUSTRALIAN COLLECTION: 'THE BEST WORK BY THE BEST MEN'.

In the 1890s the NGV began to more seriously collect works by Australian artists. Over the course of the decade, Hall acquired many key works from exhibitions by local artists. In 1895, the NGV purchased David Davies's exquisitely ethereal *Moonrise*, 1894, and Walter Withers's buttery *Tranquil winter*, 1895. In 1896, Bernard Hall very strongly urged the Trustees to acquire Streeton's '*The purple noon's transparent might*', 1896: 'As it would come under the classification of "the best work by the best men", I strongly advise the Trustees not to miss the opportunity of acquiring it, & adding to the Australian selection what is *most characteristically Australian* in the way of pictorial presentment'.[77] In 1898, a special government grant enabled John Longstaff's 1898 painting *Gippsland, Sunday night, February 20th, 1898* to be purchased, its swathe of vermilion a horrid reminder of the terrible bushfires that blazed across Gippsland. The NGV also acquired its first textiles in 1895, through the acquisition of a group of Indian block-printed textiles.

However, not all of the Australian Impressionists enjoyed the lavish praise that Hall heaped on Streeton. The first Conder was not acquired until 1932 and the first Roberts not until 1920 when the NGV bought the portrait study *Penelope*, 1920, the only work acquired by the NGV during the artist's lifetime. When the elderly Roberts held an exhibition in 1924, Hall remarked, dismissively, that there were 'some nice little things which would be in place in a house but would not hold their own in a gallery'. He spoke disparagingly of Roberts's technique, remarking that 'Roberts seems to have no individual style. He paints in so many ways that *one cannot definitely place him*'.[78]

Furthermore, the Trustees did not always support Hall's recommendations. In 1894, Hall suggested that Bertram Mackennal's dramatic sculpture of the evil sorceress *Circe*, 1893, a great success at the Royal Academy exhibition of 1894, be added to the collection. Clearly enamoured with the work, Hall wrote, 'it seems to me to be a genuine work of genius – very remarkable and impressive – (without doubt I should say Young Australia's *chef-d'oeuvre*)'.[79] The Trustees, however, perhaps put off by the risqué figures writhing their way across the base, would not agree. *Circe*, the evil enchantress, was not to find her wily way into the NGV until 1910.

The students competed valiantly to win the school's annual travelling scholarship. A condition of the bursary was presentation of a work to the NGV: John Longstaff gave *The sirens*, c.1891 in 1894, Aby Altson *The golden age*, 1893, in 1895 and James Quinn *The Virgin and Child with the young St John the Baptist*, c.1897, a work inspired by Botticelli, in 1897. Works were also shipped to Melbourne from expatriate Australian artists who enjoyed validation through their presence in Europe. Hall, for instance, who was a great admirer of Velázquez, purchased E. Phillips Fox's copy of *Los borrachos*, 1891, after the original in the Prado, and Alfred Felton gave his first gift in the form of *Sea idyll*, c.1890, a fantastical Cabanel-inspired painting by his friend Rupert Bunny, who was residing in Paris.

(above)
Arthur Streeton
'The purple noon's transparent might' 1896
oil on canvas
123.0 x 123.0 cm
Purchased, 1896

(middle)
Rupert Bunny
Sea idyll c.1890
oil on canvas
100.5 x 161.5 cm
Gift of Alfred Felton, 1892

(below)
E. Phillips Fox
Los borrachos (The drunkards) (copy of Velázquez original in the Prado, Madrid) 1891
oil on canvas
166.4 x 225.6 cm
Purchased with a Government grant, 1893

(above)
McArthur Gallery,
National Gallery of Victoria,
Melbourne c.1900

(below)
Frederick McCubbin
The pioneer 1904
oil on canvas
225.0 x 295.7 cm
Felton Bequest, 1906

AUSTRALIAN NATIONALISM: RAMMING THE SHEARS. On 1 January 1901, the Constitution of Australia came into force. What had been individual self-governing British colonies were united as a federation of states as the Commonwealth of Australia. The occasion sparked two weeks of celebrations: commemorative arches were built, processions were held, the Duke and Duchess of Cornwall attended as special guests and, on 14 May, the Duchess pressed 'send' on a telegraphic message to 7000 schools causing 7000 Union Jacks to be enthusiastically raised in unison. The process that had led towards Federation – compounded also by the experience of Australia's centennial year in 1888 – prompted Australians to begin to assert a stronger sense of national identity. This nationalistic preoccupation is also evident in Australian art and writing of the time. Roberts painted *Shearing the rams*, 1890, in the same few years that Banjo Paterson wrote *Clancy of the Overflow* and *The Man from Snowy River*. Artists of the time were actively searching for myths and images with which to define an Australian identity, and they found them in the overlanders and the drovers, the shearers and the selectors.

McCubbin's *The pioneer*, 1904, was first conceived in the year of Federation. He painted the work in a triptych format – a template usually reserved for religious subjects – and on a canvas so big he had to lower it into a trench in order to reach the top. He persuaded various locals – including his wife Annie – to model for him and valiantly tried to ignore a cranky bull in a nearby paddock. He found the job challenging, writing to Roberts: 'I am pegging on at *The pioneer* and I feel like the poor devils I am painting in the picture. Rather sad about it, however I am doing my best. Sometimes up and sometimes down'.[80] Despite the difficulties of its creation, McCubbin's painting, which was the centrepiece for his exhibition at The Athenaeum in 1904, was a great success. *The Age*'s editorial of 16 August 1905 effused: 'Those who talk despairingly or sneeringly about art possibilities in Australia would do well to study an Australian picture ... *The pioneer*, by Mr McCubbin. This picture ... is to be hailed as an irrefutable demonstration that Australia can produce a strong and beautiful national art of her own'.[81] The NGV agreed and the Felton Bequest acquired the painting in 1906, one of its earliest purchases.

It took the NGV a bit longer to become enamoured with Roberts's *Shearing the rams* – or 'Ramming the shears', as Michael Leunig humorously renamed it in the 1980s. It was not purchased until 1932, a year after Roberts's death. Roberts developed his ideas for the painting at Brocklesby Station in New South Wales. He paid a shearer (and generously) to model for him, and allegedly gave sixpences to the 'tar boy' – who was actually a girl – to keep the dust kicked up in order to create a hazy atmosphere. At the end of the nineteenth century, Australia had become the world's largest wool producer – the economy really did 'ride on the sheep's back'. For an artist trying to distil some defining essence of Australia, the shearing shed must have seemed obvious subject matter. Terence Lane comments that 'it was a national picture conceived in 1888, the centenary of white settlement in Australia. Artists were looking around for subjects that would

carry that heavy message, that *histoire*, and Tom Roberts lit upon the subject of the wool industry. He set out to paint a grand, national picture in the manner of European history paintings, and it struck a chord'.[82]

THE FELTON BEQUEST: 'WEALTH!! GET IT SPENT'. In 1865, Sir Redmond Barry had written to the Chief Librarian, Augustus Tulk, lamenting the NGV's lack of funds with which to build a collection: 'I have heard from Mr. Reed that you inform him the Collection of the Villa Albani is for sale. How on earth can we as yet presume to compete with the Emperors of France and Russia, the Rothschilds and the other opulent Israelites not to mention the dilettante of Manchester who of course will be represented in the auction room?'[83]

Lack of regular funding had constrained the young NGV. However, in 1904 this situation was irrevocably changed when local businessman Alfred Felton passed away and left an enormous fortune to the NGV. He bequeathed £383,163 – an immense sum for the time – of which half the annual income was to go to charities that supported women and children and half was to be used in perpetuity to acquire works for the NGV. In one very unexpected gesture – for Felton had not previously been a significant patron – he transformed the position of the NGV, endowing it with buying power greater than London's National Gallery and the Tate combined. As Carl Villis, Conservator, states: 'What we now embrace as the NGV is very much bigger and richer in content than it was in those early days. If you subtract the Felton Bequest's acquisitions from the collection, what is left is an old and relatively well-represented Australian and British painting collection. The Felton Bequest makes all the difference in the world'.[84]

The credit line 'Felton Bequest' is commonplace around the NGV. Since his death around 15,000 works have been acquired, valued today at more than $2 billion. The impact of the gift has been profound, as John Payne, Senior Conservator, states: 'Felton's gesture changed the NGV from a provincial gallery into an international gallery. It was an extraordinary gesture of very genuine philanthropy. A noteworthy aspect of his bequest was that it was not a gift to the NGV; it was a gift to the people of Victoria to acquire works of art for the public collection. It was really forward thinking: it was not something that directors or state governments would control, it was something that an independent body would manage for the public. It was a fascinating and fabulous thing that he did'.[85] Felton's bequest was also notable for its lack of proscription: he decreed that the works must have an artistic and educational value and be calculated to raise or improve public taste, but overwhelmingly the Felton Bequest Committee was invested with broad discretionary powers.

Alfred Felton was born in England but arrived in Melbourne in 1853, part of the general stampede to the goldfields. He ultimately made his fortune as a merchant, developing a pharmaceutical manufacturing company with his business partner, Frederick Grimwade. They soon expanded into chemicals and fertilisers and set up their own bottle manufacturing plant, a business that still operates today. Over time Felton continued to diversify his interests, including becoming part owner of the substantial Murray Downs pastoral estate, a move that saved him from financial ruin when the 1890s depression hit. He was not a high-profile Melbournian: unlike many other wealthy businessmen he did not figure largely in public life. He collected art, with a preference for conventional landscapes and nostalgic English views, and was a patron of the artist Rupert Bunny, which was possibly motivated more by friendship than artistic preoccupations. He never married and lived modestly in simply furnished rooms at the Esplanade Hotel in St Kilda. Putting his money to good use was evidently on his mind, perhaps even more so when he was diagnosed with cancer; four months before his death he wrote in his diary: 'Wealth!! Get it spent'.

BERNARD HALL GOES TO EUROPE. Fortified with the first flush of income from the Felton Bequest, Bernard Hall visited Europe in early 1905. From an exhibition of French Impressionist works in London, he made a radical choice for the people of Melbourne by acquiring Camille Pissarro's *Boulevard Montmartre, morning, cloudy weather*, 1897, for £300, one of the first Impressionist works bought

(opposite left)
Tom Roberts
Shearing the rams 1888-90
oil on canvas on composition board
122.4 x 183.3 cm
Felton Bequest, 1932

(opposite right)
Michael Leunig
Ramming the shears c.1985

(below)
John Longstaff
Alfred Felton c.1932
oil on canvas
139.4 x 95.9 cm
Felton Bequest, 1932

for a public collection anywhere. Hall returned to the exhibition numerous times, writing that he would have liked to have acquired works by Monet, Sisley and Degas but that 'apart from the best of them having been held privately, the prices were prohibitive'. After spending what seems to have been an enlivening morning with the artist Holman Hunt, he decided to purchase *The importunate neighbour*, 1895, for the not insubstantial sum of £350, though he was later 'heartily ashamed of it'.[86]

Hall also spent time in France, visiting Rodin's studio, where he commissioned a casting of the head of *Jean Paul Laurens*, 1881, and also bought the elegant marble *Minerva without a helmet*, c.1896, for which the model was Australian expatriate artist John Russell's beautiful Italian wife, Marianna Antoinetta Mattiocco. His selection included Jean-Louis-Ernest Meissonier's mid to late nineteenth-century painting *The alms giver* and Edmond Aman-Jean's *Woman resting*, c.1904, a work that artist Walter Withers said gave him 'a thrill' whenever he saw it, and two small, intense sculptures by the noted *animalier* Antoine-Louis Barye.[87] Hall was also on the hunt for another monumental bronze sculpture to complement Sir Joseph Edgar Boehm's *St George and the dragon*, 1879, which had sat proudly on the Library's forecourt since its acquisition in 1888 from the International Exhibition. While in Paris, Hall visited the studio of Emmanuel Frémiet, whom he described in a letter to the Trustees as 'without doubt the greatest living master in equestrian groups'.[88] Ted Gott, Senior Curator of International Art, tells the story: 'They first talked about doing another *St George and the dragon* so there would be two – one by Boehm, one by Frémiet – but eventually they decided they would get a Joan of Arc. However, this notion of a Joan of Arc sculpture sparked negative press back in Australia. Why should a British colony have a French anti-British heroine erected outside the National Gallery?'[89] The *Argus* called it 'an almost inconceivable stupidity' and a shameful act of 'ancestral infamy'.[90] However, says Gott, 'The press turned around. The moment the work was uncrated they changed their minds and they fell in

(opposite clockwise from above)
Camille Pissarro
Boulevard Montmartre, morning, cloudy weather (Boulevard Montmarte, matin, temps gris) 1897
oil on canvas
73.0 x 92.0 cm
Felton Bequest, 1905

Edmond Aman-Jean
Woman resting
(La Femme couchée) c.1904
oil on canvas
38.5 x 46.3 cm
Felton Bequest, 1905

Auguste Rodin
Minerva without a helmet
(Minerve sans Casque) c.1896
marble
48.2 x 26.4 x 26.7 cm (overall)
Felton Bequest, 1905

*

Why should a British colony have a French anti-British heroine erected outside the National Gallery?

love with the statue. It was an early controversy about sculpture, which has of course been followed by many others, such as Ron Robertson-Swann's *Vault*, 1980, popularly referred to at the time as "Yellow Peril"'.[91]

The NGV was also unexpectedly presented with a second sculpture. In late 1906, Frémiet wrote to Hall: 'I must tell you why a second sculpture accompanies the Joan of Arc, in a separate crate. This bronze represents a gorilla carrying off a woman, and here is an explanation of its presence. When I billed you for the Joan of Arc, I had expected the work to be gilded. After you abandoned the idea of gilding the statue, I thought I would make up the difference in price by sending my Gorilla to your Museum. It is ... my pleasure to present you with one of the great characters of my art'.[92] Frémiet had created his first gorilla sculpture, *Gorilla dragging away a dead Negress*, in 1859, the year that Charles Darwin published his groundbreaking *On the Origin of Species by Means of Natural Selection*. Frémiet's second sculpture, *Gorilla carrying off a woman,* 1887, which is the version gifted to the NGV, won him both notoriety and the Medal of Honour at the Paris Salon of 1887. 'It entered the public consciousness as one of the defining images of its time,' notes Gott, 'culminating in the immortal cinematic image of Fay Wray in the arms of the beast Kong in the 1933 film *King Kong*'.[93]

THE EUROPEAN ADVISORS – AND THEIR TROUBLES.
In the early 1900s, a succession of gentlemen took on the role of European advisor to the NGV. Hall's friend the English artist George Clausen advised on works, as did the M. Marquet de Vasselot, who worked part time for the Louvre.In 1909, the role was given to Frank Gibson, who was well known for his biography of Charles Conder. Gibson was born in Melbourne and had studied at the University of Melbourne before attending the Slade School of Art in London. In 1912, Sir Sidney Colvin, the recently retired Keeper of Prints and Drawings at the British Museum, took on the role.

Mostly they had a devil of a time. Their challenges were many: for a start, Hall declared the majority of them 'amateurs' and deplored their choices when the works arrived in Melbourne ('my worst fears are confirmed', he wrote to the Trustees after a shipment from the eternally beleaguered Frank Gibson).[94] In addition, the Melbourne public and the local community of artists were often noisily protesting – in the newspaper and to whoever would listen to them – about the inferiority of the works purchased overseas and the terrible waste of money. The local artists wanted the Felton Bequest funds spent on art produced in Australia. Nearly every shipment inspired fresh outcry.

Emmanuel Frémiet
Gorilla carrying off a woman (Gorille enlevant une femme) 1887
bronze
44.7 x 30.6 x 33.1 cm
Gift of the artist, 1907

The system for approval was also cumbersome. As Gallery Director Eric Westbrook wrote, recommendations had to 'run the gauntlet of Hall, the Trustees and the Felton

Bequest Committee and were often rejected'.[95] Furthermore, in an age of sea mail, the process could be infuriatingly slow: it took weeks, even months, for photographs and other documentation to cross the oceans. The advisors had a hard time getting dealers to hold sales open for many months, especially when the NGV, more often than not, reneged on the deal after arguments in Melbourne.

By 1913, the relationship between Sir Sidney Colvin and the NGV had become treacherous. Colvin had made many carefully researched suggestions but most were inexplicably declined, with no reasons offered. In 1915, Colvin wrote: 'I thought ... I could within a few years have done much to make the Melbourne Gallery one of the finest outside the Great European capitals. My hopes in the matter have been quite frustrated'. He tendered his resignation: the role, he said, had become 'inconsistent ... with my personal self-respect'.[96]

In 1917, the Trustee Sir Baldwin Spencer travelled to England and wrote back to his fellow trustees that, among the art community, 'there is no doubt but that a certain amount of dissatisfaction and also irritation has been caused, rightly or wrongly, in London, both by criticism of certain works selected, and by the rejection of others that are regarded as of first class importance'.[97] The NGV had not endeared itself to the London arts community.

ACQUISITIONS: 'WHY NOT THE BENT TREE LOVELY FAMOUS'. Nevertheless, despite the many tensions, some good works were acquired. Camille Corot's poetic work *The bent tree*, c.1855–60, was purchased in 1907 from a sale of accountant Alexander Young's collection at Agnew's art dealership in London. A different work by Corot, *Souvenir de Picardie,* was initially selected by advisor George Clausen for the NGV, which was only a third of the price of *The bent tree*. However, when J. A. Levey, a trustee who was visiting London, was asked what he thought of *Souvenir de Picardie*, he cabled back to Melbourne the truncated but clear message: 'Quite suitable but why not *The bent tree* lovely famous'.[98]

In 1909 and 1910, Frank Gibson's purchases included a broody landscape by English Romantic painter John Constable, a painting by Eugène Delacroix illustrating a scene from Lord Byron's poem *The Giaour* and other works by Bastien-Lepage, Fantin-Latour, Pierre Puvis de Chavannes and Henry Raeburn. When Sir Sidney Colvin started as advisor in 1912, he reviewed the NGV's collection and thought it lacking in French examples. Taking Frank Gibson with him, he set off for Paris in June of 1913 determined to hunt out works from key movements such as French Impressionism and the Barbizon School. Works by Renoir, Monet, Sisley, Degas and Boudin were recommended for the NGV and all were bought but for, alas, the Renoir and the Degas.

A notable feature of Bernard Hall's directorship was his support for Asian art. The NGV had acquired some Asian objects including basketwork, cloisonné enamels and embroideries from the International Exhibition of 1880–81, but the serious collecting of Asian art really began with Hall. In 1909, a magnificent Japanese golden screen titled *Flowering plants of the four seasons*, c.1630–40, by the school of Tawaraya Sotatsu, was acquired through Felton Bequest funds. The Japanese collection was also significantly developed in 1909 when Frank Gibson acquired a series of Japanese woodcuts from the Happer sale, an American collection sold through Sotheby's. Ursula Hoff recounted that the selection was made 'by Mr E. F. Strange of the Victoria and Albert Museum, a first-class expert and author on Japanese art, and the woodcuts form a representative collection of most aspects of Japanese woodcut-making and contains some first-class impressions of famous works'.[99] The selection included this iconic image from Hokusai's famous series *Thirty-six views of Mt Fuji*, 1826–33. Mount Fuji recedes, deep in the background, dwarfed by the great curling wave that rises – a menacing claw – above the besieged fishing boats.

An Egyptian artefact, a limestone *Head of Queen Nefertiti*, came into the collection in 1907. 'It is incredibly rare', says Curator of Decorative Arts and Antiquities Amanda Dunsmore. 'You can literally count the sculpture fragments that exist of Nefertiti on one hand. It was given to us in 1907 by the esteemed Egyptologists Norman and Nina de Garis Davies. They worked at Amarna, one of the most famous sites in Egypt. Although British, Norman Davies gifted it to Melbourne because he used to be a Unitarian minister in the church here in Melbourne before he went off to become an Egyptologist. To have the head of Nefertiti gifted to the NGV is quite astonishing.'[100]

On the home front, a ruckus was caused when *Pollice verso*, 1904, a work by twenty-five-year-old Australian artist Norman Lindsay, was acquired. His brother Daryl (who would later become Director of the NGV)

(previous above)
Camille Corot
The bent tree (Ville d'Avray, Bouleau Pond) c.1855–60
oil on canvas
44.3 x 58.5 cm
Felton Bequest, 1907

(previous below)
Alfred Sisley
Haystacks at Moret – morning light (Les Meules de paille à Moret – effet du matin) 1891
oil on canvas
73.8 x 93.1 cm
Felton Bequest, 1913

(opposite above)
Katsushika Hokusai
The great wave off Kanagawa
Edo period c.1830 Japan
colour woodblock
25.7 x 37.7 cm (image and sheet)
Felton Bequest, 1909

(opposite below)
EGYPT, el-Amarna
Head of Queen Nefertiti
1353 BC–1337 BC, New Kingdom, Dynasty XVII, Year eight of the reign of Akhenaten
limestone
34.3 x 21.0 x 20.5 cm (approx.)
Presented by
N. de Garis Davies, 1907

冨嶽三十六景 神奈川沖浪裏

(above)
Elizabeth Thompson
The 28th Regiment at Quatre Bras 1875
oil on canvas
97.2 x 216.2 cm
Purchased, 1884

(below)
St George Hare
The victory of faith c.1890–91
oil on canvas
123.3 x 200.0 cm
Gift of an anonymous donor, 1905

remembered it so: '*Pollice verso* was sent to Melbourne on exhibition and purchased for the NGV on the advice of the Director, Bernard Hall, strongly supported by Sir Baldwin Spencer, a cultivated trustee of rare discrimination. Its purchase brought forth a barrage of abuse from an unenlightened, unsophisticated press and public. Howls of agony went up that £150 of public money should be spent on this unbridled slap in the face to Christianity'.[101] The public outcry was so great that for the remainder of the exhibtion the painting was allegedly hung with its face to the wall. While the 'wowsers' found *Pollice verso* hard going, they seemed to have no problem with St George Hare's *The victory of faith*, c.1890–91, despite its rather loaded depiction of two naked girls facing martyrdom sleeping peacefully among strategically placed straw. When the *Argus* newspaper conducted a poll on people's favourite pictures in the NGV in 1907, Schenck's *Anguish* and Elizabeth Thompson's *The 28th Regiment at Quatre Bras*, 1875, scored highly, as did *The victory of faith*, which had been presented by an anonymous donor in 1905.

THE DESIRE FOR A GALLERY. While the search for knowledge and educational values may have been the principal drivers for the NGV's colonial founders, as the decades progressed, attitudes about the function of the NGV changed greatly, transformed by shifting concepts of the role of art and the museum. Even in its first decades, many fascinating debates went on about the function of the NGV. Should it hold copies of great works of art in an attempt to emulate the major museums of Europe? Should the NGV buy paintings by Europe's Royal Academicians or should it support the emerging local artists? Is the function of art to enable us 'to see *variously* and *beautifully*', as Director Lindsay Bernard Hall maintained? Or, must its purpose be directed to 'stimulating moral and spiritual facilities', as Gallery Trustee James Smith trenchantly believed? These divergent ideas about the role of art and culture absorbed the NGV from its inception – and over the next few decades this would only intensify.

THE BATTLE FOR MODERNISM

WARTIME: *A SERGEANT OF THE LIGHT HORSE*.

In late 1914, the Great War erupted across Europe. At its conclusion, a series of commemorative acquisitions were made, including Arthur Streeton's *Balloons on fire*, 1918, funded through the Gilbee Bequest, and George Lambert's *A sergeant of the Light Horse*, 1920. Artist Hans Heysen wrote of it: 'The feeling way the eyes have been painted and the expression of that sensitiveness around the mouth are truly wonderful'.[1] When peacetime returned, the Felton Bequest's purchases reflected the changing mood: Penleigh Boyd's *The breath of spring*, 1919, stands as an elegy, painted by the artist in response to his war-induced depression, while E. Phillips Fox's *The arbour*, 1910, is more purely joyous. A difficult decade closed with a severe outbreak of Spanish flu in 1919. The global pandemic impacted the NGV so badly that the entire institution closed from 20 January until 4 March, and remained closed on Sundays until 1 June.

JOHN H. CONNELL: THE WHOLE OF ARTISTIC ENDEAVOUR IS OF INTEREST TO THE NGV.

A remarkable gift was made in 1914 when John H. Connell presented his collection of decorative arts to the NGV, which included furniture, silver, ceramics, metalwork, glassware, rugs and other objects. Installed in a dedicated space adjacent to the Buvelot Gallery, the collection opened to the public in September 1914 – and with no fanfare, at the express request of Connell. This was an important gift, both because of the many fine objects acquired and also for its inspiring act of philanthropy, which the Trustees hoped would inspire others. The John H. Connell Gift profoundly impacted the depth and the position of the Decorative Arts collection, as former Decorative Arts Curator Terence Lane notes: 'The Connell collection was vital because it established, at that early time, a real presence for the decorative arts in the Melbourne collection. That was unique in Australia. It established that the whole of artistic endeavour was of interest to the NGV, and not just paintings. Melbourne never had a dichotomy between the fine and applied arts, and that is a vital part of our history'.[2]

(pp. 50–1)
George Stubbs
A lion attacking a horse
c.1765 (detail)
oil on canvas
69.0 x 100.1 cm
Felton Bequest, 1949

(opposite)
George Lambert
A sergeant of the Light Horse in Palestine 1920
oil on canvas
77.0 x 62.0 cm
Felton Bequest, 1921

(below)
Derby Porcelain,
Derby (manufacturer)
William 'Quaker'
Pegg (decorator)
Oriental poppy and great blue bottle, plate c.1815
Porcelain (soft-paste)
3.2 x 22.1 cm diameter
Gift of John H. Connell, 1929

Max Meldrum
Portrait of the artist's mother
1913
oil on canvas on (board)
58.6 x 47.4 cm
Felton Bequest, 1913

GALLERY SCHOOL: FAREWELL 'THE PROF'. Male students won the first seven of the Gallery School's travelling scholarships, but when Constance Jenkins became the first female winner in 1908 she started a winning streak for her gender that was to last twenty-seven years. ('Where are the boys of the old brigade?' lamented a fed-up 'young blood' in *The Art Student* of 1932.)[3] A rival gallery school was initiated in 1916 by a previous recipient of the travelling scholarship. Max Meldrum returned to Melbourne with tenacious – if table-thumping – aspirations. Meldrum loathed experimental approaches such as Impressionism and insisted that his students follow a strict doctrine of tonal painting. They followed him devotedly, even if a sceptical Lionel Lindsay nicknamed him 'the mad Mullah'. Meldrum presented the work *A peasant of Pacé*, 1908, under the terms of his scholarship, and the Felton Bequest bought his *Portrait of the artist's mother*, 1913, that same year.

In 1917, the Gallery School students were saddened by the death of 'The Prof' – their beloved drawing master Frederick McCubbin, who had taught at the Gallery School for the long stretch between 1886 and 1917. He was succeeded by William Beckwith McInnes, another alumnus of the Gallery School. McInnes was greatly championed by the jury of the (rather conservatively oriented) Archibald Prize, held yearly at the Art Gallery of New South Wales: they awarded him Australia's leading prize for portraiture in 1921, 1922, 1923, 1924, 1926, 1930 and 1936.

ROBBIE ROSS AND WILLIAM BLAKE: 'TO THE CELLARS'. In 1917, Robert 'Robbie' Ross, a writer and art critic, was appointed Felton Advisor. His contemporary William Rothenstein stated that he had 'a genius for friendship. No man had a wider circle of friends than he. He had a delightful nature, was an admirable story-teller, and a wit; above all he was able to get the best out of those he admired. Oscar Wilde was never wittier than when at Ross's parties, the same was true of Aubrey Beardsley and Max Beerbohm'.[4] Ross is remembered for his great friendship to Wilde throughout his hardships and was executor of Wilde's estate.

William Blake
Dante running from the three beasts 1824-1827
illustration to *The Divine Comedy* by Dante Alighieri (*Inferno*, 1, 1-90) 1824-1827
pen and ink and watercolour over pencil
37.0 x 52.8 cm
Felton Bequest, 1920

Ross soon made a stunning acquisition for Melbourne. He was the catalyst for the purchase of William Blake's visionary watercolours, regarded as some of the NGV's finest holdings. The suite of work includes two illustrations for Milton's *Paradise Lost* and a large holding of the watercolours Blake created to illustrate Dante's *The Divine Comedy*, which he was still painting - propped up in bed - during his final period of illness in 1827. When the works came on to the market in 1918, Ross devised a way to enable the sale. As Cathy Leahy, Senior Curator of Prints and Drawings, tells it: A consortium between Melbourne, the Tate, the British Museum, Birmingham and the Ashmolean in Oxford was organised to secure the set. The watercolours were then divided into three groups according to their level of finish, and selections were then made in turn by each institution. As Melbourne had the most money, we secured thirty-six of the 102 works; we have the single largest group from the last great series of watercolours made by Blake. These works by Blake are something that we are known for internationally; scholars come to Melbourne just to see them'.[5] When they arrived at the NGV, they were received with hostility by the Melbourne press. The *Argus*'s art critic wrote: 'No justification can surely be shown for the purchase of so many artistically inferior pictures, which will no doubt before long find their way to the cellars'.[6] Gallery Trustee Baldwin Spencer described the acquisition of the idiosyncratic works as 'severe tests' for which 'the Trustees stood manfully'.[7]

Other significant works bought on Ross's recommendation included a series of Whistler lithographs and two stylish Pre-Raphaelite works, Edward Burne-Jones's *The garden of Pan*, 1886–87, and Arthur Hughes's *La Belle Dame sans merci*, 1863. Although the Foreign Office in London had earlier refused Ross permission to travel on account of the war, in September of 1918 he wrote to the Trustees with the pleasing news that he had secured a passport and ticket. Sadly, he was never to make the journey to Melbourne.

Ross retired to bed one afternoon, telling his landlady he felt unwell. She found him dead later that night. His ashes were placed in Wilde's tomb in the cemetery of Père-Lachaise in Paris.

FRANK RINDER: 'UNBOUNDED ENTHUSIASM FOR THE FELTON'. In 1918, one week after the end of the First World War, the art critic and writer Frank Rinder was appointed Felton Advisor in London. He had been in the running for the role when Robbie Ross was appointed, but Rinder had refused to compete against his friend and withdrew his application. During his ten years as advisor Rinder made brilliant acquisitions for Melbourne. Early on, he inspired a rare instance of agreement between the Trustees, the Felton Bequest Committee and Bernard Hall with his acquisition in 1922 of Anthony van Dyck's *Rachel de Ruvigny, Countess of Southhampton*, c.1640. This was quickly followed by a great ruckus when he bought the fifteenth-century Ince Hall *Madonna and Child* (formerly attributed to Jan van Eyck but now attributed to an unknown follower); that £31,935 had been expended on an image only 11 by 8 inches inspired a writer at *The Herald* to make snide comments about a fool and his money, to Rinder's chagrin.[8]

Édouard Manet
The house at Rueil
(La Maison à Rueil) 1882
oil on canvas
92.8 x 73.5 cm
Felton Bequest, 1926

Subsequent important historical European purchases included Hans Memling's *The Man of Sorrows in the arms of the Virgin*, 1475–79; Titian's *A monk with a book*, c.1550; and Jacopo Tintoretto's *Doge Pietro Loredano*, 1567–70. His selection of English paintings included Thomas Gainsborough's *An officer of the 4th Regiment of Foot*, c.1776–80, and Henry Raeburn's *James Wardrop of Torbane Hill*, c.1820. Works by French artists included a group by Honoré Daumier and a series of French Impressionist works such as Gustave Courbet's *Winter*, c.1872–73, and *The wave*, c.1872. His purchase of Édouard Manet's *The ship's deck*, c.1860, so upset John Shirlow, local etcher and Trustee, that he fired off a memo describing 'expenditure on a Manet a misuse of Felton's funds'.[9] Nevertheless, the same year – and for considerably more money – Rinder bought Manet's *The house at Rueil*, 1882, and, on Christmas

Day of 1925, his *The melon,* c.1880. 'These are pictures you could never replace', Sir Kenneth Clark would later write.[10] Sculptural works secured by him included Rodin's *The thinker*, 1884, and Rinder was also the advisor who bought Puvis de Chavannes's epic cartoons on the subject of *St Geneviève provisioning Paris under siege*, 1897–98.

While this selection seems remarkable now, at the time Rinder was endlessly hounded by the press. As criticism intensified, Rinder came out to Melbourne to confer with the Trustees. Leonard Cox recalled seeing Rinder at a function and that he seemed 'unhappy and depressed'.[11] The criticism evidently upset him greatly. His English colleague Professor Thomas Bodkin wrote: 'I have constantly in mind

Hans Memling
The Man of Sorrows in the arms of the Virgin 1475–79
oil and gold leaf on wood panel
27.4 x 19.9 cm
Felton Bequest, 1924

the recollection of meeting the late Frank Rinder one cold, wet afternoon, wandering like a stricken soul in Pall Mall. I stopped to talk to him and, frightened by his appearance, asked if he was ill. He replied that he had just received a bundle of newspaper cuttings from Australia, criticising the purchases that he had negotiated for the Felton Bequest Trustees. They were so venomous as to make him physically sick. I took him to dine with me in my club nearby and it needed several hours in the company of good fellows before he was restored to his normal state of cheerfulness'.[12] In 1927, Frank Rinder cabled his resignation and refused all attempts to have him withdraw it. 'The relentless attack on the Felton advisors by the local art critics is a sad part of the NGV story', says Ted Gott. 'The greatest tragedy is Frank Rinder, who was basically crucified by the local press and forced to resign as Felton Advisor. Yet he was, arguably, the most brilliant advisor we ever had. He had the most extraordinary eye, bought fantastic works of art and wrote about them beautifully in his letters back to the Felton Bequest Committee.'[13]

Frank Rinder also contributed meaningfully to the NGV in other, more subtle, ways. Daryl Lindsay reminisced that when he was in London, 'Rinder and his beautiful wife were very kind and I was always made welcome to their charming little house in St John's Wood with first state Rembrandts, Dürer etchings, Daumier lithographs, and Rowlandson drawings in the lavatory. Rinder's unbounded enthusiasm for the Felton drew us closely together and he would telephone, pink in the face with excitement, and carry me off to see a Courbet, a Constable sketch or a Blake drawing that had come on the market ... These were exciting days to me and I was quite unconsciously laying the foundation of a knowledge of art and market value that was to stand me in good stead in the distant future when I became Director of the National Gallery of Victoria'.[14]

'CHINESE' MORRISON'S BEQUEST. Bernard Hall was deeply appreciative of Chinese art: 'the old Han, T'ang & Sung wares are some of the most beautiful & affecting things in the whole range of art', he wrote.[15] He made the acquisition of Chinese works of art a priority, and must have been thrilled when the Chinese collection was expanded in the early 1920s through the bequest of Dr George Morrison. 'Chinese' Morrison, as he was known, spent most of his life in Asia. In the 1890s, he had published a memoir called *An Australian in China, Being the Narrative of a Quiet Journey Across China to Burma*, which led to a position as Beijing's foreign correspondent for *The Times*, a role he fulfilled for more than twenty years. When his bequest was received in Melbourne it was found to be of variable quality and more modern than expected, which led to a rumour that the originals had been pilfered on the Chinese wharves and the fine wares replaced with objects from the nearby markets.[16] Nevertheless there were some good pieces, which Hall further augmented in 1926 through the acquisition of some fine Tang Dynasty funerary figurines.

Later in the decade, in 1928, local art dealer Frank Godden wrote a scathing attack in the *Argus* on Hall's curatorship of the Chinese collection. He declared many of the

pieces 'trade lines', said the Felton Bequest's money was 'wasted' and that he had imported such objects himself: 'clients bought them as decorative furnishings for their homes'.[17] In response, sixteen pieces were sent over to the British Museum to be assessed by the esteemed R. L. Hobson of the Department of Ceramics and Ethnography. Happily, he confirmed the worth of most of the works but, unfortunately, six pieces were damaged on the return voyage.

AT THE NGV: LIONS AND LOVE LETTERS. An *Argus* article of 20 June 1924 reported that the stately lions that stood sentry at the Library's entrance also doubled as letterboxes: art school students allegedly used their mouths as post boxes for the delivery of love letters. Information of a different sort was delivered by the Guide Lectures, a program initiated in 1924 and supported through funds donated by R. D. Elliott, Gallery Trustee and newspaperman. Lecturers included Max Meldrum, Norman Macgeorge and L. A. Adamson, Headmaster of Wesley College, and the initiative was so successful that the state government agreed to subsidise another series. In the same year, Bernard Hall secured the assistance of Percival Serle in the cataloguing of the Connell collection. 'I am not an expert you know', said Serle. 'We can't find an expert', was Hall's retort.[18] On that understanding, Serle undertook the work and corrected a great many inaccuracies in the catalogue.

(left)
Loan Exhibition of Australian Paintings McArthur Gallery, National Gallery of Victoria, 1925

(right)
Court lady's informal robe (Changfu)
late 19th century China
silk satin, silk, cotton, silk and metallic thread, gilt
136.5 cm (centre back);
26.0 cm (sleeve length)
Bequest of Dr G. E. Morrison, 1921

The NGV staff continued to expand with the appointment of Mr H. S. Gilkes as the Keeper of Prints in 1927. A notable event of the decade was the ambitious *Loan Exhibition of Australian Paintings*, initiated by Hall as part of an NGV objective to present large-scale exhibitions. Drawn from private collections throughout Victoria, the exhibition primarily featured contemporary works of art but also a few nineteenth-century works, including Tom Roberts's *Shearing the rams*.

While few Australian works were bought in the early 1920s, increasing numbers of local artists were collected as the decade progressed, including works by E. Phillips Fox, Hans Heysen, Sid Long, Frederick McCubbin's son Louis, Hilda Rix Nicholas, Napier Waller, H. Septimus Power and Bertram Mackennal. Several works by Bernard Hall and Arthur Streeton were acquired around 1925–26 on the advice of J. S. MacDonald, later a director of the NGV. The Irish Edwardian painter William Orpen proved to be a great favourite of the Felton Bequest: four of his works were acquired throughout the 1920s, including *Night (no. 2)*, 1907, a romantic depiction of the artist and his wife locked in an embrace. (R. D. Elliott was also enamoured with Orpen's work – his house possessed so many that his wife called it 'the Orpenage'.) The NGV was also presented with a fine gift in 1927 from Mr and Mrs E. S. Makower, who, among other items, gave the Gallery their exquisite collection of nineteen French fans, dating variously from the 1600s to the 1800s and encompassing the era of the Louis XIV – the 'Sun King' – through to the time of Napoleon.

By 1929, the Great Depression had begun. As a fiscal austerity measure, the state government significantly cut the NGV's budget for salaries and operational costs and put restrictions on overseas expenditure, causing difficulties for the international Felton advisors. In 1930, it was decided that the money left to the NGV in 1903 by Richmond grocer James McAllan, which had grown to the tidy sum of £32,000, would be used to fund a capital works program to build additional galleries and storerooms. The NGV's funding shortfall for the project was covered by a government grant of £7,000 through the Unemployment Relief Fund, a Depression-era relief measure.

***THE BANQUET OF CLEOPATRA*: 'THE STUFF OF A SPY FILM'.** Randall Davies was appointed Felton Advisor in 1931 when the Depression was at its worst. As the financial situation improved, he was able to make many strong purchases for Melbourne, often working in consultation with Sir Charles Holmes. John Hoppner's *Portrait of a lady*, c.1795, came in 1932 and Joshua Reynolds's *Miss Susanna Gale*, c.1763–64, in 1935 – a pretty portrait of a wealthy fourteen-year-old Jamaican heiress who was completing her education in England. Davies recommended works by Post-Impressionist artists such as Gauguin, van Gogh and Cézanne, but Melbourne was not yet ready for such modern works and declined them all, a particular tragedy as major works by these artists can now never be

(opposite left)
William Orpen
Night (No. 2) 1907
oil on canvas
76.5 x 64.0 cm
Felton Bequest, 1929

(opposite right)
Napier Waller
Virgil 1922
watercolour over pencil
53.2 x 71.6 cm (image)
Felton Bequest, 1922

(below)
Giambattista Tiepolo
The Banquet of Cleopatra 1743–44
oil on canvas
250.3 x 357.0 cm
Felton Bequest, 1933

acquired. One of the great treasures of Davies's advisorship was his acquisition of a late Rembrandt self-portrait (now reattributed) that came on the market from the collection of the Duke of Portland at Welbeck Abbey. Davies urged the NGV to acquire it: 'The Welbeck painting, ugly and rough as it is, is simply marvellous; a pathetic self-revelation of the artist in his very last years that is of extreme interest'.[19] Davies was also the advisor who bid on behalf of the NGV at the celebrated Oppenheimer collection auction in 1936. The NGV acquired seventeen Old Master drawings, including works by Andrea del Sarto, Parmigianino, Dürer, Rembrandt and François Boucher. These works, of excellent quality, still stand as the core of the NGV's collection of Old Master European drawings.

However, Randall Davies's finest hour, after a tip-off from Holmes, was the acquisition of Giambattista Tiepolo's *The Banquet of Cleopatra*, 1743–44, one of the great glories of the NGV's collection. It was among a group of works de-accessioned by the State Hermitage Museum in Leningrad in order to raise capital for more pressing purposes.[20] The works were sold on the open market through the People's Commissariat of Foreign Trade, an organisation set up in 1925 to raise hard currency for the USSR through the sale of antiques. The Russian government initially approached London's National Gallery, but there was opposition to the sale due to diplomatic ill will between the two countries. With London out of the running, Melbourne put forward an offer of £25,000, which was accepted on condition that payment be made using small currency only. On behalf of the Felton Bequests Committee, a Mr Sargent carried a suitcase containing bundles of small bank notes across Trafalgar Square to rendezvous with the Soviet agents. It was, as Ted Gott notes, 'the stuff of a spy film – they needed ready cash in Russia and so they got ready cash'.[21]

The Banquet of Cleopatra, a highly significant Italian work of the eighteenth century, was one of the Felton Bequest's most triumphant acquisitions. Director Gerard Vaughan also nominates it as a spectacular purchase. 'It is arguably the greatest non-Australian picture in the country. When it was bought it really put Melbourne on the map.'[22] Sir Kenneth Clark, the influential art historian and later Felton Advisor, stated during his visit to Melbourne in 1949: 'You are fortunate in having here a stunning [masterpiece] ... which, had it not been for a piece of fantastic obstinacy, would have been one of the glories of the London National Gallery'.[23] It has become an icon of the NGV and a Melbourne landmark – for example, George Peka, attendant at the NGV for more than thirty years, recounts that he has ushered countless nervous paramours to the painting over the decades, who have decided upon it as a sumptuous backdrop for their marriage proposals.[24]

GLYN PHILPOT: *OEDIPUS*. In 1932, the NGV acquired a work by Glyn Philpot, something quite remarkable for the times. Philpot was a prominent Edwardian portraitist who was much in demand for his Old Master–style portraits. However, in his

late forties he had a spiritual crisis, which motivated him to leave England and go to the Weimar Republic, where he submerged himself in the avant-garde subcultures. This led to doubts about his work, which resulted in a radical change of style. In the early 1930s, he produced a group of homoerotic modern paintings, picturing his blond German boyfriend. From his exhibition of 1932, the NGV purchased *Oedipus*, 1931–32, which has since been interpreted as a self-portrait because the Sphinx is based upon Epstein's tomb for Oscar Wilde. The story ends sadly, as Ted Gott describes: 'Philpot was dropped like a hot potato by London society and the London art critics savaged him – both for the change to a modern style but also because of his outing as a homosexual. By coming out as a gay man, he lost his portraiture business overnight and went bankrupt. He died broken-hearted several years later, after having a heart attack from the stress'. After the NGV bought *Oedipus*, Philpot wrote a letter thanking the NGV for being the only place to have faith in him at such a dark time. 'I think that letter is heartbreaking', says Gott. 'The NGV supporting a contemporary artist at a difficult time, and Philpot writing a letter like that, is a terrifically sad and fascinating story.'[25]

(previous)
Glyn Warren Philpot
Oedipus 1931–1932
oil on canvas
81.1 x 59.9 cm
Felton Bequest, 1932

(below)
Rembrandt Harmensz van Rijn
Two old men disputing 1628
oil on wood panel
72.4 x 59.7 cm
Felton Bequest, 1936

BERNARD HALL GOES TO EUROPE AGAIN: 'MOST IMPORTANT DISCOVERY'. For decades Bernard Hall had been lobbying for the role of Felton Advisor. He was convinced that he would do a better job than the European advisors and he deeply desired the opportunity: 'Nothing would please me better than to take up again the work I had a taste of twenty-four years ago', he wrote to the Trustees in 1928.[26] After twenty-eight years of campaigning, his wish was granted. However, when he arrived in London in 1934, he found it had vastly changed. The treasures he had envisaged scooping up for the NGV were not forthcoming. After a few months, he wrote back to the Trustees: 'There aren't any – I believe – We are too late – & Kings' ransomes would be required'.[27] Nevertheless, he managed to hunt down some notable acquisitions, including Luca Giordano's *St Sebastian being cured by Irene*, c.1653; Francesco Guardi's *The lock at Dolo on the Brenta: Capriccio*, c.1780; an exuberant *Flowerpiece*, 1811, by the Dutch artist Jean-François van Dael; and a fine portrait of the bespectacled *John Guthrie of Carbeth*, c.1815, by Henry Raeburn. His most important discovery, however, was in Amsterdam, where he found Rembrandt's *Two old men disputing*, 1628, in the gallery of Messrs Hoogendijk. On 4 August 1934, a cable was sent to the Felton Bequests Committee: 'Most important discovery', followed a few days later with the urgent: 'Must be now or never'.[28] After much prevarication – caused by anxiety about the painting's authenticity – the NGV accepted his recommendation.

The artist George Bell, who was living in London at the time, recounted how he had seen Hall there, and that he seemed 'lonely and depressed, and longing to return home'.[29] Bell had invited him to dinner but he failed to attend, which Bell later learnt was because Hall had died after a bout of severe pneumonia. Despite the uncertainty surrounding its provenance, subsequent scholarship has confirmed *Two old men disputing* to be an extraordinary early work by Rembrandt, making it a memorable find and a fitting commemoration of Hall's forty-three years as Director of the NGV.

J. S. MACDONALD: 'A FIGHTABLE DISPOSITION'.

Early in 1936, James Stuart MacDonald was named as the director of the NGV, a controversial appointment. MacDonald had trained at the Gallery School but gave up painting in the early 1920s to become an art critic. He held a deeply nostalgic view of Australia, the apotheosis of which he saw in the pastoral imagery of Streeton, which represented for him 'the way in which life should be lived in Australia, with the maximum of flocks and the minimum of factories'.[30] He revered the traditional lineage of European art, subscribed to many of the values held dear in the art academies and was violently opposed to all forms of modern art. He came to the NGV after holding the position of Director of the

J. S. MacDonald
Self-portrait 1922
lithograph
40.2 x 37.5 cm (plate);
51.0 x 46.5 cm irreg. (sheet)
Purchased, 1922

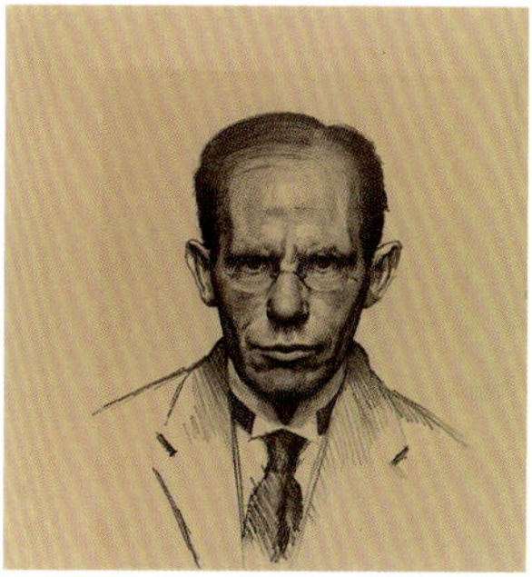

National Art Gallery of New South Wales since 1928, where he had built a reputation as a highly combative, intemperate man. Percival Serle later described him as 'a likeable man with some charm, little tact, [and] a fightable disposition when roused'.[31] MacDonald's directorship at the NGV was to be a troubled one. It also started most inauspiciously: the Trustees had selected another candidate for the position – the architect Hardy Wilson – but the government had favoured MacDonald, the Trustees' second candidate, and overrode the Trustees' recommendation. Many Trustees were displeased by the appointment; Professor Wood Jones, for instance, resigned immediately. MacDonald immediately – and irrevocably – locked antlers with Sir Keith Murdoch, the energetic Trustee and great protagonist of modern art.

THE BATTLE FOR MODERNISM. The battlelines over modern art started to emerge within the NGV early in the 1930s. An early upset was caused in 1932 when Sam Atyeo, Bernard Hall's best student at the Gallery School, unexpectedly submitted to the competition for the travelling scholarship a painting of nudes in the modern style. Hall was disgusted by the traitor within the ranks, and refused to hang the work. Atyeo responded by exhibiting it in the window of a Collins Street shop where, legend has it, it stopped traffic.

By the mid 1930s, sparks were truly flying between the moderns and the conservatives. Two rival sides emerged: the conservative Australian Academy of Art, formed in 1937, and the Contemporary Art Society, formed in 1938. The Australian Academy of Art was a (belated) attempt to create a traditional academy for Australia, and its 'prime mover' was the then Attorney-General, Robert Gordon Menzies. 'I feel definitely that some authority and body should be formed here as in other countries', he said. 'Every great country has its academy. They have set certain standards of art and have served a great purpose in raising the standards of public taste ... Great art speaks a language which every intelligent person can

(opposite above)
James Gleeson
We inhabit the corrosive littoral of habit 1940
oil on canvas
40.7 x 51.3 cm
Anonymous gift, 1941

(opposite below)
Eric Thake
Salvation from the evils of earthly existence 1940
oil on cardboard
41.8 x 52.2 cm
Anonymous gift, 1941

*

'I don't think we should have modern art in the gallery at all'

understand. The people who call themselves modernists today talk a different language.'[32] Other diehard members of the Academy included notorious table-thumpers Max Meldrum and J. S. MacDonald. The NGV's Dirërctor was very clear where the boundaries were at the NGV: 'I don't think we should have modern art in the gallery at all. It is not liked by the art galleries of Australia'.[33] The Australian Academy of Art's inaugural exhibition was held at the NGV in 1939.

The Contemporary Art Society emerged in 1938 in opposition to the Academy. The Society had grown out of earlier incarnations of contemporary art groups established in the city, such as the Contemporary Group of Melbourne initiated by George Bell in 1932. Bell was a powerful force in the development of modern art in Australia. He had trained under Bernard Hall at the Gallery School but, particularly after his extensive study trips in Europe and America, became a true convert to modernity. In 1932, he had established a modern art school in Melbourne, in collaboration with the younger painters Arnold Shore and William 'Jock' Frater, which became an important wellspring for the new breed of modern artist. The Contemporary Group of Melbourne held its first exhibition in August 1932, and included artists such as Bell, Frater, Shore, Daryl Lindsay, Eric Thake and Ada May Plante. Writing in the *Argus*, Streeton dismissed the 'misshapen representations of humanity, flowers, trees and architecture' as painting 'done just to attract attention'.[34] However, Streeton's contemporary, the seventy-eight-year-old Blamire Young, rose to the defence of the new guard: 'Under the drug of academicism we have perhaps painted with the mindlessness of the sleep-walker, but that is over. One does not necessarily go out and weep because our beliefs have been betrayed ... Forward the rebels!'[35] Bell was also the instigator behind an early exhibition of contemporary art held at the NGV in October 1937. For the *Loan Exhibition of Works of Modern Art by Artists Outside Australia* Bell assembled fifty-two privately owned works of art, including works by Picasso and van Gogh, to create an exhibition that further kindled interest in contemporary art.

At their first meeting of the Contemporary Art Society (CAS), held on 13 July 1938, George Bell was elected president; Rupert Bunny, artist vice president; John Reed, a lawyer, lay vice president; and Adrian Lawlor, secretary. Their constitution stated that their aim was to support art forms that were 'original and creative or which strive to give expression to progressive contemporary thought and life as opposed to work which is reactionary or retrogressive, including work which has no other aim than representation'.[36] The group represented contemporary artists from diverse alignments including social realists such as Yosl Bergner, classical post-impressionists such as George Bell and figurative expressionists such as Sidney Nolan. The CAS also held an exhibition at the NGV in June 1939, which was formally opened by Mr Justice Evatt of the High Court of Australia, a vocal advocate for modern art in Australia. It featured works by Sidney Nolan, Noel Counihan, Albert Tucker, Sali Herman, James Gleeson and Russell Drysdale, among others.

At the CAS's exhibition of 1940, artists James Gleeson and Eric Thake were jointly awarded the prize for the best work of art 'showing new expression of thought in art'. 'Gleeson's *We inhabit the corrosive littoral of habit*, 1940, and Thake's *Salvation from the evils of earthly existence*, 1940, are two of the very earliest surrealist paintings made in Australia,' states Kirsty Grant, Senior Curator of Australian Art, 'and there was great controversy around them. They were gifted to the NGV by an anonymous donor. The Trustees accepted them but then refused to exhibit them, contravening the usual custom for works presented as gifts. They were duly banished to the Print Room. That was a curious way for works to come into the collection'.[37]

MODERN ART: 'DEGENERATES AND PERVERTS'. Sir Keith Murdoch was appointed President of the Library Board in September 1939 and maintained a strong focus on the activities of the NGV. He also held 'almost missionary leanings' in his desire to promote modern art.[38] This manifested itself in a highly significant event of 1939: the *Exhibition of French and British Modern Art*, which brought to Australia two hundred works by artists such as Cézanne, Léger, Matisse, Modigliani, Derain, Chagall, Braque, Ernst and Picasso. Murdoch financed it through his newspaper, *The Herald*, and sent his art critic, Basil Burdett, to Europe to assemble works for the exhibition. It was housed in the Melbourne Town Hall (in recognition that any attempts to hold it at the NGV would have been over MacDonald's dead body). The public flocked to it – more than 40,000 people attended in the first few weeks – and it caused a good deal of controversy, with Salvador Dalí's *L'homme fleur* in particular inspiring conservatives to fulminate over its confusing and corrupting imagery. The painting received a more enthusiastic welcome when it returned to Melbourne in 2009 for *Salvador Dalí: Liquid Desire*, the NGV's Dalí retrospective.

The importance of the *Herald* exhibition, as art historian Bernard Smith observed, is 'difficult to exaggerate'. For the first time Australians could view an extensive presentation of avant-garde French and English works of art. This was a defining moment in Australian

*

'There is no doubt that the great majority of the work called "modern" is the product of degenerates and perverts'

art history; 'it ended', as Bernard Smith wrote, 'the dominance of the Royal Academy of London as the official arbiter of pictorial values in Australia', and contributed strongly to 'the collapse of the authority of the academic establishment in art in Australia'.[39]

Nine works were recommended for purchase by the NGV, including works by van Gogh, Braque, Utrillo and Picasso. On reading the recommendation, MacDonald's bile rose: 'They are exceedingly wretched paintings ... putrid meat ... There is no doubt that the great majority of the work called "modern" is the product of degenerates and perverts ... As owners of a great van Eyck, if we take a part by refusing to pollute our gallery with this filth we shall render a service to Art'.[40] Regardless, two works were selected by the Trustees: *Head of a man* by Vincent van Gogh (now reattributed), 1886, and Félix Vallotton's *Point du Jour, banks of the Seine*, 1901. André Derain's *Roses in blue jug*, 1920s, was also acquired through public subscription. Notwithstanding these relatively timid purchases, the NGV's failure to acquire any of the truly radical works in the exhibition remains one of the Gallery's most notorious missed opportunities.

(above)
The Netherlands / France
Head of a man
(Tête d'homme) 1880s
oil on canvas
33.0 x 40.0 cm
Felton Bequest, 1940

(opposite)
John Constable
Clouds 1822
oil on paper on cardboard
30.0 x 48.8 cm
Felton Bequest, 1938

SIR SYDNEY COCKERELL: PREVENTING 'MUSEUM-HEADACHE'. In late 1936, a few months after J. S. MacDonald was appointed, Sir Sydney Cockerell, Director of the Fitzwilliam Museum at the University of Cambridge, was appointed Felton Advisor. Cockerell arrived in Melbourne in December 1936 to meet with the NGV Trustees, accompanied by his daughter Katherine and two of her friends. A local newspaper started a column titled 'Sydney day by day' to report on their adventures, which, Cockerell recorded, included everything 'from cricket (Bradman making 270) to Koala bears'.[41]

Sir Sydney gave his opinion of the NGV most unabashedly: 'It was a shocking place ... Quite half the Committee (which was far too large) were totally ignorant – just people who were rich or important ... I was disagreeable and outspoken. But it would need the strength of Hitler ... to get anything done'.[42] Although not formally part of his Felton duties, he wrote a paper entitled the *Report on the National Gallery of Victoria, with suggestions for its rearrangement*, in which he put forward a plan for the modernisation of the NGV: 'The National Gallery of Victoria consists of twelve rooms of various sizes. The most imposing of these rooms were built in the last century, when Museums were generally regarded as dull store-houses. In those days dissimilar and inadequately labelled objects were often jumbled together: pictures were massed on the walls in bewildering confusion or deployed in the endless processions that still weary us in the older galleries of Europe. Little attempt was made to rouse the jaded visitor by attractive settings and explanatory descriptions. Dust was allowed to gather in the cases ... Boredom and museum-headache were the familiar results. We are no longer so shortsighted. The discovery having been reached that museums are made for man and not man for museums, it follows that they must be as attractive, informing, convenient and hygienic as possible ... The aim must be to welcome the newcomer, to stimulate his sense of beauty, and to induce him to come again and again'.[43] Many of his recommendations were carried out over the following decades.

While he was Felton Advisor, Cockerell bought the smart van Dyck portrait, *Philip Herbert, 4th Earl of Pembroke*, c.1634; Constable's wonderfully ethereal *Clouds*, 1822; a full-length portrait by Augustus John of Chaloner Dowdall in his role as Lord Mayor of Liverpool, complete with sword-bearer, 1909; and, from Belgium and in excellent condition, an intricate *Carved retable of the Passion of Christ*, c.1511–20. Cockerell also acquired the NGV's only paintings by Edgar Degas, *Portrait of a woman*, c.1876–80, and Paul Cézanne, *The uphill road*, 1881, the last acquired after seemingly endless knock-backs to his many other recommendations of works by the artist.

THE ART MUSEUM AND THE BEQUEST OF HOWARD SPENSLEY. In 1933, Percival Serle was made Curator of the Art Museum, a one day per week role in which he advised on the purchase of decorative arts. 'With the Felton Bequest behind us,' he wrote in December 1935, 'we could have a delightful miniature Victoria and Albert Museum'.[44] Serle found a willing advocate for the Decorative Arts collection in Sir Sydney Cockerell, and they worked closely together on the development of the collection, calling on the expertise of Bernard Rackham of the Victoria and Albert Museum with regards to European works, and Robert Hobson of the British Museum on Chinese ceramics. A strong collection of European pottery and porcelain was assembled, which was further enhanced through the gift of the Colin Templeton Collection of English porcelain in 1942. A new development at the NGV in 1938 was the opening of the new Egyptian Room. Cockerell had visited Egypt as part of his Felton duties and placed importance on the acquisition of Egyptian works, as did A. S. Kenyon, the NGV's Honorary Ethnologist, who bought seven striking mummy portraits, dating from 150 BC to 200 AD, when he was in New York in 1939.

An important development in 1938 was the Howard Spensley Bequest, a stunning gift comprising hundreds of items of European ceramics, silverware, paintings, drawings, bronzes, books and oriental works. Howard Spensley's father had emigrated to Australia in 1859 and achieved success as a lawyer and politician. In time, the family moved back to England, where Howard Spensley used some of his father's fortune to develop his remarkable collection of works of art. He evidently regarded Australia fondly, attested by his decision to bequeath his collection to the Government of Victoria, which then placed it into the care of the NGV. Standout works from his bequest include a marvellous sculpture by Rodin, *The man with a broken nose*, 1863–72; a suite of Old Master drawings, some of which are highly important; and a strong holding of bronzes from the Renaissance, which launched a new collecting focus for Melbourne.

HERBERT WADE KENT: 'VERY REFINED TASTES'. Herbert Wade Kent acquired his exquisite collection of Chinese ceramics over the thirty years that he worked for the shipping firm Butterfield and Swire. His experience in China enabled him to develop a fine understanding of Chinese connoisseurship and the unassuming, elegant taste of the Chinese scholars. 'As the years go by, my respect for him becomes greater', says Mae Anna Pang, Senior Curator of Asian Art. 'He had very refined tastes. In those days, many people were only interested in export wares but Kent was interested in presenting the Chinese taste. He built a very fine collection of Chinese ceramics, which reflected his taste for pure form and colour.'[45] In 1938, Kent presented his collection of ceramics and also became the NGV's first Curator of Oriental Art in an honorary capacity. Over the years, he also contributed to the NGV as an advisor for the Felton Bequest, going on buying trips with both Bernard Hall and Sir Keith Murdoch. Kent was particularly fond of one piece in his collection: an elegant Song vase designed to hold plum blossoms in the spring. While alive he could not part with it. During his funeral service, his wife had it placed on his coffin and later presented it to the NGV. Kent's ashes were scattered in the Pacific Ocean, midway between Australia and China.

AT THE NGV: 'TEEMING ORNAMENT' BANISHED. In 1937, an extensive reframing project was initiated; the original Victorian gilt frames were removed from the Australian paintings in the collection and replaced with the more streamlined 'Whistler frame' – a simple, matte gold construction modelled on a frame in the Art Gallery of New South Wales. Following a preview of eight paintings in their new standardised frames in 1941, the *Herald* reported: 'All of them gain surprisingly from the change. The beach scene by Rupert Bunny and the landscape by Frederick McCubbin ... look twice the pictures they did ... The lines are straight and simple, and there is none of the teeming ornament which makes some other frames in the Gallery so disturbing'.[46]

EGYPT
(Philadelphia / er-Rubayat)
Mummy portrait 170 AD-190 AD,
Roman Period
wood, pigment
35.8 x 13.2 x 1.0 cm
Felton Bequest, 1940

*

'You know, you and I are the only blokes here who would be able to cope with a mob of bullocks'

'Daryl Lindsay, the then Director of the NGV, said that he could always "pick the Phar Lap devotees by the purposeful approach and the look in their eyes."'

Eric Thake
Gallery Director or
This way to Phar Lap 1953
Linocut
20.6 x 15.2cm (image and sheet)
Purchased, 1964

From 1940 it is possible to discern the growing influence of Daryl Lindsay. Lindsay had started on 5 February 1940 as the Keeper of the Prints and Curator of the Art Museum and exerted much influence, particularly when he was made acting director for parts of 1940 when MacDonald fell ill. Lindsay carried on the reframing project, and also undertook extensive renovations. Many of these changes aligned with Cockerell's recommendations, such as the decision to create a series of bays in the McArthur and La Trobe galleries in order to give them, as described in the 1940 *Annual Report*, 'a more intimate appearance' and make them 'more adaptable for the segregation of various schools of art'.[47]

MacDonald's five-year contract ended in late 1940 and the Trustees, now with Murdoch as Chairman, did not reappoint him for another term. He was deeply angered: 'I know my ideas, particularly on some aspects of modern art, have not always met with approval, but I have tried to fill my position as best I could. I intend to make some sort of protest'.[48]

DARYL LINDSAY: 'ABLE TO COPE WITH A MOB OF BULLOCKS'. Daryl Lindsay was officially appointed Director in March 1941. Yet Sir Keith Murdoch had engineered the plan some time earlier, as Lindsay recounted in his autobiography: 'Over dinner one night, after beating about the bush, he asked me if I would consider coming on the staff and helping him pull the place together. The post of Keeper of the Prints and Curator of the Art Museum was vacant and the Directorship would be open two years later. The first would lead to the other ...'[49]

Lindsay hailed from an infamous artistic family – his older siblings included the well-known artists and writers Percy, Lionel, Norman and Ruby – yet as a young man he had decided upon a career as a jackaroo. (Years later, at an arts function, Lindsay allegedly said to Russell Drysdale, also a man of the country: 'You know, you and I are the only blokes here who would be able to cope with a mob of bullocks'.)[50] Lindsay's art career was launched almost accidentally during the First World War, when a colonel familiar with his family background said to him, 'You can draw, can't you?' and sent Lindsay to work at the facial restoration unit at Queen's Hospital. There he drew medical diagrams to help trainee surgeons. ('How was I going to translate what looked like a mess of flesh and blood into a diagram that a student could understand?' wrote Lindsay.)[51] While in this service he met Henry Tonks: 'I was struggling with a drawing and became aware of being over-looked by a tall hatchet-faced man, who looked like a cross between a Roman emperor and a wedge-tailed eagle. He asked me what I was doing and I said: "Trying to draw". He said: "I'm glad you said 'trying' which is the best that can be said of it; but I think I may be able to help you"'. Tonks was Professor at the Slade School in London and Lindsay became his student. Lindsay's artistic interests were ignited: 'Slade opened up a new world to me'.[52]

During his time in London, Lindsay also worked with Frank Rinder, Sir Charles Holmes and Randall Davies on Felton business, and enjoyed a close friendship with Gallery Trustee Sir Baldwin Spencer: 'Baldwin Spencer would sometimes come to dinner and go whistling round the house looking at pictures. He was one of the great collectors of the day, spending in his enthusiasm more than he could afford – a source of worry to Lady Spencer. With his own house full to overflowing, he would bring a picture or drawing round for me to hide away and look after'.[53] Later, Lindsay also became close to contemporary artist George Bell. The two shared opinions on art: 'We had much in common, sharing the same views on painting and the rather parochial attitude to art in Australia'.[54]

THE SECOND WORLD WAR: 'FRUITCAKES FROM THE DIRECTOR'S WIFE'. War had been declared on 3 September 1939. The NGV's ceiling was blacked out as an air raid precaution and the most precious works of art were evacuated to regional areas for safekeeping, sometimes stored within the sturdy confines of gaols. The works imported by Murdoch for his *Exhibition of French and British Modern Art* were stranded in Australia, and Lindsay took the opportunity to re-exhibit some at the NGV in 1941. By 1942, all resources were diverted towards the war effort. The staff were so depleted that all institutions within the State Library precinct were closed until 12.30 p.m. each day and the NGV did not open on Sundays. Lindsay wrote of the time: 'During the war years I had practically no staff. My wife came in three days a week to help me and among many other things dealt with ... the "Cock Eyed Mail"' – their term for the weird and wonderful requests that sometimes made their way to the NGV.[55]

In Europe, meanwhile, a Rembrandt etching, *The three crosses*, 1653, bought by the NGV in 1940 was lost 'as the result of enemy action in transit'.[56] Cockerell had ceased to advise for the NGV in 1939 and his duties were taken on by a series of consultants working for the National Art Collections Fund in London. Lindsay's wife, Joan, won hearts and some good works of art for Melbourne by sending fruitcakes over to the consultants. They were rare treats for those experiencing the privations of wartime rationing. 'That's when some of the most important items in the historic and antique furniture collection came to the NGV', states Terence Lane. 'These things often came in pairs from great houses in Europe, where whole suites of furniture were being broken up and coming onto the market. That's how we acquired the Grendey Daybed, c.1735–40, and Glemham Hall settee, c.1710–25. The advisors had connections; the V&A would choose one of the pair and the other would be sent to Melbourne. So, you know, fruitcakes from the director's wife – the art of influence.'[57]

MODERNISM WINS. Lindsay found his new job a challenge: 'The Gallery when I went there was in a deplorable condition – dark and dingy – black funereal showcases – dun coloured walls and in general appearance more like a morgue than an inviting place for the public to visit'.[58] He also struggled with the stifling bureaucracy of the public service, saying (with tongue firmly in cheek): 'Up till then I had led a moderately decent life, but faced with the frustrations and waste of time, I threw decency to the winds and embarked on a life of petty crime to gain my own ends'.[59] His 'chief' in the public service, Victorian Under-Secretary Laurie Chapman, fondly described his underling as 'Lindsay, one of my men who rings me up for my advice on something or other after he has done what he wanted to do'.[60]

In great contrast to the preceding regime, Lindsay and Murdoch enjoyed a close alliance. 'Had it not been for Murdoch's Scottish tenacity of purpose, understanding of me and adroitness in handling meetings, I would have thrown in the towel', stated Lindsay.[61] Their alliance became an unstoppable force in the battle for modernism. Together they dragged the NGV – sometimes with conservatives such as Max Meldrum and R. D. Elliott kicking and screaming behind them – into the twentieth century. Lindsay's directorship and Murdoch's chairmanship represent an historic moment in which the NGV began to shed its colonial identity to enter the modern age. Lindsay had studied modern museum administration in Europe and America and, with Murdoch's backing, he began to introduce many progressive new ideas to the NGV: 'Surely few can have brought about such profound and astonishing changes during their tenure', noted Felton Advisor John McDonnell.[62] Lindsay paid much attention to creating dynamic museum displays – he had 'a genius for display', noted John Medley – and was much celebrated for his curatorial 'eye': 'He has a great gift for hanging pictures so that they will appear at their best', wrote Percival Serle.[63] Over time, the crowded salon hang of the old European tradition, the default mode of installation during the colonial age, was replaced by the sparser hang practised by modern museums across America and Europe. Joan Lindsay also sometimes provided floral displays, as was the custom in American museums.

Hugh Ramsay Loan Exhibition,
La Trobe Gallery, National Gallery
of Victoria, March–April 1943

Across his fifteen years as director, Lindsay bought key works from all periods of Australian art. He broadened the focus of the NGV's historical collecting policy and acquired strong works such as Conrad Martens's *Elizabeth Bay and Elizabeth Bay House*, 1839; Robert Dowling's *Tasmanian Aborigines*, 1856–57; John Russell's *Dr William Maloney*, 1887; and Clara Southern's *An old bee farm*, c.1900. Works of art were often acquired from the many retrospective exhibitions mounted by Lindsay, including John Longstaff (1942), Hugh Ramsay (1943), Arthur Streeton (1944), Rupert Bunny (1946), Tom Roberts (1948), E. Phillips Fox (1949) and Frederick McCubbin (1955). Lindsay made catching up on the representation of Roberts, who had been neglected by Bernard Hall in Roberts's lifetime, a priority.

The Murdoch and Lindsay regime also ended the NGV's opposition to collecting contemporary art. The annual list of contemporary acquisitions made was usually long and broad and brilliant, peppered with names such as William Dobell, William Frater, Eric Thake, Jeffrey Smart, Yosl Bergner, Russell Drysdale, George Bell, Frank Hinder, Margaret Preston, Edward Heffernan, Margaret Olley, Clifton Pugh, Ian Fairweather, Arthur Boyd, Sidney Nolan and Roger Kemp. While in Europe on a research trip, Lindsay also bought the NGV's outstanding Florentine *Profile portrait of a lady*, c.1475.

A notable characteristic of Lindsay's ethos was his interest in Indigenous art. He purchased the NGV's first Indigenous works of art in 1946 – two watercolours by Edwin Pareroultja – and also firmly envisaged a role for Indigenous works in the art gallery, a distinct break from museum tradition. In 1952 he wrote to the Minister for the Interior requesting the loan of twenty-five Aboriginal bark drawings for display: 'Although in the past the majority of these have been collected by Natural History Museums for

ethnological purposes, it has long been my view that their artistic merit is such that a number of them should be shown in Art Galleries throughout Australia'.[64] The Minister responded to his request by presenting eight bark paintings: five from Yirrkala and three from Oenpelli. 'This was a progressive outlook', states Judith Ryan, Senior Curator of Indigenous Art. 'Indigenous work was not yet accepted as art. Prior to the referendum in 1967, Indigenous people were not even counted in the census. Why, then, would what they were making be considered art? The belief was that it belonged in an ethnographic museum, not an art museum'.[65]

A less admired aspect of Lindsay's directorship was his extensive – and now deeply regretted – program of de-accessioning works of art deemed redundant or, in Lindsay's words: 'not "surplus" pictures, but, actually, works which are not worth hanging on our walls'.[66] Many paintings, sculptures and plaster casts, mostly from the 'sentimental' period of the late nineteenth century, were deemed of 'no aesthetic value' and ignobly disposed of at various auctions conducted by Leonard Joel.[67] A *Bulletin* reporter who attended the first auction in 1941 said of the disposed works: 'Now they are as dead and unpalatable to the taste of the public as last week's dish of boarding house mutton. The only person who seemed to want them was a little priest from the New Norcia (W.A.) mission, who bought them by the dozen'.[68] The 'little priest' acquired several works for his monastery – many of which reflected religious themes – and some of the nineteenth century frames. Years later, when the NGV's ethos had changed once again and a considered program was underway to locate the old frames and reunite them with their original paintings, the NGV was able to retrieve seven of the original frames from the monastery.

A NEW HOME FOR THE NGV (BUT SIR KEITH MURDOCH SENT PACKING). Sir David Rivett, Library Trustee and eminent scientist with CSIRO, had urged his fellow trustees to consider long-range plans for the State Library and the four institutions crammed within it. A Post-War Development Committee was convened, consisting of three leading architects: Percy Everett, Leighton Irwin and John Scarborough. Their report concluded that 'the four Institutions cannot be housed on the one site' and 'favoured the suggestion that the Art Gallery, including the Art Schools, should be moved to another site, preferably Wirth's Park', on the south side of the Yarra River on St Kilda Road.[69] The report was sent to the Premier and its plans adopted. In 1944, the Trustees received the pleasing notification that Wirth's Park had been reserved for a new Combined Art Centre building. Dame Elisabeth Murdoch recalled the day that Sir Keith and others secured the site after a day of discussions with the Premier: 'It was 1944 and I had been fighting bushfires [at Cruden Farm, Langwarrin] all day when he arrived in a very jolly mood. The house was crowded with refugees from around the district who had lost their homes and I was on the roof fire-spotting. He wanted to continue celebrating his success – but I sent him packing'.[70]

*

'I had been fighting bushfires all day when he arrived in a very jolly mood ... he wanted to continue celebrating his success – but I sent him packing'

Also in 1944, and again through formidable petitioning by Sir Keith Murdoch, legislation was introduced that dissolved the single body of Library Trustees to create four separate boards of management. Through this mechanism, the NGV formally separated from the State Library of Victoria and Museum of Victoria, and the NGV Council of Trustees was inaugurated. This was an important development that enabled the NGV to assemble a board with skills appropriate to its field. It discontinued the approval process that had led Lindsay to exclaim incredulously: 'Library Trustees, Technological and Natural History Trustees, voting on pictures!'[71]

The first Board of Trustees comprised Sir Keith Murdoch (President and Chairman), John Medley (Vice-President), H. W. Kent (Treasurer), R. D. Elliott, Allan Henderson and Napier Waller, the latter in the role of Artist Trustee, a position that had been – and soon would be again – filled by Max Meldrum. Acrimony between Sir Keith Murdoch and R. D. Elliott, who enjoyed a close alliance with Max Meldrum, soon increased and the two newspapermen became bitter opponents (often using their press outlets

(opposite left)
Italy
Profile portrait of a lady c.1475
tempera and oil on poplar panel
38.0 x 25.0 cm (image)
40.0 x 26.5 cm (panel)
Felton Bequest, 1946

(opposite right)
Edwin Pareroultja
Red wall, Orminston Gorge 1946
watercolour over pencil on paper
20.4 x 37.6 cm
Purchased 1946

to fling mud at each other). Lindsay recounted: 'During one of these battles of wits, Jack Medley, who was sitting with his head in his hands and who had a witty flair for verse, passed me a note across the table':

> Birds in their little nest agree,
> But not the Gallery Trustee,
> Whose main ambition it appears
> Is setting colleagues by the ears.
> But when Death dims our Chairman's eye,
> Be the blow quick or be it tardy,
> I do not think that he will die
> Like Nelson, crying kiss me R. D.[72]

DR URSULA HOFF: 'AN ART HISTORIAN OF GREAT CALIBRE'. The Prints and Drawings Room opened in 1942, a study room modelled on the British Museum. Ever since, it has been an extraordinary research facility – the appointments book a great testimony to the extensive network of artists and teachers who have frequented it. A year later, in 1943, Dr Ursula Hoff started as Keeper of Prints and Drawings, the first professionally trained art historian to work at the NGV. Hoff was, wrote Lindsay, 'a brilliant scholar with a European reputation', who had trained with eminent scholar Dr Erwin Panofsky and completed a PhD on Rembrandt before fleeing Europe as part of the Jewish diaspora created by the Second World War.[73] Her discipline was legendary and her influence profound; she was, says Cathy Leahy, the catalyst for 'a cultural shift within the institution'.[74] She brought high standards of scholarship – she was 'first and foremost, an art historian of great calibre, an intellectual and a scholar'[75] – and was a formidable influence in the emergence of a culture of art history in Melbourne: 'there is a sense', remarked Gerard Vaughan at her memorial service held at the NGV in 2005, in which 'she has formed us all'.[76] Hoff was made Assistant Director in 1968, and also served as London advisor to the Felton Bequest from 1975 to 1983. She was a critical force behind the *National Gallery Quarterly Bulletin*, which Lindsay had initiated in 1945 and which is still published today with the title *Art Journal of the National Gallery of Victoria*. Over the years, Dr Hoff wrote many scholarly articles and commissioned a venerable list of writers, and was sometimes assisted by Joan Lindsay, an accomplished writer herself, well known for penning the novel *Picnic at Hanging Rock*. Dr Hoff's work in the Department of Prints and Drawings has been continued by Sonia Dean, Irena Zdanowicz and Cathy Leahy.

THE NGV ON THE MEDIAN STRIP IN CAMPERDOWN. The National Gallery Society of Victoria was established in 1947: 'After the war I felt it would be a good idea to form a society to help publicise the Gallery', wrote Lindsay. 'There were no funds for such a purpose so, with the Trustees' approval, I approached my friends, Norman Myer, Essington Lewis, and bankers and newspaper editors who between them contributed £1000 to start it off. Murdoch at his own expense gave a large evening party to some 400 people to launch the scheme, which proved a great success'.[77] A great success indeed: funds raised that first evening amounted to £2000, and the Gallery Society continues today, now known as NGV Members, as an active group of supporters who raise the funds and the profile of the NGV. The Society's aims, outlined at the inaugural meeting in 1947, were expressed as a desire to stimulate and sustain public interest in the NGV; to extend its influence in the community; and to enhance its cultural significance. Some of the first funds raised by the National Gallery Society were used to support Arnold Shore in the role of Voluntary Guide Lecturer, a position he fulfilled from 1948 to 1958. Today, in 2011, NGV Members has 50,000 participants.

Over the course of his tenure, Lindsay steadily built up his staff: Robert Haines started in the new role of Assistant Director in 1947 and Gordon Thomson, seconded from the Education Department, became an Education Officer in 1949, and would, a decade later, become Deputy Director. In 1949, the artist Harley Griffiths was sent abroad to learn conservation techniques. On his return, Lindsay

*

'There is a sense', remarked Gerard Vaughan, in which 'she has formed us all'

Dr Ursula Hoff

supported the formation of a research laboratory and, in 1952, Griffiths was instituted as part-time conservator, a role he would fulfil until 1974. Gilbert Docking started as an Education Officer in 1952 and trundled around the Victorian countryside in the NGV's new truck. Kirsty Grant recalls hearing the following story: 'It was Gil's job to go around, set up the exhibition, and give a talk. Once, when they were in Camperdown, the venue they were allocated was so far out of town that Gil figured no one would come. So, he checked the weather report, and then installed the exhibition on the median strip of the main street in Camperdown. It was only there for a day but everybody came to see it'.[78] Lindsay and Murdoch also devised the Chair of Fine Arts at the University of Melbourne. Murdoch stumped up £40,000 from *The Herald* to sponsor the role, which was designed to foster art scholarship and Murdoch's dearly held aim to get art 'working more strongly amongst us'.[79]

A hullabaloo was caused in 1948 by the *Henry Moore Exhibition of Sculpture and Drawings* held at the NGV. The *Argus* critic reported that, to 'the great majority' of the public, Moore's sculptures 'are ugly, meaningless things, and do not make sense'.[80] The Fashion and Textiles collection received some important windfalls: the Misses Butler presented a group of nineteenth-century costumes in 1948 and, in 1951, the costume collection of British painter Sir William Nicholson was presented to the NGV by his wife and daughter. Sir William had used the costumes as props for his painting work and among the thirty-eight costumes were five exquisite ball gowns designed by French couturier Jean-Philippe Worth. Worth had designed them for Sir William's mother-in-law but, when her husband died, she was required to put away such gay attire and adopt the black mourning costume appropriate to a widow.

AND THEN THERE WERE THREE ... GALLERY SCHOOLS. Charles Wheeler had been the Head of the Gallery School through the years of the Second World War. An ex-Gallery School student who had studied under McCubbin and Hall, he had been Drawing Master under McInnes and then moved up the ranks after McInnes's death in 1939. Wheeler resigned in October 1945, and William Dargie took the reins the following year, the first teacher in forty years who was not an ex-student. Dargie was another in a strong line of traditionalists to head the Gallery School. Yet despite his inherently conservative ethos, he made extensive changes to the curriculum, responding to feedback from students that they wanted more choice in their tuition. The Gallery School, which had been for so long the bastion of conservative painting methodology, was forced to adapt to a changed art world. The culture of the school had changed; after the war many ex-servicemen and -women entered the Gallery School under the Commonwealth Reconstruction Training Scheme, and they desired freedom and experimentation. To provide this diversity, two new teachers were appointed – Alan Sumner and Murray Griffin – and the school fragmented into three disparate 'schools'. The teachers felt this necessitated three separate end-of-year studio prizes adjudicated by three separate judging panels, a decision that Daryl Lindsay was at first reluctant to accept.

*

'He checked the weather report, and then installed the exhibition on the median strip'

SIR KENNETH CLARK AND A. J. L. MCDONNELL: 'A SMALL PICTURE OF THE GREATEST BEAUTY IN PERFECT CONDITION'. Lindsay ceased using the services of the National Art Collections Fund and returned to the old ways, instituting the appointment of a series of advisors for the Felton Bequest: he consulted the art dealership Bluetts for Chinese art, Harald Wright for prints, Sir Leigh Ashton and Ralph Edwards of the Victoria and Albert Museum for decorative arts and Sir Kenneth Clark for pictures. For Lindsay, 'the most important and far-reaching connection was with Sir

(above)
The NGV's truck – loading a touring exhibition c.1950s

(below)
Photograph of Harley Griffiths, artist and NGV restorer (1930s–1974) cleaning Gustave Doré's *Little Red Riding Hood*, c.1953

*

'We both feel it would be an ornament to the Gallery and a constant source of delight to its visitors'

Kenneth Clark, then Director of the National Gallery in London ... My relationship with Kenneth Clark is amongst my happiest memories and our collaboration over a period of years resulted in many splendid examples of old and modern masters being added to the Melbourne collection. Possibly the most erudite art scholar of the day, he is a man of impeccable taste with an unerring eye for the good thing'.[81] Clark visited Australia in 1949, during which he gave a public lecture – 'The Idea of a Great Gallery' – to a packed audience at the University of Melbourne. Clark resigned as Felton Advisor in 1951 to take on the Slade Professorship, but stayed on as principal consultant to the brilliant young Australian A. J. L. McDonnell. Together they secured a stunning collection of works, propelled along by a princely stockpile of Felton funds, accumulated during the wartime restriction on overseas expenditure.

The acquisition of Turner's *The Red Rigi*, 1842, was a brilliant start in 1947, followed shortly thereafter by Peter Paul Rubens's *Hercules and Antaeus*, c.1625–30, and Paolo Veronese's *Nobleman between Active and Contemplative life*, c.1575. Nicolas Poussin's *The Crossing of the Red Sea*, c.1634, was bought in 1948 on McDonnell's urging that it would be 'an endless source of inspiration' and 'command the continued attention of the public'.[82] A George Stubbs work was bought in 1949 thanks, it transpires, to Clark, who wrote to Lindsay: 'Pursuing our policy of buying minor English pictures, I have persuaded McDonnell to buy the Stubbs ... There is rather too much space round the central group, but the group itself is *marvellous*, and had a great influence on the Romantic Movement; Géricault actually did a copy of it'.[83]

Both McConnell and Clark became enamoured with Paolo Uccello's *St George slaying the dragon*, c.1430, and it was bought in 1949: 'An enchanting picture', wrote McDonnell. 'We both feel it would be an ornament to the Gallery and a constant source of delight to its visitors.'[84] El Greco's *Portrait of a cardinal*, c.1600–05, which was bought the following year, had similar power. McDonnell wrote: 'We

(above)
Master of the Stories of Helen
(studio of Antonio Vivarini)
The Garden of Love c.1465–70
oil, tempera and gold on wood panel
152.5 x 239.0 cm
Felton Bequest, 1948

(middle)
Nicolas Poussin
The Crossing of the Red Sea c.1634
oil on canvas
155.6 x 215.3 cm
Felton Bequest, 1948

(below)
George Stubbs
A lion attacking a horse c.1765
oil on canvas
69.0 x 100.1 cm
Felton Bequest, 1949

are both of the opinion that it is one of the most beautiful and sensitively painted portraits we know'.[85] Jacopo Amigoni's *Portrait group: The singer Farinelli and friends*, c.1750–52, acquired in 1950 was, for McDonnell, 'a picture of the greatest decorative charm' that he envisaged as 'a companion piece to the Tiepolo'.[86]

(above)
Balthus
Nude with cat 1949
oil on canvas
65.1 x 80.5 cm
Felton Bequest, 1952

(below)
Amedeo Modigliani
Portrait of the painter Manuel Humbert 1916
oil on canvas
100.2 x 65.5 cm
Felton Bequest, 1948

John Constable's *Study of a boat passing a lock*, c.1823–26, bought in 1951, had McDonnell in raptures – 'one of the most interesting and attractive pictures I am ever likely to be able to propose to your committee' – as did Simon Marmion's *The Virgin and Child*, c.1465–75, bought in 1954: 'A small picture of the greatest beauty in perfect condition', wrote McDonnell.[87] When Lindsay refocused the buying policy to enable contemporary works to be purchased, this reaped further great dividends for the NGV. Artists bought included Max Ernst, Jean Metzinger, Bernard Buffet, Paul Sérusier, Pierre Bonnard, Henri Matisse, Amedeo Modigliani, Walter Sickert, Duncan Grant, Paul Nash, Balthus and Francis Bacon.

MELBOURNE 1956: 'SOMETHING BIG WAS HAPPENING'.
The year 1956 was a defining one for Melbourne: 'I noticed', said new Director Eric Westbrook, 'that between coming in '55 for the interview to the job in 1956 that the city was beginning to realise something big was happening'. This 'something big' was partly connected to Melbourne hosting the Olympics. 'Once the foreign Olympic delegations arrived, there was a complete change', said Westbrook. 'Previously, Melbourne had had a kind of inferiority complex. It had been "Marvellous Melbourne" in the nineteenth century and then the Depression and two wars had absolutely knocked the stuffing out of it. They needed a lift and it gave them a lift.' This burst of energy had tremendous ramifications for the arts as well: 'There was a tremendous sense of euphoria', commented Westbrook; 'that same year we got the OK to go ahead with the new arts centre and new buildings'.[88] In 1956, Henry Bolte's new government proclaimed the *National Art Gallery and Cultural Centre Act* 1956, the first step in the process towards building a new NGV.

SIR THOMAS BARLOW'S DÜRER COLLECTION: 'A *FAIT ACCOMPLI*'. Another highly notable event of 1956 was the acquisition of the Barlow collection of works by Dürer. Sir Thomas Barlow was an industrialist from Manchester who, over a fifty-year period, built up an incomparable collection of work by Dürer, comprising 324 items including woodcuts, engravings, books and a solitary drawing. He developed it devotedly, upgrading works across the years until, as he wrote, 'it is safe to say that such a Dürer collection can never again be assembled ... I must therefore regard the collection, now, as a *fait accompli*'. When he decided to put it up for sale, he was adamant that it remain intact: 'I am most anxious it shall not be broken up, and there is no gallery to which I should more like it to go, than Melbourne's'.[89] Barlow had great affection for the NGV. He had visited in 1949 and was so delighted by his experience that he felt moved to write Daryl Lindsay a letter: 'I don't know why I should write to you but cannot forbear giving myself the pleasure of telling you how much I enjoyed my visit and how intense is the delight one feels when all against one's expectations one enters a gallery which so conspicuously displays an atmosphere of scholarship, judgement and intelligent buying'.[90] In 1956, his offer

(above left)
Francis Bacon
Study from the human body 1949
oil on canvas
147.0 x 134.2 cm
Purchased, 1953

(above right)
Bruno Benini
No title (Fashion illustration. Model Catherine Patchell, NGV)
(detail) 1956, printed 1998
gelatin silver photograph
40.5 x 50.4 cm; 44.0 x 52.6 cm; 50.9 x 61.1 cm
Purchased, 1998

to Melbourne was unanimously supported: Felton Advisor McDonnell called it 'the most important proposal' he would ever make, and Hoff, who was also central in the buying process, wrote of its undoubted importance and its ability to put the NGV 'among the great Dürer-owning public galleries of the world'.[91]

EVERARD STUDLEY MILLER BEQUEST: 'PORTRAITS OF PERSONS OF MERIT'. The year 1956 was also significant for the establishment of the Everard Studley Miller Bequest. Miller gifted £200,000 to the NGV, the largest bequest since Alfred Felton's in 1904. 'The terms of the bequest', wrote Sonia Dean, former Curator of Prints and Drawings, 'indicate that the donor was not so much interested in aesthetic matters but rather that his chief concern was to honour and perpetuate the memory of virtuous men and women of the past'.[92] Miller's bequest stipulated that the funds be used to purchase 'portraits, painted, sculpted or engraved prior to 1800, of persons of merit in history'.[93] Justice Sholl, also the NGV's Deputy Chairman, was asked to provide legal definitions for 'portraits' and 'persons of merit'. His report to the Trustees outlined that 'portrait' meant that the facial features of the individual must be represented, though not necessarily in full. The portrait must also be of a person of known historical character; therefore idealised likenesses, like Christ or the Buddha, would not be allowed. The definition of 'person of merit' was cause for more uncertainty: did, for instance, Madame de Pompadour, count? Could the mistress of a king really be a 'person of merit'? It provoked much discussion. However, once her 'merit' had been assured, François Boucher's delightful portrait was able to make its way into the collection. Miller's Bequest enabled the NGV to assemble a remarkable collection of portraits, with notable works including Peter Paul Rubens's *Louis XIII of France*, 1622; Nicolas de Largillierre's *Crown Prince Frederick Augustus of Saxony*, (who, incidentally, was the first owner of Tiepolo's *The Banquet of Cleopatra*, 1714–15); Thomas Gainsborough's *The Rt Hon. Charles Wolfran Cornwall*, 1785–86; and Johan Zoffany's *Elizabeth Farren as Hermione in The Winter's Tale*, c.1780.

LEONARD COX: *HUNDRED TREASURES*. Leonard Cox, the Melbourne neurologist and collector of Chinese ceramics, was one of the NGV's most ardent supporters. In 1947, he helped establish the Gallery Society; he was Chairman of the Gallery Trustees from 1957 to 1965; and Chairman of the committee that oversaw the building process from 1957 to 1964. In 1956, in recognition of his great knowledge of Chinese art, he was made Curator of Oriental Art (Honorary). His curatorship saw the collections of Japanese, Korean, Indian and South-East Asian works expand markedly. The new NGV building would also be a special time for the arts of Asia; as Mae Anna Pang commented, it 'presented a new focus on the visual arts of Asia ... [which] generated so much renewed interest and enthusiasm that there was a substantial increase in presentations and acquisitions'.[94]

(above)
Albrecht Dürer
Adam and Eve 1504
engraving
25.0 x 19.3 cm (image and sheet)
4th of 5 states
Felton Bequest, 1956

(below)
François Boucher
Madame de Pompadour 1754
pastel over sanguine and light
grey-blue washes
36.5 x 28.1 cm
Everard Studley Miller Bequest, 1965

Cox went on to write the indispensible history of the NGV – *The National Gallery of Victoria 1861 to 1968: A Search for a Collection* – published in 1970 and, in 1976, the NGV hosted *Hundred Treasures*, an exhibition of Cox's own collection, which he bequeathed to the NGV in 1976. Other notable honorary curators included Professor Dale Trendall, who had accepted the position of Curator of Greek and Roman Antiquities (Honorary) in 1957, and William Culican, who became Curator of Near Eastern Art (Honorary) in 1962.

ERIC WESTBROOK: 'A MARVELLOUS REMBRANDT AND ... A STUFFED RACEHORSE'. Eric Westbrook once commented: 'I think I may be the only man who has lectured on art from the turret of a tank'.[95] Education and open access to art were always critical to Westbrook's ethos – even, it seems, during wartime. His skills in this area would have been honed when Sir Kenneth Clark appointed him Chief Exhibitioner for the British Council, for which he managed a touring program of British art throughout Europe. At the NGV he was focused on the audience's experience, making a solid effort to redefine the general public's understanding of the art gallery from, he quipped, 'somewhere you went to keep out of the rain' to a place that generated real meaning and much excitement. 'My aim ... is simply to make art more accessible, and if I can promote a wider appreciation of all forms of culture, I'm not afraid of sticking my neck out.'[96]

'The Gallery absolutely shocked me', he said on arrival in 1956. 'For a start, it was stuck between the Library, which was constantly wishing to expand, and two museums. The storage was terrible. There were virtually no facilities for offices and administration, but then, as there were no staff, it hardly mattered.'[97] He also found the gallery experience confounding: 'You'd be looking at a marvellous Rembrandt or Tiepolo and then turn around and see a stuffed racehorse', said Westbrook. 'It was ridiculous.'[98] He also thought that the programming did not provide enough variety. In the past the galleries, said Westbrook, 'had permanent collections – and they damn well stayed permanent. If grandma took you as a child to see the paintings, you could come back in twenty-five years and find them all still there'.[99] Although the NGV had no dedicated temporary exhibition space he made space by taking down some of the permanent collection. He was also an advocate for cross-artform programs, such as holding music or performing arts events within the Gallery, which unsettled a few purists.

Eric Westbrook

Melbourne was still inherently conservative, and Westbrook was disinclined to fall in line with expected protocols: 'I was an oddity in a way. I had the right accent and the right background, but I had the wrong attitudes'.[100] This was symbolised by Westbrook's refusal to join the Melbourne Club: 'I disappointed [Daryl Lindsay] and disappointed John Medley, who was then Chairman, because I told them that I wouldn't join the Melbourne Club', he said.[101] Further feathers were ruffled by Westbrook's decision to mount exhibitions by abstract artists, including by Leonard French, also the NGV's Display Officer; by bold new painters such as John Brack and Arthur Boyd; and by social realist artists such as Noel Counihan. 'They thought of me as a communist', stated Westbrook.[102] However, he was not entirely accepted by the artistic community either: 'I really copped it from both sides. The artists thought of me as a continuation of the old regime, and the social backers, the friends of Daryl and so on, thought I was some kind of radical. So I sat in the Gallery for a long time, fairly isolated'.[103] Westbrook often found solace through art: 'After endless and often fruitless meetings, or when I had dealings with tiresome people, I would go down to the gallery and look at some of my friends among the paintings and forget the business of the day for a short time'.[104]

*

'I think I may be the only man who has lectured on art from the turret of a tank'

1961: *THE FIRST HUNDRED YEARS*. The NGV's centennial year in 1961 inspired gala events and much reflection on the past: retrospective exhibitions were held on the work of Max Meldrum and Bernard Hall – the latter augmented by fine acquisitions made during his directorship – as well as an exhibition of paintings entitled *The First Hundred Years*. Leonard Cox wrote that the opening of Hall's exhibition 'attracted a group of older people, rarely seen in the Gallery, whose tastes had been formed in the past'.[105]

With the prospect of a new and larger building in the near future, the Trustees and Westbrook campaigned to the Public Service board for more staff. In 1957 David Lawrance started as Professional Assistant to the Art Museum (and later Curator of the Art Museum); John Stringer as Assistant in the Print Room; and Leonard French as Display Officer. Gordon Thomson became the NGV's first Deputy Director in 1959. James Mollison, a future director, was appointed Education Officer in 1960; Harley Preston, Assistant Curator of Prints, in 1962; and Elwyn Dennis, Curator of the Art Museum, in 1966. For years, Westbrook and the Trustees had been campaigning for the appointment of staff in the critical areas of registration and conservation. The NGV's first registrar, John Gray, was finally appointed in 1964. The significance of his role had been made clear to the Public Service board after it was found that several pieces in the coin collection had disappeared. The police investigated and an officer in one of the other institutions was convicted of the theft. The importance of conservation was also acknowledged through the creation of a permanent position of conservator in 1965, filled by Harley Griffiths who, until then, had completed conservation work on a painting-by-painting basis.

THE NATIONAL GALLERY WOMEN'S ASSOCIATION: 'CREATIVE WOMEN'. Elizabeth Summons was an art lover who had studied arts at the University of Melbourne and attended George Bell's School of Modern Art. Years later, she found herself a member of the steering committee for the National Gallery and Cultural Centre. With an objective to raise funds for the new Arts Centre, she convened a Women's Council, handpicking twenty-four women with diverse skills across science, academia, the arts, politics, business and the land. At their inaugural meeting of 14 February 1961 they 'started work immediately', as Summons wrote, on 'an alarming goal' of raising £40,000 for capital works.[106] By 1969, with that goal ticked, they re-formed as the National Gallery Women's Association and set about raising money for acquisitions. In those early days, meetings were held at Summons's home and the dress code was formal ('certainly [no] trousers').[107] Fifty years later they remain a committed (and sometimes trouser-wearing) group, formally becoming part of the NGV in 2004 as the NGV Women's Association. Their aim is to 'seek out creative women dedicated to the NGV, with the imagination and skills to run effective fundraising events while balancing careers and families'.[108]

(above)
Elizabeth Summons on site with the construction team driving the last of 1400 reinforced concrete piles for the NGV at its new site in St Kilda Road, 12 February 1963

(middle)
Grace Cossington Smith
The bridge in-curve 1930
tempera on cardboard
83.6 x 111.8 cm
Presented by the National Gallery Society of Victoria, 1967

(below)
Brian Finemore with Mackennal's bust of Melba 1968

BRIAN FINEMORE : 'THE THRILL OF DINING WITH A PANTHER'. In 1962, Brian Finemore became the NGV's – and Australia's – first Curator of Australian Art. Finemore was a colourful character who stood out against the prevailing conservatism of Melbourne; Patrick McCaughey remarked that 'he always appeared to belong to another Melbourne than the present one'.[109] Flamboyant stories attend accounts of his life. 'Dear Madam, No.' was one of his infamous replies to a letter sent to the NGV. Of the President of the Board of Trustees he said, 'You could always tell which was the glass eye – the one with the feeling in it'. Finemore, remarked his friend Ian MacNeill, 'did not mince his words – that was part of his charm, the thrill of dining with a panther'.[110] Yet he was dedicated to the Australian collection. Finemore developed a sophisticated schedule for acquisitions and expanded the collection to include, for instance, modernist artists such as Grace Cossington Smith and Roy de Maistre. His work on exhibitions such as *The Field* (1968) and *Object & Idea* (1973) were also progressive contributions to contemporary art programming. On 23 October 1975, just eighty minutes before he was supposed to take Princess Margaret on a tour of the NGV, it was discovered that he had been murdered in his East Melbourne apartment. The crime has never been solved. As an act of memorial his colleagues assembled a publication, compiled by Jennifer Phipps, and a commemorative exhibition, both titled *Freedom from prejudice*.

FASHION AND TEXTILES: 'A WAY OF CHARTING HISTORY'. The Fashion and Textiles Department also gained momentum under Westbrook's directorship. Marion Fletcher was appointed Curator of Costumes (Honorary) in 1962, but signed on as a paid staff member in 1968 as Assistant Curator of Costume and Textiles. The area increased in prominence, particularly over those mid-century decades, as Katie Somerville, Curator of Australian Fashion and Textiles, explains: 'Textiles had been coming in since the late 1800s, but had been used more in support of the other collections – a common mode of display, for example, was to create a little vignette within a room filled with paintings. Fashion was not really collected seriously until the mid twentieth century, when there was a global shift towards collecting that was connected to an interest in fashion as a way of charting history - be that social history or art history. Initially, the collection of costume and textiles was primarily undertaken with an historical approach. However, now Fashion and Textiles has grown to be inclusive of all periods, and contemporary collecting is as vital to our collection as any other aspect of it'.[111] This reappraisal continues today; Danielle Whitfield, Assistant Curator of Australian Fashion and Textiles, comments that their department continues to 'try to change the way people look at fashion, to get them to view things in a different context. An ongoing challenge for us is furthering the idea that fashion is not always a shopping experience'.[112] A notable acquisition in this area was the purchase of the Pollen family collection of lace in 1963. The Victoria and Albert Museum expressed interest but later declined because many pieces duplicated their holdings. With examples of European textiles from the fifteenth century to the nineteenth century, and including silver, gold and cotton, Felton Advisor John McDonnell remarked, 'I cannot think it anything but a most remarkable bargain'.[113]

*

'The prevailing belief was that van Gogh and Cézanne, all that lot, were a passing phase'

JOHN BRACK: 'FAST WORK FOR THE MELBOURNE GALLERY'. In 1938, John Brack had started as a student at the Gallery School. He remembered the curriculum as an inherently conservative one: 'I used to be saddened by the general indifference of the other students to what was called Modern Art. As I remembered it, the prevailing belief was that van Gogh and Cézanne, all that lot, were a passing phase and that the only enduring tradition was naturalism. There may have been one or two wayward spirits, but the tone of the School was that of calm confidence in the visual image, with an emphasis on the picturesque'.[114] The situation remained largely the same over the ensuing two decades. In 1962, Brack was appointed Head of the National Gallery School. Over six years, he transformed the school and opened it up to bold new ideas. This experimental ethos was further assisted by Robin Boyd - the influential modernist architect, member of the artistic Boyd family and sometime business partner of Roy Grounds - who was made Chair of the school's subcommittee in 1966. Those years were

*

'It is a privilege to spend an hour with a work, to engage with it, find the visual grammar, the language, then interpret and check for congruity – shifting personal prejudices'

– Helen Brack

(above)
John Brack
The barber's shop 1952
oil on canvas
63.2 x 76.2 cm
Purchased, 1953

(below)
Geoff Hawkshaw
John Brack with the painting of Hal Hattam c.1965

also significant for the fact that sculpture classes were also offered for the first time, taught by Marc Clark. Brack resigned in 1968 to return to full-time painting, and Lenton Parr took over the role in time for the transition to the new building. The NGV acquired *The barber's shop*, 1952, from Brack's first commercial exhibition, an acquisition that prompted Arnold Shore to state: 'That's fast work for the Melbourne Gallery. It isn't often that the Gallery buys a young man's work at practically his first showing'.[115]

THE DEPARTMENT OF PHOTOGRAPHY: 'AN INTERESTING TEST CASE'. Eric Westbrook also created a department of photography in 1967, another first for an Australian public art gallery. Jennie Boddington was the inaugural Curator of Photography and Isobel Crombie took over in 1988. Crombie describes the department as 'an interesting test case' within the NGV that reflected the expanding parameters of art. Within conventional gallery practice, says Crombie, 'there is a hierarchy of art, with painting traditionally as the pinnacle'. It was a brave move for Westbrook to advocate for a photography department, and he encountered some resistance. As Crombie explains, 'It was really quite advanced thinking to have a separate department of photography in a modern art gallery. Some of the Trustees referred to it as a low form of art or a cheat's way of painting. It did get a foot in the door in those early days, but it was a very provisional foot in the door. Over the years, the acceptance of the department of photography has mirrored the acceptance of photography as an art form. Now you could say that it is shown on an equivalent basis with other art forms.'[116]

TWO DECADES OF AMERICAN PAINTING. An event of significance in 1967, and the last exhibition at the old building, was *Two Decades of American Painting*, a travelling exhibition from MoMA featuring artists such as Willem de Kooning, Jackson Pollock and Andy Warhol and which, Cox wrote, was 'finely hung' by John Stringer.[117] It generated a high degree of interest, as Stringer noted: 'Isolated and often hanging alone, paintings were presented with a reverence and authority appropriate to

(above)
William Freeman
James Freeman
Conrad Martens, January 16th, 1856 1856
ambrotype
(13.2 x 10.4 cm)
Felton Bequest, 1989

(below)
Josef Albers
Homage to the square: Autumn echo 1966.
oil and synthetic polymer paint on composition board
122.8 x 122.8 cm
Purchased with the assistance of the National Art Gallery & Cultural Centre Appeal Women's Council and the National Gallery Society of Victoria, 1967

masterpieces – it was a challenge to local taste that invited critical response, and the Australian public responded with unprecedented passion in the pages of the dailies'.[118] The NGV bought two abstract paintings – Helen Frankenthaler's *Cape (Provincetown)*, 1964, and Josef Albers's *Homage to the square: Autumn echo*, 1966 – and the exhibition was a 'significant catalyst' for *The Field*.[119]

DR MARY WOODALL, FELTON ADVISOR: 'YES, OF COURSE IT IS A CHARMING PICTURE'. After John McDonnell's death, Dr Mary Woodall – nicknamed 'Mighty Mary' by her staff – became the Felton Advisor in 1965 after retiring from her role as director of Birmingham Art Gallery. Early on, she secured Robert Delaunay's *Nude woman reading*, 1915, notable for its 'brilliant almost "fauve"-like colour and masterly drawing'.[120] A few months later she brought in a sheet of enchanting drawings of '*uomini famosi*' or 'famous men', a popular subject in the Renaissance, in what is, as Woodall described, 'a particularly distinguished acquisition'.[121] A fine pen and ink drawing by Picasso was bought in 1965, as was a brush drawing by Japanese master Hokusai. Significant acquisitions of historical painting include Perino del Vaga's *The Holy Family*, c.1545–46 and Giovanni Toscani's elegant *The adoration of the Magi*, c.1420–30. 'I am very enthusiastic about this picture', said Woodall of Toscani's *Magi*. 'I have been particularly anxious to get an Italian picture of this date, which is such a serious lacuna in the Melbourne collection.'[122] When Mattia Preti's *Sophonisba receiving the poison*, c.1675, was bought in 1968, Dr Hoff praised its 'Caravaggist features of dramatic light-dark contrast' and said: 'I recommend it warmly'.[123] *The Virgin Annunciate,* c.1645–50, was also a rare find in the same year: 'Cavallino is a rare artist and the acquisition of the picture would, in my view, add a real distinction to the collection of the National Gallery', wrote the advisor.[124] Contemporary works recommended by Dr Woodall include the op art work *Opening*, 1961, by Bridget Riley; David Hockney's *The second marriage*, 1963; and Larry Poons's *Cobone*, 1970. Opinion was divided over the large amount of money spent on Jean Ipoustéguy's

(opposite left)
Bridget Riley
Opening 1961
tempera and pencil on composition board
102.6 x 102.7 cm
Felton Bequest, 1967

(opposite right)
Henry Moore
Draped seated woman 1958
bronze
224.1 x 244.0 x 183.2 cm (overall)
Felton Bequest, 1960

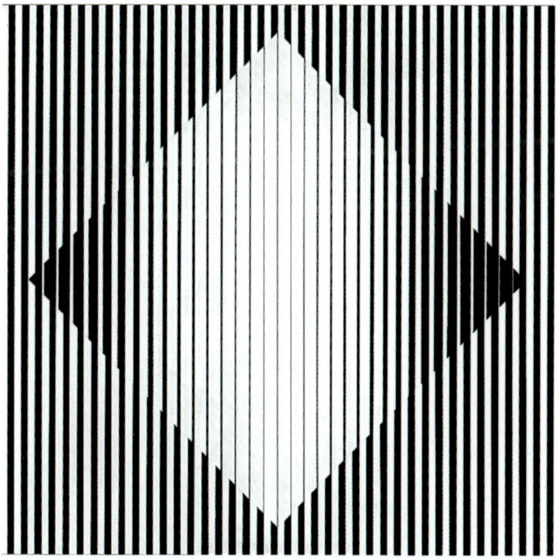

Death of the father, 1967–68, in 1972. The *Age*'s art critic, Patrick McCaughey, soon to be a director of the NGV, was not an advocate: 'What can be said about such vulgarity ... the marble drips and shines like plastic'.[125] The acquisition of a work by Claude Lorrain, however, was greatly championed. *River landscape with Tiburtine Temple at Tivoli*, c.1635, an ethereal and otherworldly landscape, was purchased in 1967 through Agnew's dealership in London. Doubts over its authenticity were dispelled by an expert, Michael Kitson of the Courtauld Institute, who wrote forthrightly to Dr Woodall: 'Yes, of course it is a charming picture. What chance is there of a better? And well worth the money'.[126]

Two remarkable sculptural works were acquired in the decade preceding the move: Gallery Trustee William Ritchie initiated the purchase of Henry Moore's *Draped seated woman*, 1958, in 1959 and the Curator of the Art Museum, David Lawrance, started the process to purchase a cast of *Balzac*, 1898, after his visit to the Rodin Museum in 1962. The Director and Trustees were behind the idea, as was Felton Advisor John McDonnell, who described it as 'a fine and commanding work of art'.[127] In 1968, the William and Margaret Morgan Endowment enabled an important collection of seventeenth- and eighteenth-century English glass to be acquired. 'It is highly significant,' says Amanda Dunsmore, Curator of Decorative Arts and Antiquities, 'one of the best collections in the world'.[128]

ROY GROUNDS: 'A WORK OF ART IN ITSELF'. In 1957, the Director Eric Westbrook wrote a brief entitled 'Spirit and Purpose', setting out ideas for the new building. In early 1959 the Trustees sought advice from Dr William M. Milliken, the Emeritus Director of Cleveland Museum of Art, one of the few directors with experience of post-war, modern museum construction. The Milliken Report advised against holding an architectural competition, and recommended that the Trustees commission 'a man willing to work closely with the professional staff' to design the building 'from the inside out'.[129] A shortlist of architects was created and each was invited to submit a proposal. On the evening of 18 December 1959, Chairman Leonard Cox and Deputy Chair Kenneth Myer offered the commission to Roy Grounds of the firm Grounds, Romberg and Boyd. 'We had interrupted his birthday party', said Cox, 'but he did not seem to mind'.[130]

In 1960, Westbrook and Grounds set off overseas to gather ideas. Of the 122 galleries and museums visited, two seem to have made a particular impression on the architect: the Castello Sforzesco in Milan, a fortified castle built out of grey stone and complete with moat, and the Museo Nazionale di Capodimonte in Naples, an eighteenth-century palace that had been redeveloped as a modern museum. Grounds's final design drew from these historical precedents, but fused them with a distinctly modern sensibility, as Gerard Vaughan explains: 'There was a tradition of monumental architecture in the 1960s that is a form of modern classicism. Some of the great examples of it are the National Library of Australia in Canberra, the Lincoln Centre in New York and the American Embassy in Grosvenor Square, London. These are large monumental buildings, very moderne in a 1960s sense but with a base in the classical tradition. The NGV belongs to a very particular moment of 1960s architecture. I think it is a great pity that the copper-sheathed conical spire of the Arts Centre never got built, because the two together would be in every textbook as significant examples of 1960s architecture'.[131]

In February 1961, the plans went public, and reactions varied greatly. There was concern that the monumental bluestone exterior would conjure up Pentridge Gaol and a section of the arts community – including Bernard Smith, John Brack and John and Sunday Reed – were critical of the five- to twelve- foot gap between the viewer and the works of art on the mezzanine level. Nicknamed 'The Cultural Gap' by the press, this feature was edited out of Grounds's final designs. The design process brought out tensions between the architect and many of the professional staff, with Leonard Cox as Chairman trying to sort through the various priorities. Many curators were concerned that the focus was on architectural vision at the expense of the needs of the art. Grounds was upfront about his priorities: 'This is not a gallery. It's a work of art in itself, or at least it's supposed to be'.[132]

Grounds conceived the building as classic and monumental: 'I had to produce a building ... that would last for an indefinite time – you don't build art galleries and pull them down like factories'.[133] However, it was also designed to be a welcoming space, as Westbrook commented: 'At that time, it was still an adventure for Australians to go to a motel [and] we wanted that welcoming feeling in the foyer, so you only encountered works of art when you went up the escalators'.[134] The building was also envisaged as a celebration of local artists and materials: Grounds used bluestone quarried in Footscray

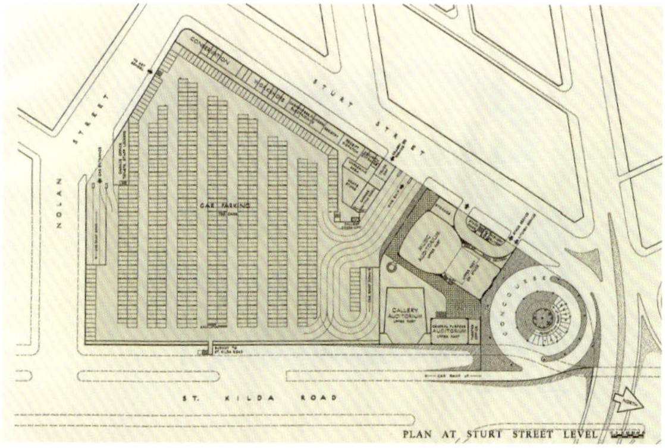

NGV during construction with design drawings from Roy Grounds's studio and Brooklyn; local hardwoods for the parquetry and mountain-ash timber for the interior detailing; local clay for the terracotta tiles; and local wool of different hues woven together to create the richly golden carpets in the foyer. The building also featured commissions by local artists: the crest over the door by Norma Redpath; the ceiling of the Great Hall by Leonard French; and the display cabinets by Grant and Mary Featherston. The building has become a Melbourne icon, and a visit to the NGV is never complete unless certain rituals are observed. Victorians are particularly enamoured with running their hands across the water wall and lying down in the Great Hall. The glass ceiling took Leonard French five years – and many cut fingers – to create it: 'My butcher's apron has blood all over it like I was doing surgery', he said. It was an all-consuming job: 'There were two other fellers working with me. But I cut all the glass: chiseled every bit ... I tried to paint, but my mind could never quite be on it'.[135]

The story goes that in 1960 Roy Grounds borrowed his wife's umbrella and drew in the dust a large rectangle with three smaller squares inside it that would become the basic plan for the NGV. To the south was the Bamboo Court, its oriental design a complement to the adjacent Asian galleries. The design very consciously privileged Asian art: 'The elgant, spacious installations made me look properly at Asian art for the first time', says Gerard Vaughan. 'The intention was a very fine one.'[136] The central court held the sculpture garden, where Henry Moore's *Draped seated woman* and, later, Rodin's *Balzac*, were marvellously installed against the zigzag walls – inspired by the Louvre Museum – close to the NGV's much-loved persimmon tree. To the north was the Playhouse Court, designed as an outdoor theatre and exhibition space in keeping with Westbrook's interest in cross-disciplinary arts, although the purpose was never fully realised.

*

'My butcher's apron has blood all over it like I was doing surgery'

THE GRAND OPENING: KNIGHTS OF MALTA AND MINI-SKIRTS. At 4 a.m. on 27 February 1968, a police patrol escorted the first truckload of works to their new home. The opening of the new building was highly anticipated:

(above)
Packing the collection to move to the St Kilda Road building 1968

(below)
Wolfgang Sievers
In the Great Hall of the new National Gallery of Victoria with Robert Garrad's Melbourne centrepiece candlesticks 1968
type c photograph
48.8 x 38.5 cm
Presented through the NGV Foundation by the artist, member, 2003

*

'I will never forget when the doors opened and the official party came in to a fanfare of trumpets'

The gala opening of the St Kilda Road building, 20 August 1968

'From an early date', wrote Cox, 'crowds had assembled before the glass panel at the front entrance, and through the soft diffuse outlines allowed by its water screen, attempted to pierce the mystery of what lay beyond'.[137] The gala opening was held on 20 August 1968 and Terence Lane was there: 'It was, in my opinion, the last great Melbourne party when everybody dressed up; many women ordered new dresses and the invitation specified that gentlemen wear decorations – their war medals or Imperial honours or whatever they had. It was, of course, the era of the mini skirt. Some daring women, such as Lady Grounds, wore one – and then there were the conservative establishment women in their furs and beaded satin dresses. It was an amazing party. I will never forget when the doors opened and the official party came in to a fanfare of trumpets'.[138] Sir Henry Bolte declared the building open, and also presented the NGV with a gift of three grand silver-gilt candelabra, 1839–40, which had been in the collection of Lord Melbourne. At a dinner in the Great Hall during that first week, it was announced that Dame Elisabeth Murdoch would become the NGV's first female trustee.

The following day, the NGV was opened to the public: 'On the next morning – the Public's day – the swelling wave of enthusiasm really broke, and bursting all bounds, became an avalanche', wrote Cox.[139] Over the next month, it was estimated that more than one million people came through the doors. 'That was such an exciting time', says Terence Lane. 'The NGV was like a bird let out of its cage. It had been cramped – kind of camping in the old building. There was the accumulation of decades – more than a hundred years of collecting – and the building was such a labyrinth. There were amazing, Piranesian stores and blankets of dust over works that had not been looked at for ages. It was so liberating to escape from that building and to have brand new exhibition halls and state-of-the-art facilities, particularly for storage. Through the process of moving, works were rediscovered – like the third panel of the Puvis de Chavannes cartoons. Two of the panels were hanging permanently on the staircase up to the art school, but another wonderful panel was uncovered that had not been seen for years.'[140]

THE FIELD: 'RADICAL FORMS OF ABSTRACTION'. While some Gallery Trustees would have preferred a grand historical survey – of Arthur Streeton, perhaps – to be mounted to inaugurate the building, Westbrook was determined to focus on the contemporary. John Stringer, Exhibitions Officer and Co-curator of *The Field*, stated that Westbrook believed that 'he had a particular responsibility to enable his constituents to understand and appreciate the culture of their own era; contemporary art, consequently, was indispensible in the exhibition line-up'.[141] The opening exhibition, *The Field*, curated by Stringer and Brian Finemore, was unapologetically modern. It featured artists such as James Doolin, Ian Burn, Mel Ramsden, Robert Hunter, Robert Rooney and Trevor Vickers, all practitioners who, said Stringer, had 'dedicated themselves to radical forms of abstraction'.[142] It was a bold and brave beginning for the new NGV, and it presented new ideas to Australian art audiences.

The works of art were mounted, most memorably, on walls that Stringer had lined with silver foil – and they stayed that way for a few years: 'It would have looked amazing – so bright', says Kirsty Grant. 'Soon after there was an exhibition called *Heroic Landscape* comprising works by Fred Williams and Arthur Streeton, and they hung it on the same foil. I remember seeing a photograph and thinking "wow, a Streeton on silver foil – that's a weird combination". Nevertheless, it was significant for Australian artists and art audiences.'[143] Stringer was a formidable presence at the NGV: 'With regards to exhibition design', says Frances Lindsay, Deputy Director, 'we have always been exuberant in taking risks, and John Stringer was an important figure in that history – he established a high benchmark'.[144]

(above)
The Field, installation shot featuring (front) Wendy Paramour *Luke* 1967 and (back) Noel Dunn *Untitled* 1967

(below)
The Field
installation shot 1968

THE VOLUNTARY GUIDES: 'THE TRANSFORMATIVE CAPACITY OF ART'. When writing his 'Spirit and Purpose' brief in 1957 for the new NGV building, Eric Westbrook wrote: 'The Gallery must be a warm and welcoming place and free from any institutional atmosphere. The people who use this building should be made to feel that it is their property and not the playground of the select few ... Culture is not to be imposed in this building, but created by the community itself'.[145] One of the initiatives introduced by Westbrook aiming to make the NGV a 'welcoming place' was the establishment of Australia's first voluntary guide program. Westbrook envisaged the guides as people who would welcome visitors and also enhance the experience for visitors who came 'not only to look but to learn'.[146]

Westbrook sought help from Gallery Society member Pat Baer, who co-opted her friend Lorli Ullin. Ullin had worked as a guide in Munich prior to immigrating to Australia. The two women collected together their art-loving friends. At the first meeting at Ullin's house, Westbrook explained his idea: 'It is distressing to see obviously interested people drifting round the Gallery and making no contact at all [with the art]'. To encourage people who may be intimidated, he said, the guides – all of whom were women at that stage – should act as 'hostesses, people ... who are nice to [the public], and smile at them, and are very concerned with their welfare'.[147] Ullin, in consultation with Westbrook, devised a program for training the guides and, by the time the building opened in 1968, a small army of voluntary guides was ready. 'I remember', recalled June Trott, part of the inaugural group, 'Eric Westbrook telling us that he wanted us to take people around the Gallery as we would show friends around our own home'.[148] In his 1969–70 *Annual Report* Westbrook wrote: 'These ladies ... now work as an integral part of the Gallery's daily program'.[149] In turn, the guides found it a rewarding experience, as Joan Shaw, one of the early guides, stated: 'It opened doors to many areas of learning and reading, rewarding us with endless hours of pleasure'.[150]

The Voluntary Guide program has grown in ambition and scope. It is an increasingly professionalised program; guides must commit to two days of training per week for eighteen months to be eligible to graduate, and their work is done for love, not money: 'The transformative capacity of art is what is so rewarding for the guides and for an educator working at the NGV', says Gina Panebianco, Head of Education and Public Programs. 'Art is fantastic for understanding yourself and the world in which you live. When you hear people's responses you realise how powerful the opportunity has been for them. If you have an interest in art and people, what better world could you be immersed in?'[151]

'Arnold Shore lecturing to an interested audience on an aspect of Higher Education.'

Eric Thake
Guide lecture 1953
linocut
20.6 x 14.4 cm
(image and sheet) (closed)
Purchased, 1964

ART
LIKE
NEVER
BEFORE

(pp. 108–9)
Gilbert and George performing
Singing Sculpture at the
NGV in 1973

(above)
Angus O'Callaghan
The NGV's forecourt, which
someone has cheekily used
as a carpark, c.1970s

(opposite)
The interior gallery spaces
of the NGV, c.1970s

I WANT TO LEAVE A NICE WELL-DONE CHILD HERE. The 1960s and '70s were a time of change and an age of protest. It was an era of great transition between old ways and new ways – and this was also true for the NGV. A sense of looking both forward and backward is immediately apparent in the NGV's exhibition program at the beginning of the 1970s. The decade opened with a trilogy of exhibitions that commemorated the bicentenary of Captain Cook's voyage up the east coast of Australia. The exhibition *Landfall: The Captain James Cook Bi-centenary Exhibition of Australian Art* was notable for its integrated presentation of Australian fine and decorative arts, something still unconventional for the time, while other interpretations of Australian history were offered by Arthur Boyd's *Australia* and Sidney Nolan's *Paradise Garden*. The three exhibitions were on the itinerary for the royal visit of 1970. Crowds of people turned out to see the Queen, the Duke of Edinburgh, Princess Anne and (for a short time) Prince Charles as they toured Australia, commemorating the moment when *Terra Australis Incognita* – 'the unknown land of the South' – was claimed for Britain.

Meanwhile, John Kaldor was masterminding – and bankrolling – something altogether different. 'I want to stretch the borders of modern art in Australia', he said at the time.[1] The fabric designer and entrepreneur initiated a series of remarkable contemporary art projects, three of which were presented at the NGV. In 1969, Christo and Jeanne-Claude presented *Wool works*, a stack of 'wrapped' wool bales presented in the Keith Murdoch Court that followed their monumental work *Wrapped coast*, 1968–69, at Little Bay, Sydney. Then, in 1971, Kaldor invited the influential Swiss curator Harald Szeemann to Australia. Szeemann spent a fortnight in Australia visiting more than seventy artists' studios, resulting in the project *I want to leave a nice well-done child here* at the NGV.

It featured the work of twenty-two artists, including Aleks Danko, Margaret Dodd, Dale Hickey, Ti Parks and Mike Parr. Alex Baker, Senior Curator of Contemporary Art, lists the Kaldor projects as notable moments that fostered an expansive definition of contemporary art: 'I think that these projects show that there are many ways of being an artist, from making large-scale sculptures to making videos to the tiniest presenting of gestures. Artists can teach us that there are no fixed ways of being in the world. I think this is one of the most important things that artists can do for us – to showcase the diversity of how humans are who they are'.[2]

'They weren't Good Artists. They weren't Bad Artists. But, my God, they were Artists.'[3] So declared Gilbert and George on their visit to Australia in 1973 for the third Kaldor Art Project. They were invited to perform their work *Singing sculpture*, for which the duo stood atop a table dressed as 'bronzes', repeatedly warbling the old music hall song *Underneath the arches* while slowly performing a sluggish soft-shoe shuffle. Melbourne was confounded, but found it impossible not to adore them. They were such polite gentlemen, who sipped most elegantly – and continually – at their gin and tonics (assuring everyone that they knew to stop drinking when they couldn't see the pink elephants on their ties anymore). When questioned, they would give charming and erudite non-answers: Is it really art? 'When you are in a gallery you must be art, otherwise you wouldn't be in there, because that's where the art is.' Is it hard to be a living sculpture? 'It is very, very difficult to be a sculpture. It's not difficult for us but it would be very difficult for someone else. I think you almost have to be born to it.'[4] Was it profitable? 'Oh tremendously. Yes. Yes.'[5] When pressed, they simply declared their work 'the most beautiful, moving, original, fascinating and serious art-piece you have ever seen'.[6] A work fit for the greatest of galleries, just like a Leonardo or a Michelangelo. 'Michelangelo's *David* is a marvel, really', said George. 'Yes', nodded Gilbert. 'A marble, really.'[7]

CONTEMPORARY ARTISTS: 'SO BLOODY MAD'. In the 1970s, the stoush between contemporary Australian artists and the NGV intensified. Research by artist Les Kossatz revealed that the NGV had spent less than 1 per cent of its acquisitions budget on contemporary Australian art over the previous seven years, which went some way to explaining the acrimony expressed by local artists. Tate Adams, Director of Crossley Print Gallery, gave the perspective of the dealers too: 'It makes me so bloody mad'. He recalled how William Lieberman, the curator at MoMA who had recently been in Australia for the *Modern Masters* exhibition, had visited his dealership: 'He bought thirty prints. The National Gallery haven't purchased as many in my lifetime. Now the New Yorkers have a better contemporary collection than we have'. He blamed Westbrook and 'these piffling social characters who act as trustees' and called the NGV 'Wirth's Circus in a new tent'.[8] There was a chasm between the NGV and the contemporary art community around it.

Director Eric Westbrook was unrepentant about the NGV's position on contemporary art: 'I am against rampant nationalism in any form. At this gallery we will never operate like some sort of local stamp collector. The only way our national art can be made universal is by Australian artists constantly coming into contact with the best overseas work. And this won't happen by sitting around in Carlton writing plays about Bob Menzies'.[9] By 1973, Westbrook was ready to focus on new challenges: after a distinguished tenure of seventeen years he left the NGV to head the team that established the Victorian Ministry for the Arts (now Arts Victoria). The National Gallery School also experienced an important transition in 1973 when it became the Victorian College of the Arts, formalised through a government order from the Premier of Victoria and Minister for the Arts, Rupert Hamer.

*

'I am against rampant nationalism in any form. At this gallery we will never operate like some sort of local stamp collector'

EXHIBITIONS: 'THE SERIOUSNESS OF 137 BRICKS'.

The NGV hosted a number of early 'blockbuster' exhibitions in the mid 1970s. The MoMA exhibition *Some Recent American Art* gave Australians the opportunity in 1974 to see works by artists such as Donald Judd, Sol LeWitt, Dan Flavin, Vito Acconci, Richard Serra and Agnes Martin. However, the broader Australian public was still resolutely closed to such art, and the media were incredulous. Carl Andre's work, in particular, greatly offended them. How could his *Lever*, 1966, consisting of 137 house bricks arranged in a line, be art? Jennifer Licht, Curator of Painting and Sculpture at MoMA in New York, did her best to explain its significance: 'If you open your head and drop your prejudices – then you might understand and enjoy it', she said. 'No work of art is made as a joke.'[10] Patrick McCaughey, writing in *The Age*, offered a different perspective in a review titled 'The seriousness of 137 bricks'. 'The value of seeing these particular objects in the flesh is immeasurable ... So far we have heard the rhetoric but not seen the art.'[11]

'Everyone who is anyone in Melbourne and the Western District' was there, said the *Herald* of the gala opening of the exhibition, *Modern Masters: Manet to Matisse* in

Crowds gathering to see *Modern Masters: Manet to Matisse*, 1975

1975. The exhibition toured 113 modern art 'masterpieces' assembled by William Lieberman, Curator of Drawing at MoMA in New York. Premier Dick Hamer called it 'a rare feast', influential art dealer Joseph Brown said it contained 'the best of everything' (and also called Modigliani's *Reclining nude*, 1917, 'the nudest nude I've ever seen') and Dame Elisabeth Murdoch called it 'the greatest thing artistically to happen to Australia'.[12] The public agreed. The exhibition sparked huge attendances: chairs were put in the foyer so people could be more comfortable during the long wait to get in, and the NGV opened seven days a week and at night to deal with the crowds. Director Gerard Vaughan, who was a university student at the time, remembers the impact: 'I never imagined I would see things like this in Australia'.[13]

The year 1977 featured one of the first blockbuster exhibitions of Chinese art. Gough Whitlam had opened up diplomatic relations with China during his time as prime minister, including establishing an embassy in Beijing in 1973. He had seen *The Chinese Exhibition* in Europe in 1973 and placed a request for an Australian visit, but it took years of diplomatic efforts and a $200 million underwriting scheme from Mobil Oil to persuade the Chinese government to allow the collection to travel here. The exhibition drew large crowds but Prime Minister Malcolm Fraser also emphasised the significant diplomatic act symbolised by the exhibition: 'The exhibition is one of exceptional significance, both artistically and in the development of relations between Australia and the People's Republic of China'.[14] The exhibition presented ancient Chinese archaeological artefacts that covered an incredible 600,000 years of Chinese history, including flint scrapers used by Neolithic man and a magnificent burial suit made of jade sewn together with pure gold wire, which had been created for Princess Tou Wan in 113 BC to magically prevent her body from decay after her death.

ACQUISITIONS: 'A WILD SPELLBINDER'. When Turner's wonderfully ethereal *A mountain scene, Val d'Aosta*, c.1845, was purchased in 1973, it caused a tremendous furore. Some Australians were not convinced that $475,000 should be spent on an almost abstract picture of air. Protestors gathered outside the NGV holding placards stating that 'half a million could be better used not abused' and calling the purchase 'another gimmick for our sick society'.[15] Daryl Lindsay, former director and perhaps Australia's most highly regarded Turner expert, did not help matters when he called it 'a very, very second rate example' that had 'practically nothing in it'.[16] Yet it worked its magic on some: McCaughey called it 'a wild spellbinder' and Joseph Burke, Professor of Fine Arts at the University of Melbourne, swooned: 'It shines, it sings'.[17] After a determined campaign by the NGV, the purchase had been enabled by a donation of $158,000 from Associated Securities, a Sydney-based finance company. Managing Director Reginald Shanahan shrugged off the controversy: 'It is an honour to be able to contribute something as worthwhile as this magnificent Turner painting to the cultural life of Australia'.[18] A year earlier, Felton Advisor Mary Woodall had bought Annibale Carracci's celebrated drawing *Study for an ignudo*, 1598. It was one of the key works listed in a sale at Sotheby's in London of works from the Ellesmere collection, which had been assembled by British Regency portrait painter Sir Thomas Lawrence.

J.M.W. Turner
A mountain scene, Val d'Aosta c.1845
oil on canvas
91.5 x 122.0 cm
Purchased with the assistance of a special grant from the Government of Victoria and donations from Associated Securities Limited, the Commonwealth Government (through the Australia Council), the National Gallery Society of Victoria, the National Art Collections Fund (Great Britain), The Potter Foundation and other organisations, the Myer family and the people of Victoria, 1973

CHANEL ADDICTS: THE FASHION AND TEXTILES COLLECTION. Works in the Fashion and Textiles collections tend to enter the NGV in a distinctive way: they are usually highly personalised collections, worn lovingly by their owners, and then passed on to the NGV. Roger Leong, Curator of International Fashion and Textiles, for instance, lists people like 'Toorak matron' Mavis Powell – ' a Chanel addict' – and Perth-based Neil Taylor – 'a collector who was mad for Vivienne Westwood' – among such sources.[19] Both were passionate collectors whose wardrobes eventually found their way to the NGV. Katie Somerville, Curator of Australian Fashion and Textiles, describes similar stories in relation to the Australian collection. Edith Ma, for example, was a host at Chequers, one of the leading cabaret venues in Sydney in the late 1950s and '60s. 'She looked amazing: she wore a blend of very fashionable Chinese cheongsams with killer, up-to-the-minute international accessories'. There was also Mr Wicking who, after his wife passed away, 'had some bags full of gowns from the 1950s made by the Melbourne fashion house La Petite and didn't know quite what to do with them. He took them to the MTC, who luckily sent him and his gowns our way'.[20]

(below)
Madame Gough, London
Scrap album, fancy dress c.1893
chromolithographic print on paper, linen, silk, cotton, metallic thread
(a) 29.3 cm (centre back); thread 26.0 cm (waist, flat) (bodice); (b) 108.0 cm (centre front); 28.5 cm (waist, flat) (skirt) (c) 61.5 x 11.5 cm (sash); (d) 81.4 x 66.4 x 3.4 cm (e-f) 9.2 x 7.0 x 24.9 cm (each) (shoes)
Schofield Collection
Purchased with the assistance of a Victorian Government grant, 1974

In 1974, the Fashion and Textiles collection was radically altered, virtually overnight, through the acquisition of the Schofield Collection. The collection comprises more than a thousand items – including coats, dresses, shawls, hats, bridal bouquets, gloves, umbrellas and parasols – dating from 1800 to 1947, which had been assembled by Anne Schofield and her husband Leo from dealers in London, Paris and Australia. Anne Schofield had started collecting in London in the 1960s, when the idea of second-hand clothes was evidently a bit repellent: 'When I told my host that the feather boa I was wearing had cost me five shillings from an antique shop, he said with horror: "My dear, I can hardly bring myself to wear my own old clothes, let alone somebody else's"'.[21] Towards the end of the decade, the Fashion and Textiles collection received another notable gift in the form of millinery. There was a time when wearing a hat was de rigueur: one did not think of leaving the house without covering one's crown. One of the period's best milliners was Thomas Harrison of Melbourne. Over a number of years Harrison gifted more than three hundred of his hats, many of which he had acquired by chasing down his old clients.

THE ARTISTS' SIT-IN. Relations between the NGV and the contemporary art community continued to be fraught; 'there was very, very serious hostility', remembers Terence Lane.[22] Things took a turn for the worse in 1975 when Domenico de Clario's ephemeral installation *Elemental landscapes* was removed over concern that a working radiator that formed part of the work was placed too close to McCubbin's *The pioneer*. Most unfortunately the artist was not consulted. This slight was further compounded by a second incident in which a project by the Art & Language collective, which was critical of the 'cultural imperialism' they felt was represented by MoMA's *Modern Masters* exhibition, was relocated to the Art School because the Acting Director, Gordon Thomson, was worried that it would embarrass the International Council of MoMA during their visit to the NGV. The local artistic community accused the NGV of censorship and disrespecting contemporary art. In the same eventful year, artist Ivan Durrant dumped a dead cow that he had named 'Beverley' at the entrance to the NGV in an attempt to raise interest in animal rights; yet it also seemed to further intensify the general atmosphere of hostility.

The contemporary artists held a meeting at which they wrote up a series of demands and organised a protest to be held in the NGV's Australian galleries. 'The authorities at the Gallery must have feared riot and arson', Ken Scarlett recalled, 'for, with one exception, the hundreds of paintings in the Australian area of the Gallery were all taken down'. The protest, however, remained peaceful. One of the outcomes of the Artists' Sit-In was the creation of the Artists' Steering Committee. Artists John Davis and Ken Scarlett were elected as representatives to negotiate with the Trustees of the NGV and the Victorian Ministry for the Arts. Initially communication did not flow easily between the NGV and contemporary artists; Scarlett recalled that 'the situation was complicated by the Trustees' refusal to reply to letters or meet a delegation'.[23] Slowly, however, their agitations were to bear fruit.

The artists found a willing listener in Eric Rowlison, the young American who started as Director of the NGV in 1975. Rowlison was progressive in his outlook. He met with the Artists' Steering Committee and his notes describe ideas such as having a dedicated curator of and space for contemporary Australian art. By 1976, Rowlison was considering the establishment of a separate art gallery for contemporary art. He also spoke out in support of Ron Robertson-Swann's beleaguered public sculpture, *Vault*, saying that 'in contemporary art it inevitably takes twenty years for public acceptance to catch up with the vision of artists'.[24]

THE ART FOUNDATION. One of the notable features of Rowlison's directorship was the establishment of the Art Foundation of Victoria (now named the NGV Foundation). By the 1970s, the Felton Bequest could no longer produce sufficient funds to acquire the kind of masterpieces which were its staple for its first fifty years, and the NGV's other endowments were also close to exhausted. Gallery Treasurer Brian Stonier said, 'We do the best we can with the funds we've got. But the existing funds are buying less and less'.[25] To combat this decline, the Art Foundation of Victoria was established in 1976 by four trustees: Sir Andrew Grimwade, President of the Council; Hugh Morgan

Peter Tyndall
The artists' sit in, 1975
(left to right) Eric Westbrook, John Davis, and Terry Smith

of Western Mining; Baillieu Myer; and Brian Stonier, Treasurer, and Chairman of Macmillan Publishers. Andrew Grimwade's tenure as president began in 1976 and was to last until 1990, making him the longest-serving President of the Council of Trustees. ('He was a superb Chairman and kept business flowing', McCaughey would later say, who also spoke highly of his 'sense of warmth, good humour and dignity'.)[26] Andrew Grimwade has dedicated a major part of his life to supporting the NGV and in recognition of his contribution the boardroom is named in his honour. (No NGV event was ever complete, recalls Gerard Vaughan, without one of his famous limericks.) Hugh Morgan's tenure has also been extensive and illustrious: he was the inaugural Chair of the Art Foundation, and maintains an interest today as president.

In the first instance, the Art Foundation aimed to raise $5 million, a target greatly assisted by Premier Dick Hamer's promise that the state government would match donations, dollar for dollar, to a maximum of $2.5 million. The Art Foundation launched its campaign, and enjoyed a positive response with very substantial donations coming in from companies such as the Commercial Bank of Australia, Alcoa, Shell and the National Australia Bank and individuals such as the very generous Mr and Mrs Henry Krongold, who contributed $200,000.

Renamed the NGV Foundation in 2000, the foundation is now the major conduit through which works of art are acquired by the NGV. As well as raising funds for acquisitions, the Foundation helps to provide an avenue for the donation of works of art. In 2011, the total value of works funded or donated through the NGV Foundation amounted to more than $100 million, some of which, such as Picasso's *Weeping woman*, 1937, are highlights of the collection. The first work acquired, and one shrouded in great secrecy until the Queen unveiled it on national television in 1977, was the NGV's first Renoir, *The guitar player*, c.1896, bought for $396,000.

In 1975, the NGV established the Life Member awards. The award of Life Member of the NGV is the highest award conferred by the Gallery, recognising people who have made an outstanding contribution to the NGV's welfare and collections. The inaugural announcement included Premier Henry Bolte; patron Howard Michell; historian Ursula Hoff; Women's Association founder, Elizabeth Summons; former director Daryl Lindsay; and architect Sir Roy Grounds. New members are announced annually at a celebratory dinner: artist Peter Booth was made a member in 2009, Fred Williams in 1978 and Lady Drysdale in 1986. In 1976, the NGV was also boosted by the establishment of the Friends of the Gallery Library. With Dame Elisabeth Murdoch as convener, an association was formed to help the NGV create a high-quality reference library to support the work of curatorial staff. The 'Friends' donated funds but also made individual bequests of books from their own libraries. A ruling of the Supreme Court of Victoria in 1977 relating to 'art gifts' also had positive impacts on the NGV. In 1972, Kenneth Myer had made a gift of $21,565 through his

NGV publications
Survey 1, 1978, and *Survey 8*, 1979

company for the purchase of four works, but the Australian Tax Office refused to grant him a tax deduction. Myer took the matter to court and the judge ruled in his favour, thus initiating a process that would enable future monetary donations to the NGV to be tax deductible and culminating in the extremely beneficial Cultural Gifts Program, which represents an ongoing Commonwealth contribution to the NGV's collecting activities.

AUSTRALIA'S FIRST CURATOR OF CONTEMPORARY ART: LETTING DOWN THE DRAWBRIDGE. Robert Lindsay became Associate Curator of Contemporary Australian Art at the NGV in 1977, the first such role in an Australian gallery. 'The Trustees told me in no uncertain terms', remembers Lindsay, 'that I had to be a public relations knight. Someone who could let down the drawbridge – because the NGV was known as "the castle", and was even complete with a moat. They literally said I was to go to as many artists' studios as possible, and go to *all* the openings. I came down to the NGV with the purpose of defusing the bad relationship between the NGV and Australian contemporary art'.[27]

Lindsay campaigned for a dedicated space in which to show contemporary art: 'The best place we could find was one of the hallways, but I was pleased: I thought, *everyone* has to walk through this space'. He then

*

'The Trustees told me in no uncertain terms', remembers Lindsay, 'that I had to be a public relations knight. Someone who could let down the drawbridge – because the NGV was known as "the castle", and was even complete with a moat'

initiated the Survey exhibitions, which presented a remarkable series of contemporary artists grouped together in pairs around specific themes. *Survey 1: John Davis* and *Survey 2: Rosalie Gascoigne* considered land art and nature, for instance, and *Survey 3: Robert Rooney* and *Survey 4: John Lethbridge* examined systems and rituals. The series generated an audience and, importantly, an expectation that contemporary art was a significant part of the NGV program. The exhibitions were also notable for their pioneering use of multimedia. 'I had always been interested in film', says Lindsay, 'and I knew Bob Weis at Open Channel. I went to Bob and said "I want to make a series of documentaries"'. Using early and 'extremely crude' video technology, Lindsay and Weis produced short interviews ('basically the twenty-seven minutes that would fit on old pneumatic cassettes') that were screened at the entrance of the exhibitions. Each Survey exhibition was presented to the public as a suite comprising an exhibition, a catalogue and the video interview, all designed to develop the audience's understanding of contemporary artists. 'What was important to me', says Lindsay, 'was not that people *liked* the work but that they made an informed decision about it. I wanted to present really good contemporary art that was about challenging the taste of the time and giving an alternative view'.[28]

THE MICHELL ENDOWMENT: 'BY THE SKIN OF ITS TEETH'. The NGV's relationship to contemporary Australian art also changed with the establishment of the Michell Endowment in 1976. After being told by their children that young Australian artists were going unsupported and uncollected, Howard and Christine Michell decided to direct some of their wealth towards remedying this situation. The Adelaide couple had initially offered their $100,000 gift to the Art Gallery of South Australia, but their offer was turned down – to the NGV's great gain. Robert Lindsay recalls how 'the Michells would come across to Melbourne and remind me that it is about *support* for young and emerging artists, and not solely about developing the collection. That took precedence over everything'.[29]

When Patrick McCaughey took over as director in 1981, he described the quarterly meetings of the Michell Endowment as 'slightly strange'. The Michells, he said, 'were the embodiment of Adelaide rectitude and restraint', and yet they sat in meetings (chaired by the very conservative Trustee Dick Austin) to studiously consider sometimes quite outré works. They 'rarely blink[ed] an eye', said McCaughey (while Dick Austin, who 'loathed' these works, was often heard to 'swallow hard').[30] In 1986, Mrs Margaret Stewart AM continued the good work of the Michells with an endowment established to focus on moments of change or innovation in Australian artists' careers. Between the two bequests, hundreds of works of art were acquired from artists such as Jenny Watson, Julie Rrap, Caroline Williams, David Larwill and Juan Davila.

One of the great contemporary works of art acquired through the Michell Endowment was Howard Arkley's *Muzak mural – chair tableau*, 1980–81. Lindsay recalls: 'I was

(above)
Howard Arkley
Muzak mural – chair tableau
1980–1981
synthetic polymer paint on canvas and wood chairs, vinyl tiles on composition board
(a-h) 240.0 x 330.0 x 90.2 cm (overall) (installation)
Michell Endowment, 1982

(below)
Indian
Dewali celebrations at Kotah
c.1690
opaque watercolour and gold paint on paper
48.2 x 43.8 cm (image)
Felton Bequest, 1980

really trying to acquire Arkley's *Muzak mural*, but it had been knocked back twice. Then it was in a show out at Banyule. Patrick had just started as director and when he saw it he said, "it's absolutely fantastic!" So he put it up for a third time. I remember the Michells saying "well, while you are on your honeymoon, we'll accept it". So it got in by the skin of its teeth'.[31]

ACQUISITIONS: A TALE OF TWO CITIES – THE GALLIA AND LANGER APARTMENTS. Sassetta was one of the greatest Sienese artists of the early fifteenth century, and *The burning of a heretic*, 1423–26, is an outstanding example of his work, despite its depiction of a very grisly scene from the 'fire and brimstone' history of Christianity. Ursula Hoff recommended the work when she was the Felton Bequest Advisor in London, and it was a find. Eric Rowlison remarked: 'It is one of the most significant pieces of work we could have bought to expand the Renaissance art collection. So far as we know this is the last Sassetta left in private hands'.[32] In 1980, Hoff also recommended that the NGV spend two years' of the Felton Bequest's budget on 274 Indian Rajput miniature paintings; after consulting experts from the Indian department at the Victoria and Albert Museum, Hoff was convinced of their importance. The acquisition radically broadened the scope of the NGV's Asian collection: previously strong on Chinese ceramics and painting, the Gallery now held one of the most comprehensive collections of this style of Indian miniature outside India.

Peter Booth
Painting 1977
oil on canvas
182.5 x 304.0 cm
Gift of the artist in memory of Les Hawkins, 1978

'During the Second World War many Jewish families migrated to Australia', says Terence Lane. 'For some it was the furthest away from Europe that they could go. There were restrictions on taking money and works of art out of countries such as Austria, but you could take household goods and chattels. So that is how quite a few collections of important twentieth-century design were brought to Australia – it was all that the families could bring.' The Gallia apartment, c.1912–15, designed by the influential designer Josef Hoffmann, was brought to Australia in 1939 and crammed into an apartment in Sydney. For decades it remained largely intact, except for Gustav Klimt's *Portrait of Hermine Gallia*, which was sold to the National Gallery in London. In 1976, after years of negotiations, Terence Lane made a world-class acquisition, purchasing around one hundred items including furniture, ceramics, jewellery, glass and leather from the Gallia descendants. Remarkably, a few decades later, in 1994, Lane negotiated the acquisition of another suite of important furniture from a Viennese apartment, this time from the Langer apartment, c.1903, designed by Adolf Loos, an architect with a very different design ethos from Hoffmann. Lane nominates these two acquisitions as high points of his forty years at the NGV: 'I was fortunate to be involved in bringing those two collections to the NGV. I think, without doubt, they would be the most important of the many collections of early twentieth-century design brought to Australia. They are now highlights of the NGV's collection'.[33]

Peter Booth presented one of his own major works to the NGV in 1978. Booth worked at the Melbourne Iron and Steel Mills in Brooklyn and in his lunchbreaks would make sketches of his workplace and surrounds. After showing them to John Brack, Head of the Gallery School, he was awarded a place and supported through a scholarship from the NGV's Women's Association. Brack was to be a formidable influence on Booth. After graduation, Booth was appointed technician of the Department of Prints and Drawings, just like John Brack two decades before him. There he became a great friend of Les Hawkins, a technician in the Department of Asian Art. Booth presented *Painting*, 1977, in memory of his friend Hawkins.

The NGV was also gifted, by gem dealer John Altmann and his wife Jan, a highly important collection of Australian silver comprising more than 120 pieces amassed with the help of dealers across the world (and the Altmanns' children, who were sometimes enticed to do the job with a $10 spotting fee). The earliest pieces were six teaspoons from the 1820s made by the Sydney convict Walter Harley. The collection also included a number of emu-egg caskets, often enlivened with Australian flora and fauna or a 'noble savage'.

THE JACK MANTON COLLECTION: 'WHAT MUST BE DONE'. Jack Manton began to assemble his collection of Australian Impressionist paintings in 1961 in commemoration of his father – a 'self-made man' whose first job at age eleven was fixing boots to the feet of skaters at the local skating rink and whose last was as the head of Manton's, the large Melbourne department store. Reflecting on the impact that his father had had upon him, Manton came to

a decision: 'Suddenly, I knew what I wanted to do, what must be done. I would form a collection of paintings covering the period of his early life. It would not only be an expression of my love for him but would also symbolise his creativity and perseverance, his quest for perfection and enthusiasm for life'. Oswald Burt – 'company solicitor, friend and patron of the arts' – was Manton's guide into art history. One night he introduced Manton to his own collection. 'It was a revelation!' said Manton. 'I drove home as if in a dream.'[34]

The two men became collecting allies, encouraging each other's passions: 'Sell the farm and buy Conder cover catalogue', Burt once cabled to Manton. When Burt died in 1969, he stipulated that Manton was to have first pick of his collection. 'I've led many friends up the Heidelberg path', he had told Manton, 'but no one stuck to it like you, nor dedicated themselves to it as much. You will have the greatest collection of the school in Australia and become the greatest authority'.[35] In 1972, the collection was loaned to the NGV where it formed the inaugural display at the Banyule Gallery, a neo-gothic mansion in Heidelberg, the suburb in which many of the artists worked. Banyule Gallery was purchased by the Victorian

Charles Condor
The farm, Richmond, New South Wales 1888
oil on paper on canvas
45.0 x 50.7 cm irreg. (image);
45.4 x 51.3 cm (canvas)
Purchased with the assistance of a special grant from the Government of Victoria, 1979

(opposite)
Swimming in the moat

government and set up as a branch museum between 1977 and 1986. In 1979, a special grant of $2 million from the Hamer government enabled the NGV to acquire the Jack Manton collection.

GLASNOST – AND BARE FEET – COME TO THE KREMLIN. When Patrick McCaughey took on the job of director in 1981, he found the place at a low ebb: 'The Gallery was at a low point in public esteem ... A state of internal tribal warfare existed among the staff. James Mollison and the National Gallery of Australia were making the running, buying twentieth-century masterworks and promising an exciting new era. Melbourne looked like being left behind in the wake. Attendance was dropping. The art world regarded the place as irrelevant and out of touch. The mixture of squabbling inaction, internally, and the solid bluestone facade, externally, earned the Gallery the title of the Kremlin of St Kilda Road'.[36]

On arrival, McCaughey 'declared *glasnost* to be the policy of the Kremlin of St Kilda Road' and then gave early evidence of it by overturning the 'bare feet ban'. On hot summer days, visitors would cool their heels in the moat and then try to wander inside, only to be stopped by a guard enforcing the 'no bare feet' rule inside the NGV. The ban had brought negative press and scorn from the community – young curator Paul Taylor, for instance, would mischievously arrive barefoot for his meetings with McCaughey to see what would happen. 'This small bureaucratic action became a metaphor for the Gallery's attitude to its public', stated McCaughey. It was intensifying the general public's perception of the NGV as an unfriendly and intimidating place. 'By welcoming the barefooted, the Gallery suddenly looked open to all mankind. *Glasnost* had begun.'[37]

EXHIBITIONS: 'A WITHERING DISPLAY OF AESTHETIC FIREPOWER'. Patrick McCaughey described *The Great Eighteenth Century Exhibition* as 'the turning point of his directorship'.[38] The project was the first of his 'internal blockbusters': large-scale exhibitions that promoted the

*

'The mixture of squabbling inaction, internally, and the solid bluestone facade, externally, earned the Gallery the title of the Kremlin of St Kilda Road'

NGV's extensive holdings. 'In the old days the Gallery had stupendous collections which were under-utilised', said McCaughey. It 'got by on snob appeal – you know, "We have the *only* Rembrandt" – but snob appeal fades rapidly'.[39] McCaughey was very aware of the breadth of the NGV's holdings of eighteenth-century objects and *The Great Eighteenth Century Exhibition* was a chance to dust them off and show them off. It was intended, McCaughey told the press, 'to be a withering display of aesthetic firepower. No other gallery in the land could muster such an exhibition of over 750 objects'.[40]

In 1983, the NGV also hosted the Chinese travelling exhibit *Entombed Warriors: Exhibition of the Terracotta Figures of Warriors and Horses of the Qin Dynasty of China* (remembered by McCaughey as 'the single most hair-raising and hilarious exhibition' of his directorship).[41] As a celebration of the tenth anniversary of diplomatic relations between Australia and China, the Chinese had agreed to loan nine 2000-year-old burial statues to Australia. The loan of these archaeological treasures was a political and artistic coup. It was planned that the Great Hall would be transformed into a Chinese tomb, with the figures and horses displayed within reconstructed burial chambers. In the end, the exhibition was a tremendous success and people flocked to see it.

McCaughey always had misgivings about the exhibition's design: 'It was truly awful and I was lucky that Melbourne forgave me this egregious error of taste'. It was also bothersome: it was meant to snap easily into place 'like a large Lego set' – except that it didn't. On the day of the exhibition the damn thing was so cumbersome that McCaughey eventually sent an 'SOS to the curatorial staff', and everybody worked like mad to set it up in time. Even as he bolted onto the stage to make the opening speech, McCaughey could hear the 'hammers going on behind us in a last desperate attempt' to get the display ready. In all the panic there was, of course, a mishap: an Iron Age sword was snapped in two by external handlers. This was, needless to say, a catastrophe. 'The Chinese government went berserk', said McCaughey, and, closer to home, the Australian government was not thrilled at having to foot the bill, the first claim made under the new indemnity arrangement.[42] It was all the more upsetting for NGV staff because, just a few months earlier, a painting had been accidentally damaged as it was being de-installed ('what was wrong with us?' lamented McCaughey).[43]

When NGV Trustee James Smith visited an exhibition of works by the Australian Impressionists in 1889, he had declared most of them 'a pain the eye' and not fit for public presentation. Almost a century later, in 1985, the works of art exhibited in *Golden Summers: Heidelberg and Beyond* were feted and adored. The project was initially proposed by McCaughey as the second 'internal blockbuster' but Jane Clark, Myer Curator of Special Exhibitions, and Bridget Whitelaw, Curator of Nineteenth-Century Australian Art, proposed a more ambitious project, which would assemble the most comprehensive exhibition of Australian Impressionism yet. Kenneth Hood suggested the project be named after Streeton's painting *Golden Summers* (but evidently the project also earned itself the nickname 'Golden Chunders' in tougher moments and 'Golden Slumbers' in more sleep-deprived ones).[44] The exhibition was critically acclaimed, with influential arts writer Bernard Smith calling it 'probably the best exhibition of Australian art that has ever been mounted'.[45] It was also a popular success, smashing attendance records for an exhibition of Australian works. The Prince and Princess of Wales were the first to see the exhibition, but unfortunately they saw the display back to front because they had to enter via the goods lift for security reasons ('Only superior beings can see Australian history backwards', McCaughey told the press).[46]

A year earlier the NGV had pulsed with a different kind of energy with the opening of Paul Taylor's 1982 exhibition *POPISM*. Robert Lindsay, now Senior Curator of Contemporary Art, had invited twenty-four-year-old Taylor, who had come to prominence through publishing the critical arts journal *Art & Text*, to put on 'something contemporary'.[47] *POPISM* rallied together what Taylor called 'the advance wing of Australian contemporary art', featuring work by Maria Kozic, Robert Rooney, Peter Tyndall, Imants Tillers, Juan Davila, Jenny Watson, Richard Dunn and Howard Arkley; performances by →↗→ and David Chesworth; and a lecture by Adrian Martin. The works were heavily influenced by popular culture and key impulses were appropriation, irony and 'second degree' statements – 'the difference', as Taylor said, 'between saying a word and then saying it in inverted commas'. The exhibition was intended as a 'political statement', said Taylor, and 'not just a survey of a period of art'.[48] *POPISM* was also groundbreaking in Taylor's insistence that the artists be paid an exhibiting fee, enabled through an arrangement with the Victorian Ministry for the Arts. Taylor said, 'Everyone else gets paid in an exhibition, but not usually the artists. That artists are getting paid this time is a breakthrough. It's never happened before at the National Gallery'.[49]

*

The project earned itself the nickname 'Golden Chunders' in tougher moments and 'Golden Slumbers' in more sleep-deprived ones

CONSERVATION: 'A PLACE OF KEEPING'. In the early days of the NGV, John Herbert's 6-metre long painting *Moses bringing down the Tables of the Law*, 1872–78, became known as 'The Barometer' because when the weather was wet the painting would become 'a mass of waving undulations'.[50] Reports by the early directors anxiously monitor the paintings, their concern perhaps heightened by uncertainty about the effects of the extreme Australian climate on paintings made in more temperate European environs. Different initiatives were undertaken to make the NGV a more protected environment: thermometers were installed; blinds fitted and glass painted to limit the strong sunlight; and hessian used to filter air ducts to keep out impurities, including the infernal flies and the infernal smoke billowing in from the hospital next door.

Two of the earliest restorers were Louis Buvelot, who was submitting quotes for conservation work to the Head Librarian, Augustus Tulk, from 1867, and Eugene von Guérard, who also undertook restoration work after his appointment as Painting Master at the Gallery School and Curator of the Gallery in 1870. When G. F. Folingsby became director in 1882 he stopped all restoration, holding the belief that it was 'a very dangerous process and in most cases unnecessary'.[51] Bernard Hall, the subsequent director, also held a non-interventionist position, stating: 'I know nothing about the methods of the professional picture-restorer, but as an artist I am afraid of him'.[52] Meanwhile, some of Melbourne's concerned citizens held the opposite view, accusing the NGV of neglect. An anonymous 1899 article in the *Argus*, for instance, titled 'Our National Gallery: Decay and Danger', warned that 'the pictures in our National Gallery are perishing for want of the skilled restorer'.[53]

While the Art Gallery of New South Wales was proactive in this field, creating Australia's first dedicated conservation studio in 1933, the importance of conservation was slow to emerge at the NGV. The painter Harley Griffiths had been employed as a sole consultant conservator since the late 1930s, and was joined in that role by former Decorative Arts curator David Lawrance in 1967. Various equipment was purchased but, generally speaking, comments John Payne, Senior Conservator, conservation was not a priority for most of the last century: 'It was a tough period – it was not easy to get it underway'. It was not until the 1980s that momentum increased, partly due to the establishment in 1978 of Australia's first conservation course at the University of Canberra, which was itself, as Payne says, part of a 'big push to get conservation underway in Australia as a professional discipline'.[54] Painting conservator Tom Dixon was brought out from the United States to teach in the course, and John Payne signed up as one of the second intake of students. By the early 1980s, both were on staff at the NGV: 'John and Tom were really the architects of the department that we have today', states Carl Villis, Conservator.[55] Dixon was influential as the first Head of Department, work on which Payne has continued to build (as well as an encyclopaedic knowledge of the NGV's collection). 'When we came along, from about 1980 onwards, it was all yet to be done', says Payne. 'There was some groundwork in place, but progress had been rocky. There was a need to start increasing the level of professionalism. This was also the time that the registration department expanded. There was an increase in knowledge about how you manage collections. An understanding, for example, that moving works of art requires a body of expertise and is not just an odd job'.[56] Villis, who started as a volunteer in 1986 and joined the staff in 1995, remembers the early days: 'We could X-ray the paintings here but we had to walk over to Prince Henry's Hospital just down the road to process the film. When the hospital closed we then had to get them processed in the coroner's mortuary nearby'.[57]

Since the 1980s the capacity of the department has steadfastly grown: in 1981 there were four conservators, and now there are around twenty, making it one of the largest conservation departments in a public gallery in Australia. While in the past the NGV deferred to international expertise – such as in 1955 when the Tiepolo had to be sent to London to be restored – the NGV has had the capacity since the 1980s to care for its collection in-house. Conservation is an abiding principle in the ethos of the institution, as Payne states: 'Conservation is a concept that is built into the notion of this institution. If you see the role of the NGV as a place of keeping, then how you keep and how you look after the works are absolutely critical. This has to be embedded in everybody's thinking'.[58]

KEITH HARING PAINTS THE WATER WALL. 'Haring was brought out by John Buckley in 1984 as an early project for the Australian Centre for Contemporary Art', remembers Ted Gott, Senior Curator of International Art, 'but the building was not yet ready. John had nowhere for Haring to exhibit, so he came to the NGV and spoke to Patrick McCaughey and Robert Lindsay, and they decided that Keith could paint the water wall'. Working to a soundtrack of hip hop emanating from a brightly coloured beat box, Haring turned the entrance to the NGV into a dynamic field of flying saucers, dancing figures, blocky dogs and his signature motif, 'the radiant child'. 'He painted inside over two days', says Gott. 'He did the white on one day and the black and the red on the second day. He had never seen the water wall before and used no preparatory drawings – he was an absolute genius.'[59]

'It was very popular', says Gott, 'and Haring interacted beautifully with people while he was here. He had boxes of catalogues from his show at the Tony Shafrazi Gallery and he would do a drawing inside it and autograph it for you. Anyone who walked by, any member of the public that got chatting to him would be given one. Of course, few people in Melbourne knew who he was'. The work was planned to be exhibited for a few months, but it had to be pulled after just a few days. Gott recalls how 'one night, only a couple of days after the window was finished, someone fired a projectile at it – and it must have been with some force because it is thick glass. A panel started to crack and they had

to shut it down because of public safety. They never found out who did it or what the projectile was. Some will remember that after dark along here in Melbourne in the late '70s and early '80s it was hoonsville. It was, however, a loss for Melbourne because it shortened the life of a great Keith Haring work'.[60]

THE ABORIGINAL AND OCEANIC GALLERIES: 'A MASSIVE CATCH-UP EXERCISE'.

When he returned from lunch one day in the summer of 1983–84, McCaughey saw a line of Aboriginal children visiting the NGV on a trip from Bathurst Island. 'I realised,' he said, 'heartsick at the thought, that they had been all over the Gallery for the last two hours and had seen neither stick nor stone of their own art or culture. I felt ashamed, as I have rarely done before or since'.[61] The experience steeled his resolve to create a dedicated space for Indigenous works of art. His predecessors had attempted similar projects, but had failed due to lack of support. The money that allowed the creation of the dedicated gallery space was eventually donated by the Japanese car company Mazda. In 1984, the NGV opened its new Aboriginal and Oceanic Galleries with *Kunwinjku Bim*, an exhibition of bark paintings from western Arnhem Land. At the launch, McCaughey was forthright: 'We are on a massive catch-up exercise, and I admit it's a terrible scandal that it has taken us so long to bring Aboriginal art out of its museum curio corner onto the public stage'.[62]

Anne Marie Brody became the NGV's first Curator of Aboriginal Art in 1981, and was succeeded by Judith Ryan in 1987. 'When I started here it was a very Eurocentric place', says Ryan. 'Even the Australian art collection was not at the forefront. Historical European art was definitely the priority. The Indigenous collection was the last big department to be founded. It seemed to me that within this important collection – which since 1861 has built up the best collection in Australia of other forms of world art – it was vital that we had an important collection of Indigenous art and that we also honoured the Pacific'.[63] McCaughey agreed, attested to by his statement from 2003: 'My generation grew up ignorant and stupid about Aboriginal art and stayed that way for half our lives. I am so glad that period of darkness and ignorance is over for good. The new public prominence of Aboriginal art remains the greatest single revolution in the past quarter-century in Australian art. We now know the names and the countries of Aboriginal artists; we know their myths, their stories, and their place in the Dreaming. And through them we have found a new way to understanding our own'.[64]

THE KEITH AND ELISABETH MURDOCH COURT OF CONTEMPORARY ART. At Patrick McCaughey's very first meeting with the Trustees in 1981, he proposed that the NGV 'roof over a dreary and useless courtyard' and transform it into a new space for contemporary art, which would replace the Survey gallery.[65] A little over six years later, on the eve of his departure, McCaughey opened the Keith and Elisabeth Murdoch Court of Contemporary Art, a $2.7 million extension funded by the Cain government and designed by Melbourne architect Peter Sanders, the first major alteration to the building since it had opened in 1968. The contemporary art court was another chance for the NGV to counter criticism that it excluded contemporary Australian artists, an accusation that had dogged the Gallery its entire history. 'I believed we really must do more for the contemporary artist', stated McCaughey at the launch. 'Of all the achievements of the Gallery, the one area where I think it has had a very spotty record is in its relationship with the living artist.'[66] The space was named in honour of Sir Keith and Dame Elisabeth Murdoch's great contributions to the NGV (something which must have made former director J. S. MacDonald turn in his grave).

The court opened with three special exhibitions. *Australian Art 1960–1986: Field to Figuration*, curated by Robert Lindsay, was 'a response to *The Field*', he said, 'but drawn from our collection'.[67] Ted Gott curated *Backlash: The Australian Drawing Revival*, which explored the remarkable

*

We know their myths, their stories, and their place in the Dreaming. And through them we have found a new way to understanding our own

(opposite)
Geoffrey Burke
Keith Haring painting the water wall 1984

upsurge of drawing during the preceding decade. The third project, *Drysdale: Photographer*, presented a hitherto unknown aspect of Russell Drysdale's work. Curator of Photography Jennie Boddington had seen some of Drysdale's photographs in 1982, published in a book about George Bell. Her interest piqued, she contacted Lady Drysdale to ask about the photographs and uncovered an extensive photographic archive, which Lady Drysdale presented to the NGV a few months later. Boddington called it 'a gift of such magnificence that it changed the character of the collection in one fell swoop'.[68]

ACQUISITIONS: FILLING GAPS IS WHAT DENTISTS DO. In contrast to the prevailing system, Patrick McCaughey was determined to concentrate funds to enable 'museum-wide' acquisitions. 'I refused', he said, 'to divide and diffuse the larger funds into departmental allocations. Instead we were going to pursue major works and look across the entire collection to see what should be acquired. We would stalwartly refuse to "fill gaps" which is what dentists do and nearly always results in museums buying "examples" instead of a substantive work of art'.[69] Within a few weeks of its introduction, this new acquisitions policy enabled the purchase of two fine Boucher pastorals, very significant additions to the NGV's eighteenth-century holdings. Under the old system, the Curator of European Painting and Sculpture, Dr Emma Devapriam, had assumed they were far outside their price range. However, on sighting the paintings in the sale catalogues, McCaughey declared them 'ravishing' and bolted up the stairs to brainstorm a way of buying them with Kenneth Hood, the Deputy Director for Collections and someone, McCaughey gratefully said, who always 'backed the high choice over the lower'.[70] McCaughey convinced curatorial departments across the NGV and the Felton Bequest to pool their funds to make this major acquisition.

McCaughey also discontinued the position of an expatriate and salaried Felton Bequest Advisor, believing that times had changed. Instead, he chose to consult with two 'men on the ground': John Elderfield, Curator of Painting and Sculpture at MoMA, advised on US-based works of art, and Gerard Vaughan, later director of the NGV, advised on works available in Europe. Elderfield helped McCaughey acquire the NGV's Mark Rothko painting, *no. 37 (Red)*, 1956, another acquisition that inspired great public outcry. The historical European collection was also added to with Thomas de Keyser's exquisite seventeenth-century portrait of a dapper couple from Amsterdam, sweetly holding hands on a patio.

The NGV's only work by Andy Warhol was acquired in 1987 – and through a series of lucky coincidences. Robert Lindsay, Senior Curator of Contemporary Art, happened to be in London at Christmas visiting his sister. He dropped in on British art dealer Anthony d'Offay, who unexpectedly was in the office despite being closed for the holidays. D'Offay had some of Warhol's self-portraits in the stockroom, which had

(above)
McCaughey showing Arts Minister Race Mathews the new Boucher works

(below)
Andy Warhol
Self portrait no. 9 1986
synthetic polymer paint and screenprint on canvas
203.5 x 203.7 cm
Purchased through The Art Foundation of Victoria with the assistance of the National Gallery Women's Association, Governor, 1987

'One of my favourite works in the collections of the NGV is this rare, early *Bodhisattva* from the great centre at Mathura. It is not only a beautiful Indian sculpture of its period. Its Hellenistic influences remind me of the enduring legacy throughout history of the cross-cultural flow between East and West along the silk roads, whether by trade or in this case the invasion of Alexander the Great some centuries before'

– Lyn Williams

featured in an exhibition that had closed two weeks earlier. On sighting them, Lindsay fell in love and reserved one – at what now seems the incredibly low price of US$35,000 – for the NGV. Back in Australia, Acting Director Kenneth Hood declared outright: 'You'll never get it through'. Luckily when Patrick, who had just flown back to Melbourne from Harvard to launch the Murdoch Court, saw it he was similarly enamoured. As Lindsay recounts: 'After the launch there was a celebratory luncheon and Patrick said to Sir Andrew, the President of the Trustees, "let's hold a Trustees' meeting and acquire this work". Not all of them were there, but they had enough to pass it. By the time I got home on Friday afternoon it was still morning in London. I rang on our home phone and said to Anthony d'Offay: "I have approval, it's *fantastic*, send it out. Yes, it's a *definite* sale". The next morning we opened the paper to read the tragic headline: "Andy Warhol: dead"'. To Lindsay's surprise, d'Offay honoured the sale, even though 'it was just my word over the phone and he could have sold it at the time for $200,000. If I had waited until Monday to call from the NGV it would have been too late'. Lindsay was also behind the acquisition of works by key figures in the 1980s trans-avantgarde movement, including the German artists Rainer Fetting, Jörg Immendorff and A. R. Penck, and the Italian Mimmo Paladino. 'Rainer Fetting is the best of the wild German painters, and *Another murder at the Anvil II* is a totally uncompromised Fetting. You won't find a better Fetting anywhere.'[71]

The NGV's collection of Indian art was greatly strengthened by the acquisition of an Indian *Bodhisattva* from the second century AD. John Guy, Curator of Asian Art of India and South-East Asia, got off the plane from London where he had seen the work and called McCaughey from Tullamarine. Half an hour later, 'an excitable, bleary-eyed John Guy was downing a scotch' and rabbiting on about the magnificence of the work, which McCaughey agreed would 'change the face and character of the collection'. It cost a princely $325,000, a price significantly higher than the Rothko. However, with Guy and McCaughey as staunch advocates, the Trustees 'took it on the chin' and found the funds.[72] The acquisition of the *Bodhisattva* also went some way to inspiring Sir James Plimsoll, diplomat and former governor of Tasmania, to present a very fine collection of Hindu and Buddhist sculptures from India, the Himalayas and Cambodia.

ACQUISITIONS: TREASURES FROM EBAY. On his very first day in office, in between being 'sandbagged ... with public service memorandums', McCaughey 'found a piece of paper and wrote letters to Sidney Nolan, Albert Tucker and Roger Kemp saying they were underrepresented in the collection and that I would like to talk to them about it as soon as possible'.[73] For McCaughey this was the first step towards addressing a major oversight: 'To my admiration and dismay,' he said, 'I had watched Canberra collect the crucial period of the 1940s in Australian art with a sweep that beggared all other public collections ... The National Gallery of Victoria had sat meek and mute as these treasures were carried off from Melbourne ... Late though it was, I was determined to rectify this crippling absence'.[74] McCaughey was pleased to discover that Nolan's *Wimmera* series was still largely available. In 1983, Sidney and Mary Nolan made the extraordinary gift of twenty-five *Wimmera* paintings, 1942–44, which the NGV augmented with the purchase of a suite of drawings. Albert Tucker had also been roundly ignored by the NGV, his hometown gallery. In 1982, five paintings by Tucker were acquired, including two studies from the *Images of Modern Evil* series, 1943–46, and the broody *Self-portrait*, 1945, in which Tucker's discontented face stands out against a blotchy, bruise-like backdrop. McCaughey also resolutely instigated the collecting of Indigenous works of art, which resulted in the purchase of works by the Papunya Tula artists, now a cherished part of the collection. The ANZ Bank made a substantial donation in 1989 to support the acquisition of Eugene von Guérard's epic *Weatherboard Creek Falls, Jamieson's Valley, New South Wales*, 1862.

(opposite)
INDIAN
Bodhisattva
Kushan period, 2nd century AD, Mathura, Uttar Pradesh, India
sandstone, pigment
Purchased through the Art Foundation of Victoria with the assistance of Hari N. Harilela OBE, Fellow and Mrs Padma Harilela, and Brenmoss Investment Pty Ltd, Fellow, 1982

(overleaf left)
Sidney Nolan
Wimmera (from Mt Arapiles) 1943
enamel paint on wood panel
61.0 x 91.6 cm
Gift of Sir Sidney and Lady Nolan, 1983

(overleaf right)
Douglas T. Kilburn
No title (Group of Koorie men) c.1847
daguerreotype, leather, wood, velvet, brass
(7.5 x 6.5 cm) (image)
9.2 x 7.9 x 1.7 cm (case) (closed)
Purchased from Admission Funds, 1983

The first of the Douglas Kilburn daguerreotypes made its way into the collection in the 1980s. 'These daguerreotypes', says Isobel Crombie, Senior Curator of Photography, 'have been a persistent element of my tenure. One was in the collection when I arrived and I bought one at auction in London. With regards to the third one in our collection, I got an anonymous tip-off from someone saying "you should check eBay". I mean, we never buy anything off eBay. But I looked it up and – lo and behold – it was a Kilburn daguerreotype in a shop in Wales. I knew that Wales was a place where a person had taken some of these daguerreotypes back in the 1840s, so the work was probably from a deceased estate that ended up in the shop. I knew that it was unverifiable because it was from eBay, but I recognised it as an extraordinary thing that must enter our collection. I found a colleague here who is really good at bidding and he got it for us. We now have three from this series, and I can't think of many other daguerreotype series of this nature in the world. They are extremely rare'.[75]

Rowena Clark, Curator of Costume and Textiles from 1972 to 1990, is notorious for an acquisition made in 1984. Travelling on the Number 6 tram one day, she noticed a punk: 'I thought, "I'm not going to let you escape me, baby", so I waited until he caught my eye and then I introduced myself. I gave him my card and offered to buy his outfit. The whole tram was in silence'.[76] Within a few days, the sixteen-year-old rang to accept her offer of $500 for the outfit. Apparently he was happy to give up his leather, as he had decided to become a vegetarian. A few years later, during a day out at the footy in 1986, Clark cajoled a Collingwood supporter to let her buy their outfit, which was complete with players' autographs. Clark is also remembered for her exhibition of infant, bridal and mourning costumes, to which she gave the spirited title: *Hatches, Matches and Dispatches.* Given its rapid growth, Fashion and Textiles split from Decorative Arts to become its own department in 1981.

A WEEPING WOMAN AND A GRIEVING MAN: THE THEFT OF THE PICASSO. 'Not a weeping woman, but a grieving man' ran many of the newspaper headlines above stories about the NGV's stolen Picasso. It was a headline always accompanied by a photograph of a dejected Patrick McCaughey, still wearing his customary bow tie but with his usually ebullient character turned down a few notches. He described the week-long ordeal in 1986 as 'a hideous perpetual burden of ignominy and shame – like having perpetual jetlag without feeling tired'. *Weeping woman*, 1937, which McCaughey described as 'a magnet of suffering' and a 'key postscript to *Guernica*', was a hugely significant work in the collection that had been bought after it featured in a Picasso exhibition at the NGV in 1984.[77] Race Mathews, the Minister for the Arts at the time, said that 'its significance, particularly to Spanish people in the context of the war, is immense. You would have to say this painting we held in trust for the rest of the world'.[78]

And now it was gone. The painting was removed from its wall on a Saturday afternoon, and replaced by a little typed card, the usual protocol for works removed for conservation. It was not until Monday morning, when the media received the ransom note, that everyone was alerted to the theft. A search of the NGV resulted in the frame being found in a nearby alcove but, alas, no Picasso. Ted Gott remembers that 'everyone

was totally mesmerised – and paralysed – with shock. It was literally unbelievable. It was like some ghastly film unfolding and you were in the middle of it as some extra. I remember that they asked to search our offices and everyone was terrified that it would turn up in their office. It was really weird. It was just amazing and horrible and one felt really sorry for Patrick – he aged overnight'.[79]

The typed card was signed the 'Australian Cultural Terrorists', who then outlined their demands in a series of ransom notes. The first stated: 'We have stolen the Picasso from the National Gallery as a protest against the niggardly funding of the fine arts in this hick State'. They demanded a 10 per cent increase in funding for the arts over the next three years and five prizes of $5000 – to be called 'The Picasso Ransom' – to be awarded to artists under thirty. Race Mathews, Minister for the Arts as well as Minister for Police, had a unique opportunity to unite his two portfolios, a fact not lost on the thieves: 'Because the Minister of the Arts is also Minister of Plod, we are allowing him a sporting seven days in which to try to have us arrested while he deliberates'.[80] Mathews received another shellacking in the second ransom note, which further proved the group to be colourful – if mischievous – letter writers. 'Dear, oh dear. Race Mathews, you tiresome old bag of swamp gas', it began. 'We have not dumped the painting in a blue-nosed funk.' They boasted that they had stolen the work with 'less risk than shoplifting cotton hankies from David Jones' and ended: 'Good luck with your huffing and puffing, Minister, you pompous fathead'.[81] A third letter, received soon after, contained only a burnt match with a note stating: 'Thank you for your support. Phase two begins shortly'.[82] On Tuesday 19 August 1986, the phone rang at the night editor's desk at the *Age* and a man claiming to be one of the terrorists stated: 'The painting is returned. It's in locker 227 at Spencer Street'.[83] McCaughey waited with bated breath as the locker door was jimmied open to reveal the painting unharmed and neatly wrapped in brown paper. A press conference was held that concluded with a champagne toast to the return of the

(previous left)
Des Kirwan (designer)
James Lynch (decorator)
Unknown (maker)
Punk outfit c. 1983–84 (detail)
leather, cotton, metal, rubber, plastic, paint, fur, found badges, wool, blood
(a) 64.0 cm (centre back), 58.0 cm (sleeve length) (jacket)
(b) 104.0 cm (outer leg), 36.5 cm (waist, flat) (trousers)
(m) 64.0 cm (centre back) (t-shirt)
Purchased, 1984

(previous right)
Pablo Picasso
Weeping woman 1937
oil on canvas
55.2 x 46.2 cm
Purchased by donors of The Art Foundation of Victoria, with the assistance of the Jack and Genia Liberman family, Founder Benefactor, 1986

(opposite left)
Patrick McCaughey at Spencer Street Station 1986

(opposite right)
Ron Tandberg
cartoon published in the *Age*

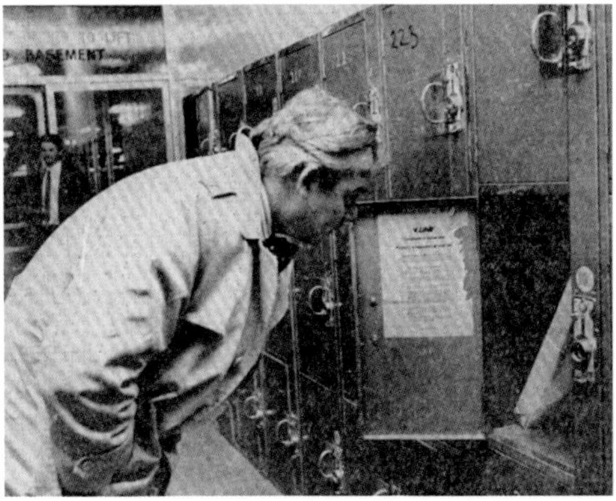

Weeping woman, who sat on her easel, as media reports quipped, looking like a million dollars (or more). Ironically, when *Weeping woman* had been proudly unveiled in 1985, McCaughey had exuberantly proclaimed: 'It is our ultimate museum-wide acquisition ... This face is going to haunt Melbourne for the next hundred years'.[84]

THE BICENTENARY AND NAPPERBY DEATH SPIRIT DREAMING. Rodney Wilson started as director in March of 1988, which coincided with Australia's bicentennial year. 'Rodney Wilson was very important', says Judith Ryan, Senior Curator of Indigenous Art. 'The bicentennial year was a time of intense protest and a watershed moment in terms of transforming opinion about Indigenous people and history in Australia. Wilson thought that the Felton Bequest should purchase one Indigenous work and *Napperby death spirit Dreaming*, 1980, was chosen. This was the first time an Indigenous work had been acquired using Felton Bequest funds. There was a very long debate at the acquisitions meeting over the cost of the work; however, a Philip Guston painting, which was $100,000 more, escaped such scrutiny. There was a prevailing idea that Indigenous art could be bought for a song'.[85]

The NGV's Business Council was also established in 1988 with the aim of bringing art and business together. Judy Williams, now the NGV's Head of Foundation, first worked for the Business Council: 'The Business Council was set up', she says, 'to look at engaging the business community with the NGV. At that time, the Gallery structure was very much that of the public service and there was no entrepreneurial activity. The Business Council aimed to engage the business community with a view to sponsorship and support for public programs and NGV initiatives. It was really the first step towards the NGV developing the structure that it now has. Today, the NGV is a pretty interesting creature: we are a museum, we are a large education provider, we are an entertainment venue, we have a commercial aspect to us and we are part of the public service'.[86]

JAMES MOLLISON: A COMPULSIVE INTEREST IN AUSTRALIAN ART. Wilson resigned after just nine months, allegedly over a housing dispute. A running joke did the rounds of the arts community: Bernard Hall's tenure had been forty-two years, Daryl Lindsay's fifteen years, and Eric Westbrook's seventeen years, but in Wilson's case the term had dwindled to only a few months. What was wrong with the NGV? By the late 1980s, it was clear that the NGV really was in the doldrums. Lack of financial support had run the place threadbare: staff turnover was high, morale was low and the carpets were shabby. In 1989 Westbrook lamented, 'It is time we stopped saying we have the greatest gallery, which we have, but we won't if it goes on like this'.[87] Appointed in October 1989, the new Director, James Mollison, agreed. 'The place needs sprucing up', he said at the time. 'People have forgotten about the place. We no longer get an enormous number of tourists ... Young people actively dislike it. For them, this look of the '50s is the equivalent of something absolutely, totally dead'.[88]

James Mollison

'They were not great years for the Gallery', Mollison says, thinking back. When asked why the NGV was languishing, he responds: 'I suppose it was complacency. There was still an overhang of the nineteenth century in the Gallery's practices. The NGV had not accepted that it was heading towards a new century and the old systems were considered good enough'. On arrival he found fault with the deficient administrative systems, the disparities between responsibilities and wages, and the lack of forward planning. He set about restructuring the NGV: 'I wanted to build confidence in what we could do if we all went in one direction'. Mollison was about to finish a long – and illustrious – stint at the National Gallery of Australia and was visiting New York, but thoughts of the Melbourne Gallery persisted: 'I sent off a cable that stated, "I am a long way from Melbourne, but I have realised that I do want the job"'. Mollison had grown up with the NGV: 'My introduction to the NGV was when I was twelve', he remembers, 'and I have been into that building every fortnight of my life – unless I was overseas – from then until now. When I was sixteen Daryl Lindsay told the man with the key "when he comes in on the weekend, let him into the picture store. He's only a boy, he can't hurt anything".

So, I learnt the fronts of all the works by heart and, when I had done that, I learnt the backs. I knew a great deal about the Gallery and its collections'.[89]

A notable quality of Mollison's directorship was a deep engagement with Australian art: 'All my life I have been a studio visitor', he says. 'My first studio visit was to Arnold Shore, my next to Jock Frater and Eric Thake, and then, when I was seventeen, to Danila Vassilieff. I have so enjoyed watching the growth of artists'.[90] This translated into a desire to present reinvigorated displays of Australian art: 'We know that Australian art is of compulsive interest to Australians', he said at the time.[91] Mollison increased the space allocated to Australian art and, in August 1991, the Rooms of Australian Art were opened on the ground floor, featuring an integrated presentation of paintings, sculpture and decorative arts with input from various curators. He also amended the invitation lists: 'When I arrived, the policy was that artists were not invited. There were also no members of the Aboriginal community invited – and that broke my heart'.[92]

Mollison also instigated a program of Australian art retrospectives, which were grouped across three tiers: significant historical figures, such as Rupert Bunny; senior contemporary artists, such as John Olsen; and mid-career contemporary artists, such as Susan Norrie. A series of research-led art historical surveys were also mounted, of which *Classical Modernism: The George Bell Circle* is a good example. It opened to solid acclaim in 1992: the *Australian*'s critic Robert Rooney said the NGV had 'got things right' and Christopher Heathcote from *The Age* said the 'initiative deserves nothing but praise, especially if it results in more exhibitions of this significance'.[93] This focus on Australian art history was complemented by a series of blockbuster exhibitions featuring artists such as Toulouse-Lautrec and Odilon Redon, artists 'high on everybody's curiosity list' who would easily garner both commercial and popular success.[94]

Many fondly remember Mollison for establishing the Access Gallery in 1991, a space for community groups to have a presence in the NGV through display of their arts and crafts. This was the first community-access gallery established by a major art institution in Australia, and the community responded eagerly. Jane Scott curated the space with assistance from David Hurlston, and a survey of the exhibition program reveals projects such as *Traditional Cosmopolitanism: Serbian Art in Australia Today* and *The Art of Making Do*, an exhibition celebrating the centenary of the Australian Labor Party. The initiative aimed to enable broad representation at the NGV: 'I wanted those kids who may have suffered a bit from chiacking in the schoolyard', remembers Mollison, 'to be able to go to the NGV and see things that their country had produced, so they could have pride in who they are as well as the pride they take in absolutely fitting in as Australians'.[95] Within a few years, the doldrums were banished. In 1990, Mollison stated: 'I am now working for a gallery which has a future, instead of working for a gallery that had a great past. That's made an enormous difference to morale here. We know how we can manage our affairs into the future'.[96]

ACQUISITIONS: 'THE QUICK AND THE DEAD'. While at the NGA in Canberra, Mollison had assembled Australia's best collection of post-war works of art, including the controversial purchase of Jackson Pollock's *Blue Poles*. In contrast, the NGV had been less active in this area. Mollison set about reversing this: in 1992, he purchased Anselm Kiefer's *Böse blumen (Evil flowers)*, 1985–91, Gerhard Richter's *Abstract painting (725-3)*, 1990, and an earlier Abstract Expressionist work, *Combat*, 1965, by Lee Krasner. When the works arrived, the international galleries were rehung with an innovative mix of modern European, American and Australian works. Australian artist Tony Tuckson's gestural abstract *White lines (horizontal) on red*, 1970–73, for instance, was hung alongside Krasner's piece, and a pale minimalist work by Australian Robert Hunter sat in an interesting dialogue next to a work by American minimalist Donald Judd. Works by Indigenous artists, such as Rover Thomas and Emily Kam Kngwarray, were also included. 'At the time', says Judith Ryan, 'there was an immense air of excitement about these juxtapositions because Mollison had embraced the notion of international twentieth-century art, and also the idea that Indigenous artists had brought a new vision to the world, expressed in an innovative style and in an aesthetic unique to their way of experiencing the world'.[97]

Mollison placed great importance on developing, with curator Mae Anna Pang, the Japanese calligraphy and painting collection as well as broadening the NGV's collection of Australian art: 'It was truly the National Gallery of *Victoria*. I don't remember the figures exactly, but there were less than fifty pictures made before 1945 by Australian artists living outside of Victoria in the collection when I began working there. I felt that the representation of artists from other Australian states was of particular importance'.[98] His staunch advocacy for collecting contemporary works by Indigenous artists was a quality cherished by Ryan: 'He had a passion for Indigenous art. He believed that we were witnessing something very important – the equivalent of Renaissance Italy or the School of Paris – and he drove me

(below)
Gerhard Richter
Abstract painting (725-3) 1990
oil on canvas
225.8 x 200.6 cm
Purchased through The Art Foundation of Victoria with the assistance of Westpac Banking Corporation, Founder Benefactor, 1992

(opposite above)
Rover Thomas
Yari Country 1989
earth pigments and natural binder on canvas
160.0 x 200.2 cm
Purchased through The Art Foundation of Victoria with the assistance of Pacific Dunlop Limited, Fellow, 1990

(opposite below)
Bill Henson
Untitled 1990–1991 from the *Paris Opera Project* series 1990–91.
type C photograph
123.4 x 123.4 cm irreg.
Purchased through The Art Foundation of Victoria with the assistance of David Syme and Co. Ltd, Fellow, 1991

to develop the collection'. This is nicely symbolised by the story behind the acquisition of three iconic works by leaders of the Warmun School of painting, Rover Thomas and Jack Britten. From an exhibition of Warmun works, Mollison and Ryan chose two powerful works by Rover Thomas and, in addition, Mollison asked Ryan to consider Jack Britten's *Purnululu country*, 1989. As Ryan recounts: 'Aware of the paucity of acquisition funds, I initially hesitated but then argued strongly for it in response to Mollison's retort that there were "two kinds of curators: the quick and the dead"'.[99] All works made their way into the collection.

One of Mollison's first actions as director was to move photography to a gallery adjacent to the entrance. A notable acquisition in this area in 1991 was a series of works from Bill Henson's romantically charged *Paris Opera Project*, 1990–91. Henson has a long association with the NGV that dates back to 1975, when he was invited to present his first solo exhibition at the age of nineteen. The NGV also came out strongly in support of Henson in 2009 when he was the target of criticism from politicians and the media over his controversial use of a thirteen-year-old model. The NGV made a public statement of support for the artist and also, says Isobel Crombie, 'in our own quiet way we supported Bill by putting more of his work up on the walls'.[100]

TIMOTHY POTTS AND THE TEMPLE OF DOOM. Mollison's successor, Timothy Potts, is an intriguing combination: part Indiana Jones and part merchant banker. Potts trained in archaeology and between 1976 and 1989 worked in the field on ancient excavations in Jordan, Greece and Iraq (apparently while Iraqi jets scorched overhead). In the early 1990s, he swapped the sand for suits: resigning from his role of Research Fellow at Christ Church in Oxford to take up a position at Lehman Brothers in New York before coming to Melbourne in 1994 to take up the position of Deputy Director, International Art and Public Access at the NGV. When James Mollison retired in 1994, Potts was clearly an heir apparent. The NGV made no secret of fact that it had aimed to develop a succession plan: President of the Trustees Will Bailey said they had encouraged Mollison 'to recruit people who would have the potential to succeed him. The practice of having a successor in the place is terrific – you get a running start'.[101]

When Potts accepted the role in 1995, he commented that it was a position that he had been 'working towards for many years'. He held a distinguished academic record, which included a PhD from Oxford in archaeology and subsequent roles at Oxford as Research Lecturer and Research Fellow in archaeology. This strong scholarly background was then supplemented by skills in business, finance and marketing, which he had honed though his experience at Lehman Brothers. 'If I was to have an advantage over others', he said at the time, 'I had to have another string to my bow'.[103] 'One thing we are going to have to face', confirmed Bailey, 'is that the role of the director has changed and is changing – they can no longer just come into the ranks as purely academics, educators or from museums ... We are in [a period of] enormous cultural change from being a totally public institution to one that has got to be more entrepreneurial to make the Gallery viable'.[104] This shift was a significant one, as Judy Williams, Head of Foundation, notes: 'Museums all over the world have had to change, and Timothy Potts instigated these changes at the NGV. His charge was to modernise the Gallery and he did that over a period of time despite a lot of resistance. I don't think he has ever been properly recognised for that, but it was a major change'.[105]

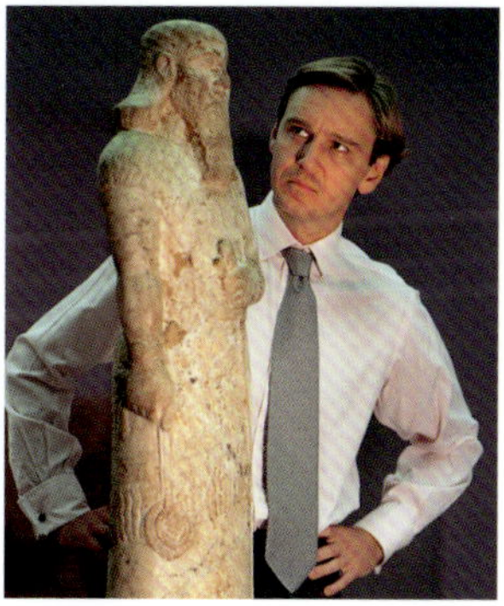

Craig Abraham
Dr Timothy Potts

Potts will also be remembered for the exhibition *Rembrandt: A Genius and His Impact*. Once again, it was his dedication to scholarship that convinced the major museums to lend their works to Melbourne. At the time, he said: 'These days you can't just front up to a museum and say "Can I borrow a Rembrandt, please, we're having an exhibition!" You have to convince the museum that the reason you want the work is that it will contribute in some substantial way to understanding of Rembrandt'.[106] Potts set up the framework for an international symposium and then enticed all twelve of the world's best Rembrandt scholars to attend. The Rembrandt exhibition must have felt like a major achievement for Potts, yet Rembrandt would become a thorn in his side.

THE *PISS CHRIST* INCIDENT: 'THE WHOLE THING WAS HORRIBLE'. 'The last two weeks', wrote Timothy Potts on 18 October 1997, 'have been the most traumatic in the National Gallery of Victoria's recent history'.[107] That fortnight had involved a heady wave of hysteria surrounding *Piss Christ*, a photograph included in the survey show *A History of Andres Serrano*. Since it was created in 1987, *Piss Christ* had become something of a cause célèbre, inciting a roadshow of religious rage wherever it went. The photograph depicts a crucifix bathed in a golden and Godly light. Except it's not light, it's piss, with the work's title, *Piss Christ*, ensuring that no one misses the punchline.

A month before the exhibition, the NGV had started receiving abusive phone calls. A few days before the opening, the Archbishop of Melbourne, George Pell, went to the Supreme Court of Victoria seeking an injunction to stop the exhibition on the basis that *Piss Christ* was blasphemous and/or obscene. Potts and the NGV fought back and Pell was unsuccessful, but nevertheless he used the opportunity to galvanise support for a campaign against what he felt was the 'remorseless slippage towards obscenity, pornography and permissiveness' in western society.[108] His words evidently stirred passions. Christians of many denominations congregated in the forecourt to 'atone for the public blasphemy', as vigil organiser Ben O'Brien described it.[109] Shortly after the exhibition opened a man tried to walk out with *Piss Christ* and, in the ensuing tussle with security guards, the work was damaged. The work was rehung and security was increased. A week later, an eighteen-year-old youth made a flying kick at one of the Klansmen works, providing the perfect decoy for his sixteen-year-old associate, who had gained entry to the exhibition using fake ID, to attack *Piss Christ* with a sledgehammer, breaking the Perspex, ruining the print and injuring a security guard.

Up to this point, Potts had staunchly defended the artist's right to freedom of expression; however, he was evidently privy to threats serious enough to dent his resolve. Though the details remained 'necessarily confidential' for security reasons, the words 'death threats' and 'bomb threats' figure repeatedly in statements made at the time.[110] While injury to people was obviously a key concern for the NGV, another concern was the potential of injury to the priceless works by Rembrandt on display at the same time. International lenders were growing increasingly uneasy, as was the federal government, which had indemnified the Rembrandt exhibition at a breathtaking $800 million. Reluctantly, Potts and the Trustees decided to close the Serrano exhibition a mere two weeks into its run. Potts issued a statement: 'The decision to close was a very anguished one, aware as we were that it could be interpreted by the vandals and others as a moral victory ... In the final analysis, we had no doubt that anything less than closure would involve more serious injury and perhaps even fatality. This I could not accept'.[111] On hearing the news, Serrano released a statement: 'I denounce the National Gallery's cancellation of my exhibition, I denounce the Director Timothy Potts's spineless lack of support, I denounce any and all acts of terrorism and violent dissent, and most of all I denounce the cowardice of those unable to fight for and defend the principles of their democracy'.[112] Some NGV staff felt betrayed by Potts's capitulation, and were furious at his lack of consultation with them or the artist. Isobel Crombie, curator of the exhibition, remembers that: 'The whole thing was horrible. The NGV had backed down on the two things that I value most of all as a curator: support for artists and freedom of expression'.[113]

Potts was clearly having a few very bad days at the office: 'It's by far the most unpleasant thing I've ever been involved in, and the saddest day for the arts and for freedom of expression in this city'.[114] He went on to say, 'I've done more than any other person in this

(above)
Wayne Taylor
Christians protesting
outside the NGV

(below)
Sebastian Costanzo
Andres Serrano press
conference

whole episode to defend and promote Serrano's right as an artist, and the principle of freedom of artistic expression in a public space ... It would be a great irony and a great historical inaccuracy if I ended up being portrayed as the one who's compromised artistic freedom of expression'.[115] Speaking at a public forum, the art critic John McDonald gave a succinct summary of the incident: 'We've ended up with Andres as a martyr, we've ended up with Timothy Potts as a villain, and the world's just not like that. We don't have all these heroes and villains – it's obviously something that's very, very difficult and has to be looked at in a more subtle way'.[116]

ACQUISITIONS: IN MEMORY OF A BRILLIANT GREEK SCHOLAR. Timothy Potts found an outstanding work for the antiquities collection in 1997: the Graeco-Roman *Torso of athlete* from the first century BC – first century AD. The acquisition aligned with Potts's area of expertise and also commemorated the contribution of Professor Dale Trendall who, from the 1950s, was a driving force behind the development of the NGV's celebrated Greek and Italian vase collection. Former director Daryl Lindsay described him most memorably as 'that brilliant Greek scholar, Professor Dale Trendall ... with his puck-like whimsical face and every-ready, devastating crack at some dullard. Asking him one night who was the strange-looking bearded scientist at dinner, he replied: "A Martian, I think, arrived on a saucer last night'.[117] Felton Advisor (and soon to be Director) Gerard Vaughan also purchased for Potts at auction in London a bewitching Egyptian funerary head-covering, embellished with brilliant gold and totemic patterning, for the Antiquities collection. A few years later, the European painting collection was enriched by Jean-Baptiste Regnault's *Venus preparing herself*, 1815, a sumptuous neo-classical representation of Venus adorning herself with help from a coterie of maidens.

A major work also came into the Australian collection when Janet and Donald Holt gifted Emily Kam Kngwarray's 8-metre masterpiece *Anwerlarr anganenty (Big yam Dreaming)*, 1995. The Holts decided to donate the work to a public gallery and the NGV successfully negotiated the acquisition. The Gallery also acquired a series of strong contemporary Australian works including Constanze Zikos's *Fake flag*, 1994, a sleek concoction of plastic laminate assembled to create a striking – and easy to clean – Australian flag; Fiona Hall's *Paradisus Terrestris Entitled*, 1996, which won the inaugural $100,000 *Contempora5* Art Prize initiated by the Kennett government and presented at the NGV; Patricia Piccinini's large-scale future-scape *Psychogeography*, 1996; and Ricky Swallow's *Model for a sunken monument*, 1999, the melting mask of Darth Vader purchased with the assistance of the Joan Clemenger Foundation.

THE NGV GETS STUFFED. 'Every corner of the place is stuffed', said Timothy Potts in 1997.[118] 'The collection has outgrown the infrastructure, it's cannibalising exhibition space. We have collected about 800 objects a year since the gallery opened and [have] no extra space. Because things are crammed in so much, ultimately that endangers the objects.'[119] When Potts started in 1995, he had declared the NGV 'the most scandalously underfunded gallery in Australia', echoing the sentiments of directors past.[120] Only 5 per cent of the collection could be exhibited at any one time, storage space was insufficient, systems were archaic and it looked dowdy. Victoria's great gallery was in crisis and Potts and John Gough, President of the Council, were campaigning for change: 'Well as it has served us in the past, in a number of key functional areas the building has become inadequate for the needs of a major art gallery as we approach the twenty-first century'.[121] Potts was also tired of watching people get lost. While the 'wonderfully strong' exterior was still a marvel for him, the foyer was 'an ill-defined and eccentric space. Look at people when they come in', said Potts. 'Nearly everyone stops and scratches their heads because it is not clear which way to go.'[122] John Gough, President of the Council, made a determined campaign for the NGV. There had not been a visit by a premier to the Gallery for many years, but Gough invited Jeff Kennett in to impress upon him the dire need for an upgrade.

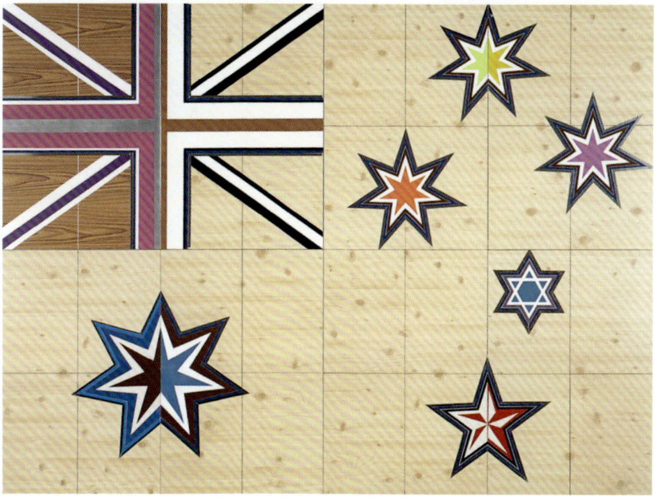

(above)
GREECE/ITALY
Torso of athlete 1st century BC–1st century AD, Hellenistic/Roman period
marble
102.6 x 52.1 x 27.4 cm
Felton Bequest, in memory of Professor A. D. Trendall, 1997

(below)
Constanze Zikos
Fake flag 1994
thermo-setting laminate, enamel paint, crayon, metallic and plastic self-adhesive tape on composition board
(a–h) 198.1 x 262.2 cm (overall)
Purchased, 1999

The NGV then found advocates in two ministers for the arts: first in Haddon Storey and then in Premier Jeff Kennett, who took on the arts portfolio after Storey's retirement. In the election year of 1996, the Coalition government's arts policy earmarked $80 million for refurbishments. This came (somewhat controversially) from casino income: 'It allows us to give to the people of Victoria, in return for dollars lost on gaming through the casino, another asset which will be provided to them at no debt whatsoever', said Kennett.[123] Potts was thrilled: 'The $80 million puts in place the keystone of our strategy to reposition the NGV as the best [gallery] in Australia within five years'.[124] Potts had also campaigned tenaciously to remove entrance fees to the NGV, submitting business models to successive ministers to support his case. The Coalition ultimately agreed and the decision to scrap entry fees caused attendances to increase dramatically. In 1997, one million people went to the NGV, making it the most frequently visited visual arts institution in Australia. In the end, the state government would contribute a total of $93 million, allocating an extra $13 million from the general budget.

THE NGV GETS GOING. In 1996, the Trustees launched an international design competition seeking proposals for the refurbishment of the interior and the construction of additional buildings at the St Kilda Road site. After a highly competitive process, in late 1996, Italian architect and design luminary Mario Bellini, in association with Melbourne-based Métier3, was appointed as architect. To his credit, Potts decided – perhaps a little against his temperament – that the redevelopment process should be as public as possible: 'The Gallery is owned by all Victorians and their interest in, and commitment to, the overall aims and objectives of such a major project are fundamental'.[125] Early proposals from Bellini that contemplated removing the water wall (or 'the shower', as Kennett called it) and modifications to the Great Hall inspired outrage, causing the National Trust to go straight on the defensive. Interestingly, the brief outlined that the spaces allocated to the contemporary, Asian and Indigenous art collections were to be doubled, while the European collection received an increase of only 16 per cent in floor space, a fascinating reflection of the recent development of the NGV's own collection.

THE NGV GETS … ANOTHER NGV! The parameters of the project changed radically when Premier Kennett unexpectedly declared there would be a second NGV at Federation Square. Kennett, who earned himself the nickname 'the Medici of Melbourne' for his ambitious program of building works throughout the 1990s, had previously mused about art spaces at Federation Square. In 1996, for instance, he said: 'I'm very keen to put the Albert Tucker collection in one of them and I'd like to get the Joseph Brown collection in another'.[126] He was also considering plans for a dedicated gallery for contemporary art, the establishment of which had been argued for very persuasively by a large lobby group. However, Potts had also campaigned strenuously on behalf of the NGV, arguing that the government should move 'from a very focused display to a sort of display that doesn't exist anywhere else in the country, and do something for Australian art that really needs to happen'.[127] Kennett seemed to take almost everybody by surprise with his offer to fund the 'Museum of Australian Art' at Federation Square.

It was news to the architects, for instance. Lab Architecture Studio had not included it in their first prize-winning design of Federation Square in 1997. Even Potts, who had been lobbying for years for more space, seemed pleasantly surprised. He had said to Kennett: 'If you really want to do something major and important, and something that will last, a dedicated museum will celebrate the coming of age of Australian art, which will mirror the coming of age of Australian politics to be commemorated at the centenary of Federation'. This idea evidently caught the Premier's imagination: 'From that moment,' said Potts, 'it was a done deal'.[128] The new gallery was to be designed by London's Lab Architecture Studio, headed by Sydney-born Peter Davidson and Texan Donald Bates, working in conjunction with Melbourne's oldest architectural firm, Bates Smart. Lab had won against 177 proposals entered in the extensive international competition to design the $393 million, 3.8 hectare development.

The decision to divide the NGV's collection into a 'Museum of Australian Art' and a gallery of international art polarised the arts community. There were those staunchly against the concept: Daniel Thomas, Director of the Art Gallery of South Australia, for instance, warned against creating a 'protected ghetto for the contemporary end of Australian art'.[129] However, others championed the idea of a dedicated space for Australian art. Jan Senbergs, formerly the artist representative on the NGV's Board of Trustees, spoke for those in support: 'I don't think we ought to be apologetic or thought of as chauvinistic or provincial if we show off our art in a prominent way. The more I see of the various art centres of the world, the more I realise how strong and vivid our own contemporary and past art scene has been and is, and how unknown it is in the centres of world art and to

*

'In one sense, the creativity of individuals over time is a very true reflection of the development of Australia'

visitors coming here'.[130] Timothy Potts was unequivocal, stating that it would enable 'the country's finest and most comprehensive experience of Australia through its art'.[131] Jeff Kennett echoed these sentiments: 'If we were going to have a major civic space, it seemed to me that it should have a natural drawcard. In one sense, the creativity of individuals over time is a very true reflection of the development of Australia'.[132]

GERARD VAUGHAN: 'A VERY, VERY INTENSE PERIOD'. Timothy Potts resigned in 1998 to take up the role of director of the Kimbell Art Museum in Texas. To find a suitable candidate, the President of the Council, Steve Vizard, and the Deputy President, Jim Cousins, met with applicants from around the world. 'The standout applicant', Vizard recalled, 'was Dr Gerard Vaughan, an Australian who had studied at the University of Melbourne under Professor Margaret Manion and was known to the Felton Bequest'. After completing his studies Vaughan taught at the universities of Monash and Melbourne before going to Oxford to write a doctoral thesis exploring eighteenth-century attitudes to antiquity. Although he imagined he might be in England for three years, he stayed for eighteen. Subsequently, he became Deputy Director of Oxford's major fundraising campaign, and the CEO of the newly formed British Museum Development Trust, responsible for facilitating the Norman Foster rebuilding project after the transfer of the British Libary to its new home. The Council were thrilled: 'To have an Australian with a background in large-scale fundraising and a specialist degree in Fine Arts with an employment pedigree that included the British Museum seemed like a dream come true'.[133]

'When I first came to the NGV in July 1999, it was an odd time', says Gerard Vaughan, 'because we were in the process of closing the building down and then emptying it. There were four building projects underway: the St Kilda Road building, Federation Square, our temporary base in the new Public Record Office in North Melbourne and the temporary gallery space in the State Library building in Russell Street. I remember doing an interview with a journalist who said, "Well, you are in for an easy time, aren't you, Dr Vaughan? Just as you arrive at the NGV you are closing down for four years, so you can put your feet up, can't you?" It was a great irony because, you know, I had never worked so hard – and not just me. We were probably, in those first few years, working eighty- and ninety-hour weeks. It was a very, very intense period, but a satisfying one'.[134]

Vaughan admits that at times 'it was daunting; I'd sit down and think "cripes, how the hell am I going to get my head around this?"' He emphasises the input of 'an extremely capable Buildings Committee', chaired by the Deputy President of the Council, Jim Cousins, and also the 'very assiduous' Barry Sweeney, Redevelopment Manager. In order to tackle the tasks, Vaughan appointed two deputy directors, both of whom had extensive museum-building experience. On 21 February 2000, Frances Lindsay had her first day as Deputy Director of Australian Art, managing the project at Federation Square, and Tony Ellwood started as Deputy Director of International Art, managing the St Kilda Road project. Another key

person was Daryl West-Moore, Redevelopment Design Manager, who worked across the two projects. 'Once we settled it down it worked extremely well,' says Vaughan, 'but you can imagine how difficult it was during those years to have two separate building projects. They were happening at the same time; they had different architects, different building firms and different funding sources. When I look back on it now I sometimes wonder how we managed it. I think it is a great tribute to everybody. It was achieved through a lot of hard work on the part of a team of dedicated, exceptional people. Frances Lindsay and Tony Ellwood each did an amazing job in delivering the building and related curatorial projects for which they had direct responsibility'.[135]

THE BIG PACK. On 27 June 1999, a mizzly Sunday afternoon, a crowd gathered to watch as Jeff Kennett and Bethany England – a nine-year-old helper picked by Kennett from the audience – turned off the water wall. The closing of the St Kilda Road site was symbolised by Kennett and England turning a large, and slightly ungainly, model of a tap. ('It was made out of foam', said Bethany, perhaps slightly incredulous about the chain of cause and effect.)[136] Nevertheless, the water stopped falling and a curtain was pulled across Victoria's beloved wall of water. A few days and one gala 'send-off' dinner later, the NGV shut its doors, leaving the staff to continue packing the 60,000 or so works that were to be temporarily housed, along with the NGV staff, in the new Public Record Office in North Melbourne. A team of twenty worked for months gently packing the collection, using kilometres of foam and tissue paper. The public had an opportunity to see the move-in-progress at an open day. Documentation from the day shows visitors peering at works of art that had been carefully dressed in their moving outfits.

RATS AND PHAR LAP: THE NGV AT RUSSELL STREET. In November 1999, the NGV moved into its new temporary digs – or, rather, its old haunt. In a whimsical revisiting of the past, the NGV found itself back in its former home at the State Library of Victoria,

(previous left)
Gerard Vaughan with
Bertram Mackennal's *Circe*, 1893

(previous right)
Jerry Galea
Jeff Kennett turning
off the water wall
27 June 1999

where it had resided for the long stretch from 1861 to 1968. When the Melbourne Museum vacated the building, architects Ancher, Mortlock & Woolley had carried out an extensive restoration project, but one dedicated to remain true to the materiality of the building. In McCoy Hall, for instance, the original glazed skylights were reinstated (though blacked out for conservation reasons) and the floor, badly scuffed from its previous inhabitants – dinosaurs, whales, apes and their hordes of visitors – had its constituent parts turned over so that its 'good' side was showing. Six hundred of the NGV's 'icons' were installed at the Russell Street site, and some people were delighted to see the collection back in its original home. The art critic Ronald Millar wrote a nostalgic piece in *The Age*: 'Back to the old Museum', he effused. 'Back to that dank smell of country-hospital disinfectant, attendants' old boots, waxed parquet floors ... the proper bronze statue of Sir Redmond Barry, his noble skull always dripping with pigeon dung ... and the seductive smell of oil paint ... The old gallery had character', he said, 'and rats', which he alleged had made themselves useful as target practice for the night security guards.[137]

Rehousing the NGV in the State Library precinct saved the Victorian government around $19 million in rental costs, and the 'downtime' during the two-year rebuild enabled the NGV to undertake extensive conservation projects, most notably the opportunity for conservators Carl Villis and John Payne to spend 2500 hours cleaning *The Banquet of Cleopatra*. The NGV also used the opportunity to tour the exhibition *European Masters: Six Centuries of Paintings from the National Gallery of Victoria* to the Auckland, Cincinnati, Kimbell, Denver, Portland and Birmingham (Alabama) art museums. The NGV has loaned many works to institutions, but opportunities to present a consolidated collection are rare. This exhibition was, as Gerard Vaughan remarked, formative in putting Victoria's collection 'on the world map'.[138] At the official opening of the Russell Street site, new Premier Steve Bracks inadvertently touched a raw nerve when he said to the crowd: 'We don't have a water wall here, but I understand we have Phar Lap'.[139] Australia's most beloved taxidermy racehorse was indeed in residence. In the past, when the Museum and the Gallery were housed together, there used to be a curious tension between the two institutions, symbolised by the figure of Phar Lap. In 1951, Robert Haines, Assistant Director, complained to the *Argus* newspaper that 'Phar Lap's body should be placed in the centre of an intricate maze, through which people must pass the whole gallery of paintings to find it. It is disappointing to be working in a gallery and to find so many people come here only to see a horse'.[140] However, it was also pleasing for the NGV to be reunited with some of its own works. The forecourt of the State Library houses a number of sculptures still owned by the NGV, such as Emmanuel Frémiet's *Joan of Arc* and Sir Joseph Edgar Boehm's *St George and the dragon*. They may be securely affixed but Gerard Vaughan eyed them off nonetheless. 'I'd love those for the sculpture garden at the NGV', he said, 'but I daren't ask'.[141]

LAB ARCHITECTURE STUDIO: IMAGINING THE FUTURE. For a time the only subject that quelled discussion of Melbourne's infernally changeable weather was the Federation Square development. Melbournians loved to love it, or loved to loathe it. It had its high-profile champions such as Dame Elisabeth Murdoch: 'We can't just build another repeat of something from the last century ... we should be very excited and get behind it and believe in it'.[142] However, it also had its high-profile detractors: 'Frog spawn', harrumphed Barry Humphries, 'getting used to it is like getting used to leprosy'.[143] There were budget blow-outs, trashed timelines and shards that were sliced down by the government. Lab Architecture's Donald Bates described the fatigue induced by 'being told for five and a half years that you were building a monstrosity'.[144]

The twin buildings of the NGV tell a fascinating story about different historical conceptions of the art museum. 'The Roy Grounds building', says Gerard Vaughan, 'was very much the idea of the museum as the temple of culture, as a fortified treasure house. It even has a moat and an implied drawbridge – the forecourt. Lab approached their architecture very differently. They were interested in the idea of the Melbourne laneway, and they were also, of course, deeply influenced by American architect Daniel Libeskind's ideas about the need for informality in the new museum of art. I think that the Federation Square concept brilliantly captured the new thinking about what a museum could be in the context of a new urban space'.[145] Architect Peter Davidson echoes these sentiments: 'The gallery on St Kilda Road resembles a fortress, right down to its moat. Now, thirty years ago that seemed right. Art then was a treasure to be protected, but today galleries are different. They're open places and that's what we're trying to address'.[146] In sharp contrast to Grounds's largely impenetrable castle, NGV Australia is the very model of permeability. Lab stated that they were interested in architecture that 'violates the role of the edge, boundary, surface or wall'.[147] The architects took inspiration from the artist Giacometti, whose sculptures and drawings comprise energetic squiggles that resolve to loosely define their subject. Giacometti's border is always provisional and Lab admired the artist's ability 'to insinuate a wholeness out of disparate, disordered elements'.[148]

(above and middle)
The Ian Potter Centre:
NGV Australia

(below)
First hang at
Federation Square
showing Julie Gough
and E. Phillips Fox

The architects were adamant that the building 'imagines the future, not the past'.[149] Their design process interrogated many ideas around the concept of the art museum and involved much experimental thinking. As Daryl West-Moore, Exhibition Design Manager, recalls: 'I remember one of their original concepts was for leaning walls – but, you know, how do you hang works on a tilting wall? There was also an idea for a huge doorway in the shape of an elephant. But how do you get a door to work in there? How do you keep the environment closed? We knew, however, that we wanted a groundbreaking piece of architecture and that we had to adapt the way that we thought. As a designer it was a fantastic time, because Lab questioned our team and our practice and our process. You know: "Why do you do it like this? Have you ever thought of doing it this way? Can we try it this way?" There was an opportunity to try new things'.[150]

THE GALLERY FLOOR PLAN: 'A NEW ORDER OF THINGS'. While Bates and Davidson worked collaboratively on the exterior of Federation Square, they split the interiors: Bates was principal architect for the interior of ACMI, and Davidson for the Ian Potter Centre. Frances Lindsay describes how they aimed to develop a floor plan that opened up possibilities for interpretation and did not just present one neat – but fictional – linear narrative. 'I felt that we should not have chronology as the tyranny of the curatorial endeavour', she says. 'Peter Davidson was very good at articulating the way in which you could use the architecture to support the story you want to tell as a curator. The interrelationship of the building and the collection established a new paradigm for the way in which you can be more inventive in terms of displaying the collection.'[151] The design of the galleries is intended to empower the visitor to make their own associations. 'The building's design', wrote the architects, 'suggests the means for visitors to inscribe their own experiences of the collection through a shifting matrix of gallery view lines and cross connections'.[152] Davidson has commented that 'art speculates about a new order of things, how things might be, not just what they are now. Architecture is the same. A speculation'.[153]

When designing the first hang of the Australian collection, Lindsay describes how the curators 'were very conscious of the problem of not having a collection of nineteenth-century Aboriginal Australian art. So we got around this by using interventions, and this meant using contemporary Aboriginal art alongside historical works'.[154] The result was a series of striking curatorial interventions in which contemporary Indigenous artists responded to works of art from the western lineage of Australian art history. Julie Gough, for instance, responded to E. Phillips Fox's grandiose history painting *The Landing of Captain Cook at Botany Bay, 1770*, 1902, which had been commissioned by the NGV Trustees on the occasion of Federation. Gough's installation *Chase*, 2001, challenged Fox's view of Australian history, and presented a different experience. 'I think our role as curators is to constantly reinterpret collections', says Lindsay. 'History needs reinterpretation as we increasingly enlarge our understanding of the past, and the artist's voice is paramount to this process.'[155] On a more whimsical note, the interior floors of the gallery spaces are made largely from wood recycled from an old three-storey woolshed in West Footscray, the Goldsborough Mort Woolstore. Wonderfully, a gallery dedicated to Australian art has been built out of an old woolshed; *Shearing the rams* is back in its original habitat.

GRAND PHILANTHROPIC GESTURES. 'Everyone commiserated with me when I arrived', remembers Gerard Vaughan. 'They said, you have just arrived to take up this new job and they expect you, on day one, to raise $70 million for the building projects.' The NGV had an existing pledge of $94 million from Kennett's state government and then, beyond that, says Vaughan, 'two big grants gave us the edge': $15 million from the Ian Potter Foundation and $25 million from the Commonwealth government through the Centenary of Federation fund. 'Those two things gave us the head start we needed. From that point on we sought donations in the Melbourne community, and we got them.'[156]

The tradition of grand philanthropic gestures that has so powerfully impacted the history of the NGV continued, with many people giving generously to the redevelopment campaign. Headlines were made when the Ian Potter Foundation announced that it would contribute a hefty $15 million. 'The grant from the Ian Potter foundation was transforming', says Vaughan. 'At the time it was the largest grant that had ever been made by a private foundation to an arts institution in Australia. It was decided that the best way to commemorate it was to offer the naming opportunity for the Federation Square building to the Potter Foundation. In 1999, $15 million was an enormous amount of money.'[157] Sir Ian Potter would likely have been supportive of the contribution. The businessman and stockbroker had been a proud supporter of the arts who sat on numerous boards and was a member of the Bolte government's National Gallery and Cultural Centre Building Committee in 1964, a key group behind the development of the St Kilda Road site. Other philanthropists also rallied: Peter Clemenger, through the good offices of Clemenger BBDO, donated $2 million for the Clemenger Auditorium; media figure James Fairfax's $1 million pledge gave him naming rights to a gallery of eighteenth-century works of art; the Myer family contributed $1 million to a gallery of Asian art; the Pratt Foundation donated $1 million for access programs; and Dame Elisabeth Murdoch made yet another significant contribution.

'THE GREAT FOCAL POINT OF VISUAL CULTURE IN AUSTRALIA'. Australia's first major gallery dedicated to Australian art opened with three days of festivities in late November 2002. Across twelve permanent galleries and eight temporary spaces, the Ian Potter Centre presented the largest collection of Australian art anywhere in the world. 'We've had the collection building up since 1861 when we were founded', said Director Gerard Vaughan, who predicted that the Ian Potter Centre would be 'the great focal point of Australian visual culture'.[158] The new museum – the only one dedicated to Australian

art – would encourage a deeper understanding of the trajectory of art in this country. This more complex understanding of Australian art history could have far-reaching social implications. Frances Lindsay gave a neat summary: 'People will understand Australian life and culture and identity in a new way by looking at these works'.[159] Steve Vizard, President of the Trustees, echoed this sentiment: 'There's no collection like it anywhere. Anybody wanting to know what we are dreaming and thinking, where we are going and where we have been, *this* will be the place to go'.[160]

The NGV has always celebrated the fact that it enjoys one of the highest rates of local audience attendance in the world. From the start, the Ian Potter Centre was similarly 'owned' by its local population. Huge numbers poured through: while the Centre Pompidou and Musée d'Orsay museums average around four thousand visitors per day, in its first few weeks the Ian Potter Centre was averaging eight thousand people per day. 'It has to be one of the most visited art museums in the world just now', said an understandably pleased Vaughan.[161] Within a year there had been an incredible two million visitors. And entrance was still free. When the government wobbled on the issue of free entry for the new site, Steve Vizard stated unequivocally: 'It's a matter of social justice. I don't want to see anyone forced to squint through the outside window to look at the people's art

Lady Potter painting 'Open' on the Art Relay canvas, assisted by John Landy, Governor of Victoria, 2002

William Barak
Untitled (Ceremony) 1900
earth pigments, watercolour
and pencil on paper
50.5 x 63.0 cm
(image and sheet)
The Warren Clark Bequest, 2001

collection just because they might be out of work'.[162] Attendances had doubled when Jeff Kennett removed fees at the St Kilda Road site in 1997, and it seemed especially critical that the Australian collection be freely accessed by its local population.

CEREMONY: THE OPENING OF THE INDIGENOUS GALLERIES. One month earlier, a profound event had taken place in Australian art history. On 26 October 2002, the Indigenous galleries opened on the ground floor of NGV Australia, making it the first public Australian art museum to have a suite of galleries dedicated to exhibiting the work of Aboriginal and Torres Strait Islander artists. The floor plan was designed to enable a nuanced understanding of the complexity within and interrelatedness between Indigenous nations, as Judith Ryan explained: 'We were excited by the idea of having an open-plan design. The collection is about diversity and representation across all art-producing areas and communities. We felt that it was important to concurrently display different iconographies, discrete visual traditions and individual language groups. You can see connections across the space, there is constant dialogue – nothing is closed off or separated'.[163]

The Indigenous galleries were also symbolically sited on the ground floor: 'It was considered vital that Indigenous art be on the ground floor. Indigenous art is the longest continuing living tradition; it pre-dates settlement, it is ex-Europe. It cannot just be integrated into the European displays. The ground-floor site was also important because of the profound relationship that Indigenous people and their art have with country. There is an important connection with land. This was a *paen* (freshwater) meeting place for the Wurundjeri people, known as Birrung Marr, and that was very important to acknowledge'.[164] Respectfully placed on the entrance wall was William Barak's drawing *Untitled (Ceremony)*, 1900, which had been purchased by the NGV in 2001 specifically for the opening of the Indigenous galleries. Barak, the first Indigenous artist of renown, was a leader of the Wurundjeri who is said to have witnessed the signing of the spurious Batman Treaty. He was an influential figure in the push for Indigenous rights, leading four deputations to parliament to plead the case for Wurundjeri self-management of Coranderrk.

***FIELDWORK*: 'A DISPUTED FIELD'.** The first temporary exhibition at NGV Australia reflected upon the Gallery's own history. The exhibition *Fieldwork* drew from the NGV's own collection to explore developments in Australian art history from 1968 to 2002. The title referenced *The Field*, the groundbreaking exhibition that launched the St Kilda Road building in 1968, but it was also, as Frances Lindsay said, 'a perfect title for contemporary art and its exploratory nature'.[165] As with most historical surveys, the various movements refused to conform to a neat trajectory. This inherent complexity was a guiding principle for curators Charles Green and Jason Smith. The exhibition aimed to show, said Green, 'that there weren't smooth transitions from one movement to another, that art has been a disputed field'.[166] If any overarching message radiated from the diverse exhibits, it was that Australian art history is assertively diverse and divergent: 'Rather than amplifying particular ideologies', wrote Jason Smith, 'the works reaffirm art as a practice, as a type of work – as *Fieldwork* – that is above all an emphatically open enquiry into ways of being in the world ... The curatorial and audience-oriented processes of occupying a newly constructed art gallery ... insist, more than usual, that the first role of the art gallery is to enable its visitors to inhabit the world *imaginatively* as well as in *fact*'.[167]

ST KILDA ROAD: 'A PARTICULARLY CRANKY ICON'. From the minute it was made public, Roy Grounds's design for the NGV on St Kilda Road polarised opinion: it was hailed as both masterpiece and monster. Early on, locals disparagingly nicknamed it 'Pentridge', but over the decades grew so fond of it that the mere suggestion of removing the water wall in 1996 when the brief was under discussion inspired a testy 'hands off our gallery' protest, with hundreds of Melbournians vigorously waggling hand-shaped placards in the NGV's forecourt. Patrick McCaughey called it 'the Kremlin'; Vaughan 'the mothership'. Whatever your position, Grounds's bold, brutalist monument has undeniably become an iconic building in Melbourne. Tony Ellwood recognised the significance of the site: 'Victorians are justifiably very sentimental about the St Kilda Road building. Many of us have grown up with it and affectionately recall many phases of the interior spaces'.[168] However, after three decades of heavy use and unending changes to accommodate the rapidly growing collections, it desperately needed renovations. 'The building was bursting at the seams when I was there ten years ago', said Patrick McCaughey, former director. 'Those bluestone walls must be falling into the moat.'[169] Yet how to proceed? 'Reworking an iconic building is a risky thing to do', commented Paul Walker, Associate Professor of Architecture at the University of Melbourne, and this building is 'a particularly cranky icon'.[170]

MARIO BELLINI: 'AN EMOTIONAL, TRANSPARENT SPIRAL WALK'. 'We knew from the outset that we could not satisfy everyone', says Ellwood, 'but we also knew that we were delivering a consistent treatment across a large building and not a disjointed one only in a few wings, which for practical and funding reasons had been the case over many years'.[171] While Bellini and Métier3 left the exterior largely untouched, they performed a complete 'inside-out' rebuild of the building. A guiding principle for Bellini was the belief that 'good architecture can have a series of new lives'. The architect was appreciative of Roy Grounds's architecture: 'I consider, and have always considered, this building a masterpiece'. However, he said, 'inside is a different matter'.[172]

The crux of the new design was to construct two freestanding towers within Grounds's bluestone exterior to the north and south. These towers are placed 'off-grid' to the exterior, set at a dynamic angle inside Grounds's elegant modernist rectangle. Built of translucent glass and silvery metal, they contain high, spacious exhibition rooms that visitors access via a walkway that winds around the outside of each tower, in a structure set between the bluestone walls of the original building and the new towers. For Bellini, these towers offer 'a new solution to the insufficient circulation across the gallery, with an emotional, transparent spiral walk through sun and shadows between the old courtyard's skin and the new building'. The new interior also encapsulates Bellini's materials-forward approach, as Tony Ellwood comments: 'I worked very closely with the architects at Bellini's studio in Milan. They had very interesting ideas about the palette of materials for this building, aiming constantly to keep it as simple as possible. The use of stone, furnishings and wall colours was all very deliberate and pared back. It taught me a lot about reducing ideas to the minimum in order for a building to flow. They were very sophisticated thinkers and had enormous experience around Europe'.[173]

NGV INTERNATIONAL: *EVERYTHING IN ITS RIGHT PLACE*. After four years of construction, NGV International officially opened on 3 December 2003. As well as gala events there was also a special ceremony for the restarting of the water wall. This time it was Premier Steve Bracks who watched as Bethany England, now thirteen, issued instructions via walkie-talkie to the control room to turn on the water wall again. The crowd held its breath as water slowly welled at the top, and exhaled as it began to fall – more evenly than ever before. When the doors opened, art aficionados swarmed into the building to be reunited with loved works of art. 'There has been a profound sense of people wanting to catch up with what they missed', said former Trustee Rupert Myer. 'It is a most loved institution and, during the period of redevelopment, there was a palpable sense of missing part of Melbourne's cultural traditions.'[174]

Vaughan also recalls a hair-raising incident – and one that 'has probably been expunged from the records'. At the preview for the major donors – 'a special occasion for a very special group' – a catastrophe occurred. As Vaughan and Council President Steve Vizard

were proudly introducing the new building to their guests, who were standing in Federation Court, some workmen moving furniture on the first-floor balcony accidentally knocked one of the fire prevention nozzles in the ceiling. In Vaughan's words: 'Suddenly there was the most awful roar and gush, and then water sprayed everywhere. It flowed over the floor and began to run over the edge behind me, like a waterfall. I could not see it happening because I was facing the audience. There was a look of horror on the faces of our guests and their mouths were open. I thought, what have I said or done? Soon I realised we were in the middle of a mini crisis. Everyone was very nice about it, but it did slightly take the edge off the festive feel for a few moments, I can tell you'.[175]

The opening of the new building was marked, appropriately enough for a gallery of international art, with the exhibition *World_Rush* that was, in part, a meditation on the nature of globalisation. Four international artists – Eija-Liisa Ahtila from Finland, Lee Bul from South Korea and Doug Aitken and Sarah Sze from the USA – contributed in different ways to a sense that, in co-curator Charles Green's words, 'a luminously new and dangerous unstable globalisation has arrived'.[176] For co-curator Jason Smith, Curator of International Art at the time, it was important that NGV International be

(above)
Antiquities gallery,
NGV International

(overleaf)
Yinka Shonibare
Reverend on ice 2005
semi-opaque synthetic
polymer resin, cotton (Dutchwax),
wool, leather
160.0 x 402.3 x 601.5 cm (overall)
Purchased with the assistance of
NGV Contemporary, 2006

launched with an unequivocal message of support for contemporary art practices: 'I think this show is sending an extraordinarily strong signal. This marks the reinvigoration of the NGV's contemporary art programming. There's a huge sector of the community that's coming back to see Old Masters and old favourites but we also want there to be a strong sense that the NGV is a contemporary museum'.[177] Sarah Sze's *Everything in its right place*, 2002–03, and Lee Bul's *Untitled*, 2003, were acquired for the NGV's permanent collection.

EXHIBITIONS: *REVEREND ON ICE*. The next few years presented two opportunities to mount ambitious exhibitions of contemporary art, which were created in collaboration with NGV Australia's neighbour, the Australian Centre for the Moving Image. The first was a large interdisciplinary exhibition, *2004 Australian Culture Now*, from which the NGV acquired Nick Mangan's *In the crux of the matter*, 2003, a motorbike turned host-body for elegant, crystalline forms. The subsequent exhibition *2006 Contemporary Commonwealth* presented a survey of international artists on the occasion of the Commonwealth Games. Frances Lindsay admitted that the curators were, at first, hesitant about working with a potentially hackneyed idea such as the 'Commonwealth', but she stated 'we realised that the artists were contributing wonderful material that wasn't about the old notion of the Commonwealth and Britain as "The Empire". It was something quite different'.[178]

The NGV purchased a work by the Nigerian-British artist Yinka Shonibare, *Reverend on ice*, 2005, but lacked the money to buy the accompanying film *Un ballo in maschera (A masked ball)*, 2004. Yet it was bewitching audiences. As Lindsay recalls: 'We asked if we could keep *A masked ball* on extended loan and did an installation with it and *Reverend on ice* in the eighteenth-century galleries. People loved it. Walking through the galleries with Joan and Peter Clemenger I said, "Come and I'll show you the Shonibare". We were looking at the video and Joan said, "I just love this film, it's amazing". And of course in the galleries everyone was sitting in front of it – they were not looking at the Tiepolo, they were looking at the Shonibare. When I told her that the work was not in the collection she asked how much it was. I told her the price and she said, "Well, I'll buy it for you". It was like a Christmas present. I loved it – this instant support for contemporary art'.[179] The Clemengers have long been passionate supporters of contemporary art at the NGV. In 1991, they instituted the Clemenger Contemporary Art Award, a series of six exhibitions spanning twenty years designed to celebrate and profile contemporary Australian art, and the Joan Clemenger Endowment, established in 1999, provided an annual fund for five years to acquire works by young artists identified as priorities for the collection. Additional contributions include travel grants for staff and support for the NGV's new project space for contemporary art, to be opened in 2011. They further endeared themselves by being the first contributors to the fund that enabled John Brack's *The bar*, 1954, to be acquired in 2009.

NGV International has also hosted the Melbourne Winter Masterpieces, a new tradition of blockbuster projects supported by the Victorian government, which bring high-profile works of art to Melbourne and inspire a broad audience to experience art. In 2004, the inaugural project, *Impressionists: Masterpieces from the Musée d'Orsay*, attracted more than 370,000 visitors, making it the most visited exhibition in the NGV's history. Subsequent years saw *Dutch Masters* (2005); *Picasso: Love and War 1935–45* (2006); *Guggenheim Collection: 1940s to Now* (2007); *Art Deco 1910–1939* (2008); *Salvador Dalí: Liquid Desire* (2009); *European Masters: Städel Museum, 19th–20th Century* (2010); and *Vienna: Art and Design – Klimt, Schiele, Hoffmann, Loos* (2011).

Ted Gott, Senior Curator of International Art, is particularly proud of the Dalí exhibition: 'We thought that Dalí should be celebrated. It was a show that we generated, we did not buy it in from somewhere else'.[180] It was also notable for the '24-hour Dalí' event, which saw the NGV stay open – for the first time in its history – for a full twenty-four hours, giving people one last, late-night opportunity to catch the exhibition before pack-down. 'It was absolutely Gerard's idea', says Judy Williams, Head of Foundation. 'When he first mentioned it, we all looked at him slightly incredulously and said "Gerard, um, perhaps we could stay open until midnight, but right through the night?" However, he championed the idea.[181] The event generated huge queues and a great sense of festivity: 'It was an extraordinary "happening"', says Gott.[182]

(above)
Salvador Dalí: Liquid Desire
24-hour opening, 2009

(opposite left)
Deborah Paauwe
Double Tresses 2006 from the *Crying room* series 2006
type C photograph
109.0 x 109.0 cm (image)
Purchased with funds arranged by Loti Smorgon for Contemporary Australian Photography, 2006

(opposite right)
Fred Williams
Red cliff landscape 1981
oil on canvas
182.4 x 152.0 cm
Presented through the NGV Foundation by Rio Tinto Limited, Honorary Life Benefactor, 2001

PHILANTHROPY: 'SOMETHING WORTH CELEBRATING'. 'I could no more go out and buy an Impressionist or any twentieth-century modernist masterpiece now than fly to the moon', lamented Gerard Vaughan in the early days of his directorship. The NGV had indeed had its good days, when the Felton Bequest had made the NGV a world-class purchasing power. 'When the Felton agents walked into an auction room, everybody sat up and took notice. "Melbourne's at it again", they would say', said a wistful Vaughan. A remarkable characteristic of the NGV is that its collection is overwhelmingly the result of private philanthropy. As Vaughan notes: 'It is amazing: the NGV holds thousands of works of art and almost every one of them has been given by a private individual, a family or a foundation – someone in the community. I think that is something worth celebrating'.[183]

Throughout his directorship, Vaughan has demonstrated that fundraising is one of his strong suits, a skill he refined in his previous role as the CEO of the British Museum Development Trust. 'I do enjoy fundraising', says Vaughan. 'In my view, you can't be credible as a fundraiser unless you believe passionately in what you are doing, and convey that to others and bring them with you. And we have been lucky – so many wonderful people have come forward and done so much.'[184] While a decade ago the state government's annual operational grant comprised around 80 to 85 per cent of the NGV's gross revenue, the ratio is now closer to 50 per cent government grant and 50 per cent funds from the private sector and the NGV's own revenue-earning activities. 'It is not that the government is giving less', states Vaughan, 'but we have become more entrepreneurial and also more successful in encouraging the private sector and philanthropists to give us more money. That is a really good position to be in. It has made things possible that would not have been possible otherwise, and it really injects energy into the place'.[185] Over the past few years, the NGV Foundation has also created a series of 'supporter groups', recognising that supporters are usually very specific about their passions. In order

to offer supporters more choice and control of how their donations are spent, the Supporters of Indigenous Art group was established in 2001; NGV Contemporary in 2002; the Supporters of Asian Art in 2007; the Supporters of Decorative Arts in 2008; and the Supporters of Prints and Drawings in 2009.

The NGV has also been the beneficiary of corporate donations. When Shell Australia moved to new corporate headquarters in 2002, for instance, the NGV was donated a suite of contemporary works worth around $1 million, comprising thirty-nine paintings, two sculptures and seven Aboriginal bark pieces. Alcoa World Alumina Australia displayed similar vision and largesse. In 2003, they presented *Landscape (Salt Lake)*, 1966, a work by Sidney Nolan in four parts, then estimated to be valued at around $1 million. However, it was Rio Tinto's donation of Fred Williams's Pilbara series, comprising eighteen gouaches and thirteen paintings, which really set the benchmark for corporate donations. The gift, valued at the time at $6 million, is believed to be the largest corporate donation of Australian art ever made to a gallery in Australia. 'When Rio gave us the Fred Williams collection for the Ian Potter Centre', says Vaughan, 'it transformed our collection. It's one of the great achievements of twentieth-century Australian art'.[186] The NGV also holds a collection of Williams's prints that Cathy Leahy, Senior Curator of Prints and Drawings, describes as the 'greatest distinction of our Australian holdings'. She says: 'One of the things that I feel should be acknowledged is the collection of Fred Williams's prints, which is unique in Australia for its comprehensiveness. This has been established through the generosity of Fred's widow, Lyn Williams, and it is the definitive study collection of Fred Williams's printmaking. It is an extraordinary resource'.[187]

THE NGV – FULL OF FAKES! Throughout the NGV's history most directors have had to endure the experience of a daily newspaper printing a photograph of them beside a work of art with a headline screaming 'Titian – a fake!' or 'Rembrandt – a fake!' While it may seem like big news in the media, within the NGV reattribution is just part of the daily business of the art gallery. 'That external conversation about attribution is one that you can't necessarily spend a lot of time listening to', says John Payne, Senior Conservator.[188] Senior Curator Ted Gott agrees: 'How can something be a famous and celebrated picture one day, and then the next day utterly fall from grace? There is a lot of misunderstanding about it'.[189]

A recent and high-profile example of reattribution occurred in 2007 when *Head of a man*, 1880s, bought in 1939 as a work by Vincent van Gogh, was reattributed by the Van Gogh Museum and is now considered a work by an as yet unidentified contemporary of van Gogh. It hit news headlines in a predictable way: *The Age* ran a photograph of Gerard Vaughan alongside the work with the headline 'NGV's "Van Gogh" a fake'.[190] ('It is not a fake', says Gott somewhat exasperatedly. 'It is by an artist working in the 1880s – it was not done in the twentieth century to deceive.'[191]) An interesting example of attribution moving in the opposite direction was the NGV's portrait of Lucrezia Borgia. The oval Italian painting was long regarded as a portrait of an unknown male youth by an unidentified northern Italian artist. 'There was almost nothing known about the picture', states Carl Villis, Conservator. 'It was a blank canvas, so to speak. I am interested in Italian painting and it was one that I was beguiled by.'[192] The art historical and technical enquiries undertaken by Villis over many years led him to conclude that the work was probably painted by one of the well-known Dossi brothers and, furthermore, that the portrait is possibly the only surviving painted image of Lucrezia Borgia, Duchess of Ferrara, one of the most high-profile women of the Italian Renaissance.

Carl Villis, Conservator of European Paintings before 1800, at the media conference for the reattribution of *Lucrezia Borgia*

Developing art scholarship is an objective at the heart of the NGV, and the conservator's examination of works contributes greatly, as Gott notes: 'I think a lot of people don't realise that our conservators are scholars as well as fantastic art restorers. They publish regularly and widely on their scientific findings. That might be a side of the NGV that the general public is not really aware of'.[193] The last few decades have seen an important shift in the NGV's capacities for scholarship, states John Payne. 'Often there were pronouncements made about works in the NGV's collection – people would say "well, clearly, this is this" – but they were working externally to the institution and often just referring to black-and-white photographs. They seldom actually came to the Gallery to view the material itself. These days the NGV expresses an opinion about works of art based on technical evidence collected here, which then affects ideas about connoisseurship and who painted what and when. That has been a turning point.'[194]

'THE NEED TO SUPPORT LIVING ARTISTS'. In November 2002, Labor's Minister for the Arts Mary Delahunty launched the Victorian Foundation for Living Australian Artists (VFLAA), a fund established to support contemporary Australian artists by purchasing their art. 'Artists represent one of the lowest-earning sectors in the community', she said, 'yet provide so much to the State we love'.[195] Her position had been informed by the recently released Myer Report, an inquiry undertaken by Rupert Myer into the health of the arts sector. Myer's report had emphasised the need to support living artists. The State government pledged $5 million, which the NGV Foundation was to match through private donations to create a $10 million acquisition fund. Since 2002, the fund has acquired works by artists such as Paddy Bedford, Jon Cattapan, Julie Dowling, Siri Hayes, Akira Isogawa, Toni Maticevski, Laith McGregor, Mike Parr, Patricia Piccinini, Sally Smart and Ricky Swallow. The NGV was also greatly assisted in 2006 by the Victorian government's decision under Steve Bracks to create a $2 billion art indemnity scheme, something that Gerard Vaughan had lobbied vigorously for. This initiative has assisted the NGV to work independently to develop large-scale international projects, allowing all profits to be re-invested in the exhibitions program.

ACQUISITIONS: 'THE SOCIAL HISTORY OF A WORK OF ART'. 'I am deeply interested in the history of collections', says Gerard Vaughan. 'The social history of a work of art – who owned it, why they owned it, when it was sold, why it was sold, who purchased it – the passage of works of art. This institution is a massive compilation of histories of collecting. Every work of art has its own history and they intersect, they coalesce, they cross over and that is the thing that I find fascinating.'[196] In 2003, the NGV acquired an exquisite fourteenth-century devotional painting by the Florentine painter Agnolo Gaddi, which was unveiled by Dame Elisabeth Murdoch at the NGV's re-opening dinner, and the same year, Nathaniel Dance's enchanting eighteenth-century picture of John Pybus and his family. It had hung over a fireplace in Victoria's Western District and had been passed down through successive generations until a direct descendant brought it to the NGV's attention and allowed the Felton Bequest to purchase it on very generous terms. In 2006, a majestic work by the Venetian Renaissance painter Paris Bordone, *Rest on the flight into Egypt with Saint Catherine and angels*, c.1527–30, entered the European painting collection as a gift from Council President Allan Myers and his wife Maria, requiring them to purchase at the highest price ever paid for a work of art in the NGV's history. Two years later Allan and Maria Myers, with support from an equally generous anonymous donor, provided funds for the purchase of Jusepe de Ribera's early seventeenth-century masterpiece, *Martyrdom of St Lawrence*, 1620–24. A greatly celebrated acquisition in 2009 was *Mother and child*, 1624, an exquisite family portrait by the Flemish Baroque painter Cornelis de Vos, a sometime collaborator with Peter Paul Rubens, with the majority of the funds gifted by Alan and Mavourneen Cowen.

The contemporary collection was augmented by the acquisition of Canadian photographer Jeff Wall's monumental light-box work, *Untangling*, 1994, an acquisition that made headlines because it was the first time the NGV had paid $1 million for a photograph. Senior Curator of Photography Isobel Crombie says, 'I remember waking up on a Saturday morning to read a headline saying something like "*How* much did they buy it for?" They never tire of it. This acquisition took a long time to bring in and a million dollars for it seemed fine to me'.[197] William Kentridge's enchanting homage to early filmmaker Georges Méliès, the black-and-white silent film *7 fragments for George Méliès*, 2003, was acquired in 2003 with the assistance of the NGV Contemporary supporters' group, and Bill Bowness's love of contemporary photography translated into an endowment that has purchased, among others, works by German artists Thomas Struth, Thomas Ruff and Thomas Demand, and Japanese photographer Hiroshi Sugimoto.

Roger Leong, Curator of International Fashion and Textiles, lists the John Galliano for Dior commission of 2002 as one of the most significant in this area. 'It's the only couture garment that the NGV has ever commissioned, and it was enabled by the donors, Norma and Stuart Leslie, supporting us to buy serious avant-garde fashion.' Leong says: 'As a designer, Galliano interrogates the way you cut, shape and make clothes for the body. This idea of taking a garment and twisting it so radically is very interesting'.[198] The department of Australian Fashion and Textiles also acquired Australian costume designer Lizzy Gardiner's infamous *American Express ® gold card dress wrap*, 1995–98, which made headlines when she wore it to the Oscars in 1995.

Christopher Menz, former Senior Curator of Decorative Arts, was behind the acquisition of a rare piece of Christopher Dresser, the great reform designer of the end of the nineteenth century, which was funded by the NGV's Women's Association as a re-opening gift. A highlight for Decorative Arts over the past few years has been the gifts from Dr Robert Wilson, a prominent collector of English Minton ceramics, who also works at the NGV in the role of Programs Coordinator, Education and Public

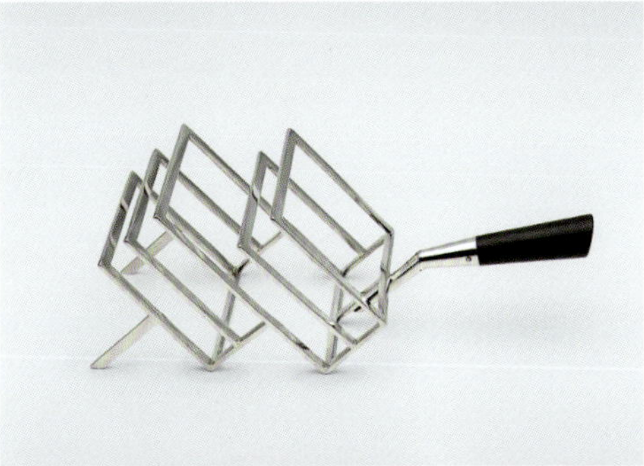

(previous clockwise from top left)
Jeff Wall
Untangling 1994, printed 2006
Purchased with the assistance of NGV Contemporary, 2006

Christian Dior, Paris (couture house)
John Galliano (designer)
Dress, hat and boots model no. 39
Presented through the NGV Foundation by Norma and Stuart Leslie, Governors, 2002

Minton, Stoke-on-Trent, Staffordshire (manufacturer)
Monkey teapot 1874
The Dr Robert Wilson Collection. Presented through the NGV Foundation by Dr Robert Wilson, Honorary Life Benefactor, 2001

Paris Bordone
Rest on the flight into Egypt with Saint Catherine and angels c.1527–1530
Purchased through the NGV Foundation with the assistance of Allan and Maria Myers, Honorary Life Benefactors, 2006

Cornelis de Vos
Mother and child 1624
Purchased with funds donated by Alan and Mavourneen Cowen, two anonymous donors and donors to the Cornelis de Vos Appeal, 2009

Christopher Dresser (designer)
James Dixon & Sons, Sheffield (manufacturer)
Toast rack c.1880
Presented by The National Gallery Women's Association, 2003

(below)
Joseph Brown at home
Australian Magazine 1990

Programs. 'Over the years, Robert has built up one of the most significant collections of Minton in the world,' says Amanda Dunsmore, Curator of Decorative Arts and Antiquities, 'large parts of which he has gifted to the NGV. There is an astonishing range of ceramics in all sorts of styles that display amazing technical virtuosity'.[199]

Gus Nossal retired as Chairman of the Felton Bequest Committee in 2004, ending an involvement with the NGV that began in 1977. One of Australia's most highly regarded medical researchers, Sir Gus also holds, in the words of Gerard Vaughan, 'a deep love of the visual arts'. Nossal had appointed Gerard Vaughan as the London-based Felton Advisor in 1984, and the two enjoyed a long working relationship. 'I have valued Gus's counsel and sound advice on many issues. The NGV, and the people of Victoria, have much to thank him for.'[200] Nossal was succeeded by Andrew Grimwade, the former President of the Council of Trustees, someone who has a strong family connection to the Felton Bequest – Alfred Felton was the business partner of his great-grandfather, Frederick Sheppard Grimwade. In 2004 QC Allan Myers AO was appointed President of the council of Trustees and, in 2005, the NGV Foundation also experienced a change of leadership when Bruce Parncutt, NGV Trustee and Principal of the investment banking firm Lion Capital, became Chairman.

JOSEPH BROWN: 'IT BELONGS TO THE PEOPLE'. When Joseph Brown received his first pay cheque at age sixteen, he used some of it to buy art, thus initiating what was to become one of Australia's most remarkable collections. Brown's family had migrated from Lodz, Poland, in 1933. He attended Napier Waller's art classes but life was tough in Depression-era Australia, especially for Jewish immigrants from Eastern Europe, and he left school for a job at Helmer's fashion house in Bourke Street. Making art was an enduring love for Brown, however, and he never gave it up. His art practice evidences his lasting interest in abstraction, with Brown undertaking formal explorations in painting and sculpture.

Brown also turned out to be an astute businessman. After a few years in the rag trade he established his own successful business, J. Brown Mantles, which specialised in evening gowns. In 1967, he transferred these business skills to developing his art dealership. The Joseph Brown Gallery was to become a formidable influence in Australian art. From the 1970s into the 1990s, Brown was one of Australia's most respected art dealers, contributing to – and, in many ways, driving – an increased appreciation of Australian art. He also amassed an exceptional private collection: uninterested in opportunities found in overseas markets, Brown set his sights squarely on Australian art. In 2004, he gifted more than 150 works to the people of Victoria, the most generous single gift of works of art in Australia, worth more than $30 million at the time of presentation. The Joseph Brown Collection is now on permanent display at the Ian Potter Centre where it complements the NGV's collection. Brown was driven by a democratic spirit, and this ethos is evident in the following statement made on the day his gift was announced. 'I am often very surprised to meet people who have never visited the Gallery', he said. 'I stress to them, this is their property. It's their gallery, they should feel it is theirs. It's not mine; it's not the government's; it's not Gerard Vaughan's; it belongs to the people.'[201]

JOHN BRACK: THE ONE THAT GOT AWAY (AND THEN CAME BACK). John Brack's *Self-portrait*, 1955, was part of the same solo exhibition of 1955 from which the NGV bought the iconic painting *Collins St, 5 pm*, 1955. When the self-portrait came on the market in 2000, it was snapped up by the NGV, one of the first works brought into the collection by new Director Gerard Vaughan. The NGV was not so lucky with Brack's *The bar*, 1954. That was the one that got away. When Vaughan discovered it was to go to auction in 2006, he was determined to acquire it. The NGV had only two months to raise the more than $2 million that they expected the painting to go for. Vaughan was unashamed: 'I begged', he said.[202] He begged the NGV Foundation and its key supporters, and then went on ABC Radio and begged the public: 'It's not something that I would normally do', he said, but the circumstances were 'exceptional'.[203] Unfortunately, $2 million was not even in the ballpark. In the Sotheby's auction room, the price escalated until the painting was sold for $3,172,000 to an anonymous telephone bidder, setting a record for the highest price paid anywhere at auction for an Australian painting. Photographs of the evening depict an ashen-faced Helen Brack and a clearly despondent Gerard Vaughan. 'The painting was a natural for us', lamented Vaughan. 'There's no point beating around the bush, we are deeply disappointed. Deeply, deeply disappointed.'[204]

When Vaughan discovered that David Walsh, Tasmanian art collector and professional gambler, had bought it, he lost no time expressing his hope that, if Walsh were ever to sell, that the NGV might have first claim. When the painting was loaned to the NGV for the John Brack retrospective of 2009, Walsh said: 'I saw them together and thought they were meant to be together'.[205] In 2009, he generously offered the painting to

John Brack
The bar 1954.
oil on canvas
97.0 x 130.3 cm irreg.
Purchased with the assistance of Peter Clemenger AM and Joan Clemenger, Elena Keown Bequest, Spotlight Foundation, NGV Foundation, Ross Adler AC and Fiona Adler, Bruce Parncutt and Robin Campbell, Marc Besen AO and Eva Besen AO, the Bowness Family, Lindsay Fox AO and Paula Fox, Dorothy Gibson, Rino Grollo and Diana Ruzzene Grollo, Ian Hicks AM, the NGV Women's Association and donors to the John Brack Appeal, 2009

(below)
A visitor at the *Ron Mueck* exhibition

the NGV for $3.2 million, the price he had paid for it himself. Vaughan was delighted and very cognizant of Walsh's good will: 'I believe this is a special moment for the people of Victoria, who now own this great painting of Melbourne life ... Posterity would never forgive us for missing it twice', he said. 'We're a little like the Canadian Mounties – the NGV eventually gets its picture.'[206]

THE NGV: THE VIRTUAL CAMPUS. In the twenty-first century, a significant global shift is occurring that positions the museum as a virtual as well as a physical space. This move towards the ethereal can be traced in the amplified role that multimedia and new technologies perform in mediating the gallery goer's experience. Jean-Pierre Chabrol, Head of Multimedia, says: 'I think the NGV has changed its way of thinking about the collection and that is because the user has changed a great deal. The user is willing to access data in different forms and in different mediums to understand the works of art. There used to be a fear – "let's not show them much online because they will stop coming to visit us" – but now that mentality has changed because we know that concept is untrue. We now know that the more you share the content, the more people will come inside'.[207] The 'third campus' of the NGV is a virtual one. The NGV's content is

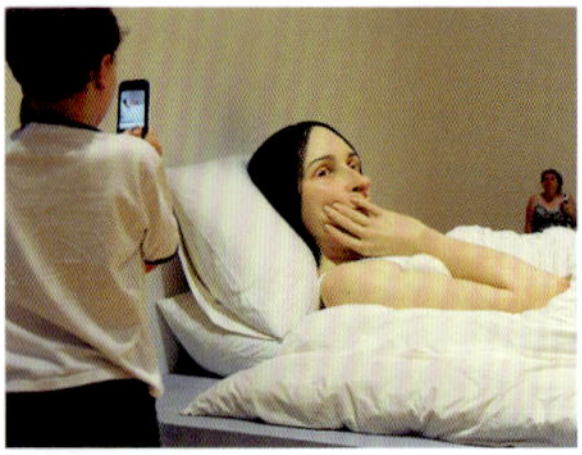

delivered and shared in diverse ways: the Dalí exhibition inspired 14,000 tweets; the Ron Mueck exhibition, which did not have the customary gallery restriction on taking photographs, inspired thousands of creative photographic responses; and the NGV's collection is used as the raw material for digital projects such as *The Floating World*, an interactive educational resource built around animated versions of the NGV's fine collection of Japanese *Ukiyo-e* prints.

Education is also an important mediator for experiencing the NGV. The education program has hugely expanded from the inaugural program of Guide Lectures in 1924. In 2010, over 257,000 people participated in public programs including artist talks, school programs, the 'Kids' Corner' spaces and community access programs aimed to make those who have never before set foot in a gallery feel welcome. The programs are predicated on contemporary understandings of the role of the museum, as Gina Panebianco, Head of Education and Public Programs, states: 'There are interesting philosophical changes across both education and museum practice Traditionally the gallery was positioned as a repository for works of art that perhaps a limited or elite group would come to experience – there was perhaps a sense that prior historical knowledge was required. Now we see a shift towards museums and galleries being part of people's everyday life and experience. There is a shift from the authoritative to the participatory. People are empowered to have their own ideas about art – it's much more inclusive, open-ended, enquiry-based and personalised'.[208]

LOTI SMORGON: 'IT'S AWKWARD BECAUSE SHE HATES MONEY BEING MENTIONED'.
The story goes that Loti Smorgon set out one day to buy a raincoat but returned home with a new work of art instead: *Rider*, 1945, by Italian sculptor Marino Marini. The bronze was placed in her living room where, allegedly, it provided a favourite hiding spot for her great-grandchildren. To celebrate the NGV's 150th birthday, Smorgon has donated the work to the Gallery, as well as works by Pablo Picasso, Alexander Calder and John Perceval. 'Loti has believed in the NGV', states Gerard Vaughan. 'It's a little awkward because she hates money being mentioned, but we worked it out on the back of an envelope in response to enquiries from journalists and the aggregated value of Loti Smorgon's gifts to the NGV – of cash and works of art – is now pushing $40 million. It's utterly extraordinary and very inspiring'.[209] The birthday present is yet another act of great generosity from the Smorgon family: the Loti and Victor Smorgon Fund for the purchase of twentieth-century and contemporary art has enabled the acquisition of works such as Antony Gormley's *Inside Australia*, 2002, and Bill Viola's *Ocean without a shore*, 2007, while the Loti Smorgon fund for Contemporary Australian Photography has purchased works by Pat Brassington, Jane Burton, Selina Ou, David van Royen, Susan Fereday and Deborah Paauwe. Loti has also been a part of the life of the NGV, something nicely symbolised by loaning her double portrait by Warhol to the NGV to celebrate the re-opening of the NGV St Kilda Road building.

MASTERPIECES FOR MELBOURNE. In May 2008, the NGV Foundation launched the 'Masterpieces for Melbourne' campaign. Led by Bruce Parncutt, Trustee and Chairman of the NGV Foundation, the campaign aimed to acquire significant new works of art but also to build a powerful corpus of funds that would enable acquisitions of master works into the future. The goal was set to secure $150 million of new money by the end of 2011, the NGV's 150th anniversary. Loti and Victor Smorgon spearheaded the campaign with the largest cash gift ever made to an Australian public art gallery from an individual source. Generous support and leadership gifts have followed from Allan and Maria Myers, the Bowness family, Alan and Mavourneen Cowen, Ian Hicks, John Higgins, Baillieu and Sarah Myer (through the Yulgilbar Foundation), Bruce Parncutt and Robin Campbell, Jason Yeap and Min Lee Wong, Nigel and Patricia Peck (through their Foundation), Peter and Joan Clemenger, and many other individuals, some of whom have chosen to remain anonymous. Masterpieces acquired or gifted through the fund since 2008 include two late eighteenth-century portraits by William Beechey and Tony Tuckson's *Untitled – yellow*, 1970–73, which is being purchased through the Loti and Victor Smorgon Fund. The NGV is in the process of acquiring Francesco Francia's High Renaissance masterpiece *Virgin and Child with the young Saint John in a garden of roses*, c.1515; Sean Scully's magisterial *Queen of the night*, 2008; and Ron Mueck's *Drift*, 2009, is a promised gift. The state government also generously presented the NGV with Sidney Nolan's *Kelly with horse*, 1955, a leadership gift to the campaign.

The Felton Bequest is also celebrating the NGV's 150th anniversary through a series of spectacular gifts: 'Great anniversaries demand special recognition', writes Andrew Grimwade, Chairman of the Felton Bequests Committee. As well as the gift of a French Impressionist work by Gustave Caillebotte, the Felton gift is distinguished by a special focus on Indigenous works of art, comprising sixty-three shields from the nineteenth and early twentieth centuries, 107 contemporary paintings from the Far Western Desert, and three Kimberley master works: *Yunurr* by Rover Thomas and two *Wanjina* by Alec Mingelmanganu. Furthermore, in deciding how they would celebrate the NGV's 150th anniversary, Grimwade states that the Felton Committee considered questions including: 'What was Indigenous art at the time when the NGV opened its doors?' and 'Who was the pre-eminent Indigenous figure in Victoria?'[210] The Felton Committee identified William Barak, the Wurundjeri leader and artist, and it was decided that his legacy should be honoured through The Barak Commissions, a series of contemporary artworks by Brook Andrew, Jonathan Jones and Vernon Ah Kee.

THE FUTURE: 'A MUSEUM OF ART IS AN ORGANIC MACHINE'. 'This is a significant moment for the NGV', reflects Allan Myers, President of the Council of Trustees. 'Since 1861, the NGV has grown from a small space at the State Library into an extraordinary collection, spanning many centuries and cultures in two architecturally renowned buildings. On this exciting occasion of the 150th it is important to not only look back to our past, but forward too, and ensure that we continue to build upon the constantly evolving role that we play in bringing access to the visual arts to the whole Victoria community.'[211] Considering the future, Gerard Vaughan states: 'Above all we need more space. We have wonderful things that cannot be displayed. When it comes to big-picture ideas for the future, we always knew – even when the first planning for the new building was done in the mid 1990s – that we were probably going to need a third building within twenty years if the growth of the collection, and the growth in visitor numbers projected, continued at the same rate. And that has certainly been the case'. Specific aims have been outlined for a new building, as Vaughan notes: 'Expanded space will be important for global contemporary art, including Australian Indigenous and non-Indigenous art and contemporary Asian and Pacific art, which in turn would dovetail with new galleries for the Asian historical collections'. Additional space for Indigenous art – interest in which, as Vaughan says, has 'grown at a pace beyond our wildest dreams' – will be essential. 'There is a huge demand for it, with both local audiences and overseas visitors wanting to see the contemporary manifestation of what is indisputably the oldest continuing visual tradition on earth.'[212]

The NGV is already developing its future plans for a new building under the project title: 'A big idea for Melbourne'. 'A new building would support these current priorities and position the NGV as a hub of museums in a broader cultural precinct', says Vaughan. 'A similar precinct with this concentration of related performing arts organisations would be very hard to find anywhere else in the world.' Importantly, it would enable the NGV to maintain its relevance in a changed – and rapidly changing – world: 'The NGV in its next phase of evolution should collect and display art from our regional perspective – and that is very important. The point is that it will be our own; it will be Australian, regional and global, reflecting our own viewpoint. We will maintain the great European strengths of the NGV, but we will also privilege the visual cultures of Asia, of the Pacific, and Australia'.[213] Deputy Director Frances Lindsay expresses similar priorities, keenly feeling the need for the NGV to 'position itself in a much more meaningful way with regards to the art of Asia and the Pacific' and to solve the 'ongoing problem of having enough space to display contemporary art'.[214] Reappraisal and growth will continue into the future: 'A museum of art is an organic machine', says Vaughan. 'It is something that needs to be constantly rethought and evolved, so that we respond thoughtfully to what is happening around us.'[215] Lindsay also echoes these sentiments: 'The NGV is not standing still. It never has, and it never will.'[216]

*

NOTES

THE DESIRE FOR A GALLERY

1 Archibald Michie quoted in S. Miriams, M. Davidson, S. Gordon, *Imagining Australia*, Thomson Social Science Press, Melbourne, 2006, p. 34.
2 Ann Galbally, 'For the Instruction and Amusement of the Inhabitants', in Ann Galbally & Alison Inglis, *The First Collections: The Public Library and the National Gallery of Victoria in the 1850s and 1860s*, exh. cat., University Gallery, The University of Melbourne Museum of Art, 1992, p. 8.
3 Sir Redmond Barry quoted in ibid., p. 8.
4 Bernard Smith (ed.), *Documents on Art and Taste in Australia 1770–1914*, Oxford University Press, Melbourne, 1975, p. 141.
5 Alexander Sutherland, et al., *Melbourne and its Metropolis*, vol. 1, McCarron, Bird, Melbourne, 1888, p. 388.
6 *The Book of the Public Library, Museums, and National Gallery of Victoria: 1856–1906* (hereafter *BPL*), vol. 1, Ford & Sons, Melbourne, 1906, p. 3.
7 Thomas Woolner, 'Life on the Diggings', 1852–53, in Smith, *Documents on Art and Taste in Australia 1770–1914*, p. 123.
8 Robert Hughes, *The Art of Australia*, Pelican, Norwich, 1970, p. 46.
9 Frederick McCubbin quoted in Jane Clark, 'The Art Schools', in Jane Clark & Bridget Whitelaw, *Golden Summers: Heidelberg and Beyond*, National Gallery of Victoria (hereafter NGV), exh. cat., 1985, p. 31.
10 *BPL*, p. 3.
11 ibid., p. 9.
12 Eric Westbrook, 'Introduction', in Ursula Hoff, *The National Gallery of Victoria*, Thames & Hudson, London, 1973, p. 8.
13 Sir Redmond Barry quoted in Geoffrey Serle, *The Golden Age: A History of the Colony of Victoria 1851–1861*, Melbourne University Press, Melbourne, 1963, p. 354.
14 Sir Redmond Barry to Sir Charles Eastlake, 26 December 1863. Appendix of *Second Progress Report of the Commission on the Fine Arts*, Victoria, 1864–65, no. 58, Shaw Library, NGV, p. 16.
15 *BPL*, p. 12.
16 Sir Henry Barkly quoted in Sutherland, p. 502.
17 James Smith quoted in Ann Galbally, 'Sculpture, and Casts of Sculpture, Friezes, Ornaments, etc.', in Ann Galbally & Alison Inglis, *The First Collections*, p. 80.
18 *Second Progress Report of the Commission on the Fine Arts*, p. A 2.
19 Professor Wilson to Sir Redmond Barry, 3 September 1863. *Second Progress Report of the Commission on the Fine Arts*, p. 14.
20 W. W. Wardell, Esq., to the Secretary of the Royal Commission, 15 October 1863. *Second Progress Report of the Commission on the Fine Arts*, p. 15.
21 Sir Redmond Barry to Sir Charles Eastlake, 26 December 1863. *Second Progress Report of the Commission of the Fine Arts*, p. 16.
22 Sir Charles Eastlake to Sir Redmond Barry, 19 May 1864. *Second Progress Report of the Commission of the Fine Arts*, p. 18.
23 Sir Charles Eastlake to Sir Redmond Barry, 19 May 1864. *Second Progress Report of the Commission on the Fine Arts*, p. 18.
24 *The Australasian News*, 25 January 1865, p. 11.
25 Leonard B. Cox, *The National Gallery of Victoria 1861 to 1968: A Search for a Collection*, NGV, Melbourne, 1970, p. 13.
26 Sir Charles Eastlake to Sir Redmond Barry, 19 May 1864. *Second Progress Report of the Commission of the Fine Arts*, p. 18.
27 Sir Redmond Barry to Augustus Tulk, 23 January 1865; Sir Redmond Barry to Augustus Tulk, 23 February 1865. Sir Redmond Barry: Papers 1798–1935, State Library of Victoria (hereafter SLV).
28 *The Age*, 24 December 1864, p. 5.
29 Sir Redmond Barry to Augustus Tulk, 21 January 1865, Sir Redmond Barry: Papers 1798–1935, SLV.
30 Sir Redmond Barry to Alfred Thomson, 26 November 1866. Records 1864–1965, SLV.
31 Sir Redmond Barry to Alfred Thomson, Commission on the Fine Arts file, 1866, ibid.
32 Alfred Thomson to Sir Redmond Barry, 26 January 1867, ibid.
33 John West, 'The Fine Arts in their intellectual and social relations', 1848, in Bernard Smith (ed.), *Documents on Art and Taste in Australia 1770–1914*, p. 77.
34 Hughes, p. 48.
35 Bernard Hall to the Chairman of the Gallery Trustees, 20 April 1900. Lindsay Bernard Hall: Papers, 1894–1935, SLV.
36 Gerard Vaughan, interview by the author, March 2011.
37 Sir Redmond Barry quoted in the *Catalogue of the Works of Art: Ornamental and Decorative Art*, exh. cat., Mason, Firth & Co., Melbourne, 1869, p. B.
38 *Annual Report*, 1873–74, NGV.
39 Letter to Trustees from students in the School of Painting, 2 December 1880 in Jane Clark, 'The Art Schools', Clark & Whitelaw, p. 32.
40 Eugene von Guérard quoted in Frances Lindsay, *Von Guérard to Wheeler: The First Teachers at the National Gallery School 1870–1939*, Victorian College of the Arts Gallery, 6–21 April 1978, exh. cat., unpaged.

41 Frederick McCubbin quoted in Jane Clark, 'The Art Schools', Clark & Whitelaw, p. 32.
42 James Smith, *Argus*, 6 November 1883, p. 9.
43 *Photographs of the Pictures in the National Gallery Melbourne*, photographed by T. F. Chuck, Marcus Clarke (ed.), F. F. Bailliere, Melbourne, 1875, SLV.
44 Sir Redmond Barry, 'Resolution on behalf of the Trustees', in Margaret Thomas, *Memoir of Charles Summers*, 1878, p. 48. Margaret Thomas: Australian Art and Artists file, SLV.
45 Vaughan, interview.
46 Terence Lane, interview by the author, January 2011.
47 Frederick McCubbin quoted in Jane Clark, 'The Art Schools', in Clark & Whitelaw, p. 32.
48 W. Moore quoted in ibid., p. 32.
49 O. R. Campbell quoted in ibid., p. 32.
50 Alexander Colquhoun, quoted in ibid., p. 32.
51 Frederick McCubbin quoted in ibid., p. 31.
52 Minutes of the Trustees, 7 December 1880. Records 1864–1965, SLV.
53 Garryowen quoted in Peter Ryan, 'Barry, Sir Redmond (1813–1880)', *Australian Dictionary of Biography*, p. 111.
54 Legislative Assembly, 4 July 1883, Cox, p. 42.
55 *Argus*, 7 October 1880.
56 George F. Folingsby quoted in Frances Lindsay, unpaged.
57 Alexander Colquhoun quoted in Jane Clark, 'The Art Schools', in Clark & Whitelaw, p. 33.
58 Bernard Smith, *Australian Painting: 1788–1970*, Oxford University Press, Melbourne, 1971, p. 191.
59 Ruth Zubans, 'Folingsby, George Frederick (1828–1891)', *Australian Dictionary of Biography*, p. 194.
60 Arthur Streeton, 1886, quoted in Hughes, p. 55.
61 Gerard Vaughan, interview by the author, February 2011.
62 James Smith, 'An Impressionist Exhibition', *Argus*, 17 August 1889, p. 10.
63 Tom Roberts, Charles Conder & Arthur Streeton, 'Concerning "Impressions" in Painting', *Argus*, 3 September 1889, p. 7.
64 Lane, interview.
65 Trustee's Report, 1891, quoted in Lindsay, unpaged.
66 Minutes of the Trustees, interview with Mr L. Fagan, 12 February 1891. Records 1864–1965, SLV.
67 Cathy Leahy, interview by the author, August 2010.
68 Arnold Shore, *The Age*, 12 December 1959.
69 Smith, *Australian Painting: 1788–1970*, p. 161.
70 Bernard Hall to E. Langton, 18 November 1892. Lindsay Bernard Hall: Papers, 1894–1935, SLV.
71 Bernard Hall to the Chairman of the Gallery Trustees, 20 March 1900. Records 1864–1965, SLV.
72 Bernard Hall to the Trustees, 25 May 1911, ibid.
73 Bernard Hall to the Trustees, 20 April 1910, ibid.
74 Bernard Hall to the Trustees, 29 November 1894, ibid.
75 Bernard Hall to the Trustees, 20 April 1910, ibid.
76 Trustee James Smith to the Trustees, undated, quoted in Cox, p. 60.
77 Bernard Hall to the Trustees, 3 December 1896. Records 1864–1965, SLV.
78 Bernard Hall to the Trustees of Felton Bequest, 23 July 1932. Felton Bequest file, NGV.
79 Bernard Hall to the Trustees, 22 January 1894. Records 1864–1965, SLV.
80 Frederick McCubbin to Tom Roberts, 3 September 1903. Letters to Tom Roberts, vol. 2. Mitchell Library.
81 'Editorial', *The Age*, 16 August 1905.
82 Lane, interview.
83 Sir Redmond Barry to Augustus Tulk, 23 March 1865. Sir Redmond Barry: Papers 1798–1935, SLV.
84 Carl Villis, interview by the author, March 2011.
85 John Payne, interview by the author, March 2011.
86 Bernard Hall to Chairman of National Gallery Committee, *Report on recent mission to Europe and acquisitions resulting therefrom, with recommendations with regard to the continuous spending of funds derived from the Felton Bequest*; Bernard Hall, *Memorandum to the Trustees on Purchasing*, 15 June 1911. Records 1864–1965, SLV.
87 Walter Withers in 'My favourite gallery pictures: The view of the artist', William Moore, *Studio Sketches*, 1906, p. 17.
88 Bernard Hall, *Report to the Chairman of the National Gallery Committee*, 27 July 1905. Records 1864–1965, SLV.
89 Ted Gott, interview by the author, August 2010.
90 *Argus,* 26 November 1906.
91 Gott, interview.
92 Emmanuel Frémiet to Bernard Hall, 13 December 1906, quoted in Ted Gott, 'An iron maiden for Melbourne', in *The La Trobe Journal*, no. 81 (Autumn 2008), p. 62.
93 Gott, interview.
94 Bernard Hall to the Trustees, 25 May 1911. Records 1864–1965, SLV.
95 Eric Westbrook, 'Introduction', in Hoff, pp. 11–12.
96 Sidney Colvin to Trustees, 2 March 1915. Records 1864–1965, SLV.
97 Sir Baldwin Spencer to Trustees, March 1917, ibid.
98 J. A. Levey to Gallery Trustees, 13 March 1907, ibid.
99 Ursula Hoff to Leonard B. Cox, 11 February 1965, quoted in Cox, p. 428.
100 Amanda Dunsmore, interview by the author, August 2010.
101 Daryl Lindsay, *The Leafy Tree: My Family*, F. W. Cheshire, Melbourne, 1965, p. 57.

THE BATTLE FOR MODERNISM

1 Hans Heysen quoted in Anne Gray, *George W. Lambert Retrospective: Heroes and Icons*, exh. cat., National Gallery of Australia, 2007, p. 154.
2 Terence Lane, interview by the author, January 2011.
3 *The Art Student*, May 1932, p. 35.
4 *Men and Memories: A History of the Arts 1872 to 1922, Being the Recollections of William Rothenstein Part One*, Tudor Publishing, New York, 1931, p. 187.
5 Cathy Leahy, interview by the author, August 2010.
6 *Argus,* 1919, Cox, p. 84.

7 Baldwin Spencer to Frank Rinder, 11 October 1918. Felton Bequest: Records 1885–1996, SLV.
8 Attributed to Clewin Harcourt in the *Herald*, quoted in Cox, p. 94.
9 John Shirlow, memo, 20 October 1926, reported in Cox, p. 104.
10 Sir Kenneth Clark, *The Idea of a Great Gallery*, The Specialty Press, Melbourne, 1949, p. 16.
11 Cox, p. 104.
12 Professor Thomas Bodkin quoted in Franz Philipp & June Stewart (eds), *In Honour of Daryl Lindsay: Essays and Studies*, Oxford University Press, Melbourne, 1964, p. 27.
13 Ted Gott, interview by the author, August 2010.
14 Daryl Lindsay, *The Leafy Tree: My Family*, F. W. Cheshire, Melbourne, 1965, p. 126.
15 Bernard Hall, memo on a letter from Captain Collins to W. H. Gill, 20 June 1924. Lindsay Bernard Hall: Papers, 1894–1935, SLV.
16 Cox, p. 95.
17 Letter to the editor, 'National Gallery ceramics', Frank Gooden, *Argus*, 23 March 1918.
18 Geoffrey Serle, *Percival Serle 1871–1951 Biographer, Bibliographer, Anthologist and Art Curator – A Memoir*, Officina Brindabella, Canberra, 1988, p. 35.
19 Randall Davies to Felton Bequest Committee, 9 February 1933. Felton Bequest: Records 1885–1996, SLV.
20 Jaynie Anderson, *Tiepolo's Cleopatra*, Macmillan, Melbourne, 2003.
21 Gott, interview.
22 Gerard Vaughan, interview by the author, August 2010.
23 Sir Kenneth Clark, *The Idea of a Great Gallery*, 1949, reprinted to accompany the exhibition *The Idea of a Great Gallery*, exh. cat., NGV, 1981, p. 15.
24 George Peka, interview by the author, August 2010.
25 Gott, interview.
26 Bernard Hall to Sir Leo Cussen, 22 November 1928. Felton Bequest: Records 1885–1996, SLV.
27 Bernard Hall to Chief Librarian, Ernest Roland Pitt, 12 April 1934. Lindsay Bernard Hall: Papers, 1894–1935, SLV.
28 Cable from London Agents to Felton Bequest Committee, 4 August 1934; Cable from Bernard Hall to Chief Librarian, Ernest Roland Pitt, 7 August 1934. Felton Bequest: Records 1885–1996, SLV.
29 As recounted by George Bell to Leonard Cox, recounted in Cox, p. 137.
30 J. S. MacDonald, 'Arthur Streeton', *Art in Australia*, October 1931, p. 23.
31 Percival Serle quoted in Cox, p. 436.
32 Robert Menzies quoted in *Argus*, 28 April 1937.
33 J. S. MacDonald quoted in *The Sun*, 5 June 1937.
34 Arthur Streeton, *Argus*, 17 August 1932.
35 Blamire Young, *Herald*, 17 August 1932.
36 Contemporary Art Society's *Constitution*, published in exh. cat., NGV, 1939.
37 Kirsty Grant, interview by the author, August 2010.
38 Cox, p. 165.
39 Bernard Smith, *Australian Painting: 1788–1970*, Oxford University Press, Melbourne, 1978, p. 207.
40 J. S. MacDonald, report, 31 October 1939. Records 1864–1965, SLV.
41 As reported in Cox, p. 144.
42 ibid., p. 144.
43 Sir Sydney Cockerell, *Report on the National Gallery of Victoria, with suggestions for its rearrangement*, 1936, Shaw Library, NGV.
44 Geoffrey Serle, p. 40.
45 Mae Anna Pang, interview by the author, August 2010.
46 Kenneth Wilkinson, 'Pictures at gallery being reframed', *Herald*, 21 June 1941, p. 8.
47 *Annual Report*, 1940, NGV, p. 7.
48 'Director not reappointed', *The Sun*, 29 December 1941.
49 Daryl Lindsay, pp. 143–4.
50 ibid., p. 152.
51 ibid., pp. 113–14.
52 ibid., p. 118.
53 ibid., p. 134.
54 ibid., p. 134.
55 ibid., p. 152.
56 Daryl Lindsay, *Annual Report*, 1941, NGV, p. 32.
57 Lane, interview.
58 Daryl Lindsay, p. 151.
59 ibid., p. 145.
60 ibid., p. 153.
61 ibid., p. 145.
62 John McDonnell, 'Daryl Lindsay, Director of the National Gallery of Victoria 1924–1955', *Quarterly Bulletin of the National Gallery of Victoria*, vol. X, no. 1, 1956.
63 John Medley, ibid.; Percival Serle, *A Life of Good Fortune: An Autobiography*, Melbourne, 1948. Terence Lane's archives, NGV, unpaged.
64 Daryl Lindsay to the Honourable W. S. Kent Hughes, Minister of State for the Interior and for Works and Housing, Parliament House, Canberra, 18 February 1952, NGV Archives.
65 Judith Ryan, interview by the author, August 2010.
66 Letter from Daryl Lindsay, Curator of the Art Museum and Keeper of the Prints to the Abbot of New Norcia, Benedictine Abbey, New Norcia, WA. Terence Lane's archives, NGV, unpaged.
67 Daryl Lindsay, *Annual Report*, 1941, NGV, p. 36.
68 *Bulletin*, 15 October 1941.
69 Report of the Post War Development Committee, 1943.
70 Dame Elisabeth Murdoch quoted in Anthony Dennis, 'Melbourne gets square', *Sydney Morning Herald*, 19 October 2002, p. 51.
71 Daryl Lindsay, p. 145.
72 ibid., p. 147.
73 ibid., p. 146.
74 Leahy, interview.
75 Irena Zdanowicz, 'Remembering Dr Ursula Hoff', in *A tribute to Dr Ursula Hoff AO OBE*, 24 February 2005, Shaw Research Library, NGV, p. 23.
76 Gerard Vaughan quoted in ibid.
77 Daryl Lindsay, p. 152.
78 *Grant*, interview.
79 Sir Keith Murdoch, transcript of broadcast interview, 4 July 1943, ABC Radio.
80 *Argus*, 13 March 1948.
81 Daryl Lindsay, p. 156.
82 John McDonnell to Felton Bequest Committee, 21 January 1948. Felton Bequest file, NGV.
83 Sir Kenneth Clark to Daryl Lindsay, 4 April 1949. Felton Bequest file, NGV.

84 John McDonnell to Felton Bequest Committee, 3 June 1949. Felton Bequest file, NGV.
85 John McDonnell to Felton Bequest Committee, 22 November 1949. Felton Bequest file, NGV.
86 John McDonnell to Felton Bequest Committee, 3 June 1949. Felton Bequest file, NGV.
87 John McDonnell to Felton Bequest Committee, 17 November 1950; John McDonnell to Felton Bequest Committee, 7 January 1954. Felton Bequest file, NGV.
88 Eric Westbrook quoted in Anna King Murdoch, 'Melbourne 1956: a golden moment in Australian art', *The Age*, 11 August 2000, p. 4.
89 Sir Thomas Barlow to John McDonnell, 19 July 1956. Felton Bequest file, NGV.
90 Sir Thomas Barlow to Daryl Lindsay, 23 June 1949. Felton Bequest file, NGV.
91 John McDonnell to Felton Bequest Committee, 28 July 1956; Dr Ursula Hoff to Felton Bequest Committee, 28 July 1956. Felton Bequest file, NGV.
92 Ursula Hoff, 'Everard Studley Miller Bequest, NGV memorandum, 1956, NGV.
93 ibid.
94 Mae Anna Pang, interview by the author, August 2010.
95 Eric Westbrook quoted in Phillip Jones, 'Driven by an artistic passion: Eric Westbrook, Director of the National Gallery of Victoria, 1915–2005', *The Age*, 11 November 2005, p. 13.
96 Eric Westbrook quoted in John Currey, 'Marrying Melbourne's arts', *Walkabout*, November 1965, p. 28.
97 Eric Westbrook quoted in Kevin Childs, 'Westbrook reveals a gallery of memories', *The Age*, 17 October 1987, p. 3.
98 Eric Westbrook quoted in Jones, p. 13.
99 Eric Westbrook quoted in Currey, pp. 29–30.
100 Eric Westbrook quoted in Childs, p. 3.
101 Eric Westbrook quoted in ibid., p. 3.
102 Eric Westbrook quoted in Jones, p. 13.
103 Eric Westbrook quoted in Childs, p. 3.
104 Eric Westbrook quoted in Corrie Perkin 'Serious fun', *The Age*, 26 June 1999, p. 7.
105 Cox, p. 297.
106 Elizabeth Summons, undated ms, NGVWA Archive.
107 Mary Archer & Naomi Morell quoted in *Celebrating 50 Years of the NGV Women's Association*, NGV, Melbourne, 2011, p. 5.
108 Mission statement, ibid.
109 Patrick McCaughey quoted in Ian MacNeill, 'Brian Finemore 1925–1975: the first Australian art curator', *Art Monthly Australia*, no. 183, September 2005, p. 40.
110 MacNeill, p. 40.
111 Katie Somerville, interview by the author, August 2010.
112 Danielle Whitfield, interview by the author, August 2010.
113 John McDonnell to Felton Bequest Committee, 23 July 1963. Felton Bequest file, NGV.
114 John Brack quoted in Sasha Grishin, *The Art of John Brack*, vol. 1, Oxford University Press, Melbourne, 1990, p. 9.
115 Arnold Shore, 'He got into a lather ... then he painted the barber', *Australasian Post*, 5 March 1953, p. 37.
116 Isobel Crombie, interview by the author, August 2010.
117 Cox, p. 380.
118 John Stringer, 'Cultivating *The Field*', in Charles Green & Jason Smith, *Fieldwork: Australian Art 1968–2002*, exh. cat., NGV, 2002, p. 18.
119 ibid., p. 18.
120 Mary Woodall to Felton Bequest Committee, 26 January 1966. Felton Bequest file, NGV.
121 Mary Woodall to Felton Bequest Committee, 14 April 1966. Felton Bequest file, NGV.
122 Mary Woodall to Felton Bequest Committee, 9 June 1966. Felton Bequest file, NGV.
123 Report, Dr Ursula Hoff, 5 December 1967. Felton Bequest file, NGV.
124 Mary Woodall to Felton Bequest Committee, 15 March 1968. Felton Bequest file, NGV.
125 Patrick McCaughey, *The Bright Shapes and the True Names: A Memoir*, Text Publishing, Melbourne, 2003, p. 137.
126 Michael Kitson to Dr Mary Woodall, 3 April 1967. Felton Bequest file, NGV.
127 John McDonnell to Felton Bequest Committee, 14 October 1963. Felton Bequest file, NGV.
128 Amanda Dunsmore, interview by the author, August 2010.
129 The Milliken Report, 11 June 1959. Shaw Research Library, NGV.
130 Cox, p. 289.
131 Gerard Vaughan, interview by the author, February 2011.
132 Roy Grounds quoted in editorial, 'At last, a gallery for our time', *The Age*, 30 November 2003, p. 14.
133 Roy Grounds quoted in Virginia Trioli, 'Grounds for complaint', *The Bulletin*, 6 July 1999, p. 44.
134 Eric Westbrook quoted in Raymond Gill, 'Gallery marks a quarter-century', *The Age*, 21 August 1993, p. 7.
135 Leonard French quoted in Michael Shmith, 'Raising the roof with Melbourne's glass ceiling', *The Age*, 27 November 2003, p. 6.
136 Vaughan, interview.
137 Cox, p. 385.
138 Lane, interview.
139 Cox, p. 386.
140 Lane, interview.
141 Stringer, p. 16.
142 ibid., p. 25.
143 Grant, interview.
144 Frances Lindsay, interview by the author, February 2011.
145 Eric Westbrook, *The Spirit and Purpose of a Cultural Centre*, 1957. Shaw Research Library, NGV.
146 Eric Westbrook, *Annual Report*, 1969–70, NGV.
147 Eric Westbrook, quoted in *Bringing People and Art Together: Voluntary Guiding at the National Gallery of Victoria 1968–2008*, NGV, Melbourne, 2008, p. 13.
148 June Trott quoted in ibid., p. 15.
149 Eric Westbrook, *Annual Report*, 1969–70, NGV.
150 Joan Shaw quoted in ibid., p. 9.
151 Gina Panebianco, interview by the author, August 2010.

ART LIKE NEVER BEFORE

1 John Kaldor quoted in Michael Ryan, 'As sculptures they are the living end', *The Age*, 29 August 1973, p. 8.
2 Alex Baker, interview by the author, August 2010.
3 Gilbert and George quoted in Jill Graham, 'Living what?', *Weekender*, 20 September 1973, p. 22.
4 Gilbert and George quoted in Chris Hector, 'They keep stiff for hours', *Nation Review*, 6 September 1973, p. 5.
5 Gilbert and George quoted in Lenore Nicklin, 'And here come the living sculptures', in *Sydney Morning Herald*, 14 August 1973, p. 3.
6 Gilbert and George quoted in Graham, p. 22.
7 Gilbert and George quoted in Ryan, p. 8.
8 Tate Adams quoted in Paul Slickey, 'Rumbles amid the Gallery glories', *Melbourne Observer*, 11 February 1973, p. 11.
9 Eric Westbrook, ibid., p. 11.
10 Jennifer Licht quoted in John Hamilton, 'These are pebbles – they are art', *Herald*, 7 February 1974, p. 2.
11 Patrick McCaughey, 'The seriousness of 137 bricks', *The Age*, 13 February 1974, p. 7.
12 Gail Franzmann, 'The night the Modern Masters came to Melbourne', *The Herald*, 17 May 1975, p. 17.
13 Gerard Vaughan, interview by the author, January 2011.
14 Malcolm Fraser quoted in John Monks, 'China gives us a taste of its jade diplomacy', *The Australian*, 19 January 1977, p. 5.
15 '$158,000 gift for that painting', *The Sun*, 16 June 1973, p. 4.
16 Daryl Lindsay quoted in John Messer, 'Expert lashes Turner canvas', *The Age*, 28 June 1973, p. 8.
17 Patrick McCaughey quoted in John Messer, 'Expert lashes Turner canvas', *The Age*, 28 June 1973, p. 8; Joseph Burke quoted in Sue Boyce, 'State to help buy painting', *The Sun*, 13 July 1973, p. 2.
18 Reginald Shanahan quoted in 'ASL's $158,000 towards Turner painting', *Financial Review*, 17 July 1973, p. 8.
19 Roger Leong, interview by the author, August 2011.
20 Katie Somerville, interview by the author, August 2011.
21 Anne Schofield quoted in Pat von Wolff, 'Looking to the past for fashion', 29 July 1977, p. 20.
22 Terence Lane, interview by the author, February 2011.
23 Ken Scarlett, *The Sculpture of John Davis: Places & Locations*, Hyland House, South Yarra, 1988, p. 95.
24 Eric Rowlison quoted in Alan Attwood, 'Review of Geoffrey J. Wallis's *Peril in the Square: The Sculpture that Challenged a City*', *The Age*, 19 June 2004.
25 Brian Stonier quoted in Adrian Blackburn, 'Experiment in free-form art financing', *The Age*, 5 May 1977.
26 Patrick McCaughey, *The Bright Shapes and the True Names: A Memoir*, Text Publishing, Melbourne, 2003, p. 183.
27 Robert Lindsay, interview by the author, February 2011.
28 ibid.
29 ibid.
30 McCaughey, *The Bright Shapes*, p. 229.
31 Robert Lindsay, interview.
32 Eric Rowlison quoted in Maureen Gilchrist, 'Drawing has a freer, broader line', *The Age*, 30 June 1976, p. 7.
33 Lane, interview.
34 Jack Manton 'Genesis' in Patrick McCaughey, *Australian Painters of the Heidelberg School: The Jack Manton Collection*, Oxford University Press, Melbourne, 1980, p. 147.
35 ibid., p. 150.
36 Patrick McCaughey, *The Bright Shapes*, p. 183.
37 ibid., pp. 185–6.
38 ibid., p. 216.
39 Patrick McCaughey quoted in '"Big show" tells a palatable story', *Melbourne Winners – Entertainment*, 24 March 1986, p. 8.
40 McCaughey, *The Bright Shapes*, p. 216.
41 ibid., p. 201.
42 ibid., pp. 202–4.
43 ibid., p. 249.
44 Anthony Clarke, 'Heidelberg's golden summers fill our eyes', *The Age*, 26 October 1985, p. 4.
45 Bernard Smith, 'New light on old light: Impressionism and the *Golden Summers* exhibition', *The Age Monthly Review*, July 1986, p. 25.
46 Patrick McCaughey quoted in Carolyn Ford, 'Royals look back on Heidelberg School reunion', *The Australian*, 30 October 1985, p. 3.
47 Robert Lindsay, interview.
48 Paul Taylor quoted in Susan Tate, 'The Mediated Image: "Something in the air"', in *The Virgin Press*, 14 June 1982, p. 2.
49 Paul Taylor quoted in 'The National Gallery goes pop', *The Age*, 22 June 1982, p. 8.
50 'Our National Gallery', *The Leader*, 24 September 1892.
51 George Folingsby quoted in Alexandra Ellem, '"Danger and Decay": A restoration drama concerning the National Gallery of Victoria, 1899', in Carl Villis & Alexandra Ellem (eds), *Paintings Conservation in Australia from the Nineteenth Century to the Present: Connecting the Past to the Future,* NGV, Melbourne, 2008, pp. 14–15.
52 Bernard Hall quoted in ibid., p. 14.
53 ibid., p. 11.
54 John Payne, interview by the author, April 2011.
55 Carl Villis, interview by the author, April 2011.
56 John Payne, interview.
57 Carl Villis, interview.
58 John Payne, interview.
59 Ted Gott, interview by the author, August 2010.
60 Ted Gott, interview.
61 McCaughey, *The Bright Shapes*, p. 226.
62 Patrick McCaughey quoted in Trudi McIntosh, 'Aboriginal art moves out of the curio corner', *The Australian*, 12 December 1984, p. 10.
64 Judith Ryan, interview by the author, August 2011.
64 McCaughey, *The Bright Shapes*, p. 227.
65 ibid., p. 188.
66 Patrick McCaughey quoted in Mike Daly, 'Connoisseurs meet at the gallery', *The Age*, 21 February 1987, p. 1.
67 Robert Lindsay, interview.

68 Jennie Boddington, 'Preface', *Drysdale: Photographer*, exh. cat., NGV, 1987, p. 7.
69 Patrick McCaughey, *The Bright Shapes*, p. 192.
70 ibid., p. 187.
70 Robert Lindsay, interview.
71 McCaughey, *The Bright Shapes*, p. 192.
72 ibid.
73 ibid., p. 184.
74 ibid., p. 194.
75 Isobel Crombie, interview by the author, August 2010.
76 Rowena Clark quoted in Sue Green, 'Out of the closet', *Sunday Herald*, 13 May 1990, p. 6.
77 McCaughey, *The Bright Shapes*, p. 248.
78 Race Mathews quoted in Andrew Bolt, Bill Ayres, Penelope Debelle & Peter Coster, 'Stolen Picasso is not insured', *The Herald,* 5 August 1986, p. 1.
79 Gott, interview.
80 'Ransom note one' from the Australian Cultural Terrorists quoted in Christobel Botten & Simon Clarke, 'Picasso ransom demand refused', *The Age*, 5 August 1986, p. 1.
81 'Ransom note two' from the Australian Cultural Terrorists quoted in Jane Phillips, 'Ransom tip: picture safe in Victoria', *The Sun*, 11 August 1986, p. 3.
82 'Ransom note three' from the Australian Cultural Terrorists quoted in Kevin Childs, 'Masterpiece manoeuvres', *The Age*, 4 October 1986, p. 5.
83 Margaret Simons & Tom Noble, 'Picasso found safe in locker', *The Age*, 20 August 1986, p. 1.
84 Patrick McCaughey quoted in Michael Shmith, 'Anguish in green replaced by faces of red', *The Age*, 5 August 1985, p. 1.
85 Ryan, interview.
86 Judy Williams, interview by the author, March 2011.
87 Eric Westbrook quoted in Bobbi Mahlab, 'From greatness to mediocrity', *The Age,* 2 November 1989, p. 5.
88 James Mollison quoted in Corrie Perkin, 'Mr Mollison's grand plans for the Gallery', *The Sunday Age*, 26 November 1989, p. 3.
89 James Mollison, interview by the author, March 2011.
90 ibid.
91 James Mollison quoted in Michael Shmith, 'The Mollison manifesto', *The Age Saturday Extra*, 1 December 1990, p. 3.
92 Mollison, interview.
93 Robert Rooney, 'Long overdue but Bell strikes the right note', *The Australian*, 24 June 1992, p. 11; Christopher Heathcote, 'New light on a neglected era', *The Age*, 24 June 1992, p. 14.
94 James Mollison quoted in Shmith, 'The Mollison manifesto', p. 3.
95 Mollison, interview.
96 James Mollison quoted in Shmith, 'The Mollison manifesto', p. 6.
97 Ryan, interview.
98 Mollison, interview.
99 Ryan, interview.
100 Crombie, interview.
101 Will Bailey quoted in Virginia Trioli, 'A change of direction at the National Gallery', *The Age*, 4 March 1995, p. 19.
102 Timothy Potts quoted in Susan McCulloch, 'Gallery director plans to revive "sense of pride"', *The Australian*, 1 March 1995, p. 3.
103 Timothy Potts quoted in Trioli, 'A change of direction at the National Gallery', p. 19.
104 Will Bailey quoted in ibid., p. 19.
105 Williams, interview.
106 Timothy Potts quoted in Angela Bennie, 'Two coups for Dr Potts', *The Sydney Morning Herald*, 9 December 1996, p. 13.
107 Timothy Potts, 'Anguish in the fight for freedom', *The Age*, 18 October 1997, p. 11.
108 George Pell, 'In respect of sacred symbols', *The Age*, 11 October 1997, p. 11.
109 Kim Wilson, 'Archbishop refuses to meet artist', *Herald Sun*, 11 October 1997, p. 9.
110 Timothy Potts, 'We could not reveal full extent of threats', *The Australian*, 6 November 1997, p. 12.
111 Timothy Potts, 'Anguish in the fight for freedom', p. 11.
112 Andres Serrano, 'I protest', *Herald Sun*, 14 October 1997, p. 4.
113 Crombie, interview.
114 Timothy Potts quoted in Greg Burchall & Rachel Gibson, 'We couldn't take a chance, says director', *The Age*, 14 October 1997, p. 16.
115 Timothy Potts quoted in Virginia Trioli, 'Holy War', *The Age*, 18 October 1997, p. 3.
116 John MacDonald as quoted in transcript from 'Andres Serrano Forum', a public forum recorded 13 October 1997 at The Continental Café, Prahran, Melbourne, broadcast on Arts Today, 10 am, 14 October 1997, Radio National.
117 Daryl Lindsay, *The Leafy Tree: My Family*, F. W. Cheshire, Melbourne, 1965, p. 194.
118 Timothy Potts quoted in Rebecca Lancashire, 'Lack of space: the final frontier', *The Age*, 21 March 1997, p. 4.
119 Timothy Potts quoted in Rebecca Lancashire, 'Potts's vision for the future', *The Age*, 6 December 1996, p. B5.
120 ibid., p. B5.
121 'Gallery update Number 1', statement issued by Timothy Potts, Director, and John Gough, President, 30 April 1997, NGV, p. 2.
122 Timothy Potts quoted in Robin Usher, 'The new priority', *Herald Sun*, 28 January 1997, p. 42.
123 Premier Jeff Kennett quoted in Kimina Lyall, 'Water wall in doubt as gallery shuts', *The Australian*, 12 May 1997, p. 8.
124 Bryce Hallett, 'Kennett pledge heartens NGV', *The Australian*, 29 March 1996, p. 8.
125 'Gallery update Number 1', statement issued by Timothy Potts, Director, and John Gough, President, 30 April 1997, p. 1.
126 Susan McCulloch 'New galleries for Melbourne', *The Australian*, 19 November 1996, p. 10.
127 Rebecca Lancashire, 'A new place to hang', *The Age*, 25 July 1998, p. 9.
128 Timothy Potts, interview by the author, April 2011.
129 Daniel Thomas 'The case against', *The Australian*, 1 August 1997, p. 15.
130 Jan Senbergs, 'The case for', *The Australian*, 1 August 1997, p. 15.

131 Timothy Potts, 'Oz art deserves its own space', *Sydney Morning Herald*, 29 July 1997, p. 13.
132 Jane Freeman, 'New home for icons', *The Sydney Morning Herald*, 29 June 1998, p. 17.
133 Steven Bedwell, *Vizard uncut: the full story*, Melbourne University Press, Melbourne, 2007, p. 266.
134 Gerard Vaughan, interview by the author, February 2010.
135 ibid.
136 Gabrielle Costa, 'For art's sake, turn off that tap!', *The Age*, 28 June 1999, p. A4.
137 Ronald Millar, 'The art of nostalgia', *The Sunday Age*, 22 February 1998, p. 4.
138 Vaughan, interview.
139 Gabriella Coslovich, 'Gallery at home again after 100 years', *The Age*, 17 November 1999, p. 12.
140 Robert Haines quoted in *Argus*, 4 January 1951.
141 Gerard Vaughan quoted in Raymond Gill, 'New gallery chief puts himself in the picture', *The Age*, 17 August 1999, p. 6.
142 Rebecca Lancashire, 'Great space for Australian art', *The Age*, 27 June 1998, p. 9.
143 Marianne Betts, Matt Johnston & Stephen McMahon, 'Barry Humphries calls for "eyesore" Federation Square to be demolished', *Herald Sun*, 26 October 2010, p. 3.
144 Donald Bates quoted in Anthony Dennis, 'Melbourne gets square', *Sydney Morning Herald*, 19 October 2002, p. 51.
145 Vaughan, interview.
146 Peter Davidson quoted in Simon Plant, 'The big picture', *Herald-Sun Weekend*, 2 March 2002, p. 6.
147 Stephen Varady, 'Federation Square' in *Architectural Review Australia*, Summer 1997, pp. 51–2.
148 ibid.
146 Peter Davidson quoted in Plant, p. 6.
150 Daryl West-Moore, interview by the author, August 2010.
151 Frances Lindsay, interview by the author, February 2011.
152 'Federation Square: NGV Australian Art' at <www.labarchitecture.com>.
153 Peter Davidson quoted in Plant, p. 4.
154 Frances Lindsay, interview.
155 ibid.
156 Vaughan, interview.
157 ibid.
158 Gerard Vaughan quoted in John Mangan, 'Party time for an art gallery with a split personality', *The Age*, 25 November 2002, p. 3.
159 Frances Lindsay quoted in Michael Shmith, 'Bringing the collections to life', *The Age*, 12 September 2001, p. 7.
160 Steve Vizard quoted in Plant, p. 4.
161 Gerard Vaughan quoted in Robin Usher, 'New art centre is picture-perfect with the public', *The Age*, 24 February 2003, p. 6.
162 Steve Vizard quoted in Robin Usher, 'Vizard calls for square gallery to be free for all', *The Age,* 1 February 2002, p. 1.
163 Ryan, interview.
164 ibid.
165 Frances Lindsay, interview.
166 Charles Green, 'The discursive field | home is where the heart is' in *Fieldwork: Australian Art 1968–2002*, exh. cat., NGV, 2002, p. 12.
167 Jason Smith, 'No compass? A postscript to *Fieldwork*', in *Fieldwork: Australian Art 1968–2002*, exh. cat., NGV, 2002, p. 120.
168 Tony Ellwood, interview by the author, March 2011.
169 Patrick McCaughey quoted in Robin Usher, 'Scare claims on gallery changes', *Herald Sun*, 18 March 1997, p. 47.
170 Paul Walker, 'NGV International', in *Architecture Australia*, March/April 2004, vol. 93, no. 2, p. 64.
171 Ellwood, interview.
172 Mario Bellini quoted in Plant, p. 4.
173 Ellwood, interview.
174 Rupert Myer quoted in Muriel Reddy, 'First impressions', *The Age*, 21 November 2004, p. 17.
175 Vaughan, interview.
176 Charles Green, '_World recognition' in *world rush _ 4 artists*, exh. cat., NGV, 2006, p. 27.
177 Jason Smith quoted in Gabriella Coslovich, 'Seeing the bigger picture', *The Age*, 4 December 2003, p. 4.
178 Frances Lindsay, interview.
179 ibid.
180 Gott, interview.
181 Williams, interview.
182 Gott, interview.
183 Vaughan, interview.
184 ibid.
185 ibid.
186 ibid.
187 Cathy Leahy, interview by the author, August 2010.
188 Payne, interview.
189 Gott, interview.
190 Dan Harrison, 'NGV's "Van Gogh" a fake', 3 August 2007.
191 Gott, interview.
192 Villis, interview.
193 Gott, interview.
194 Payne, interview.
195 Mary Delahunty, State Minister for the Arts, media release, 'Victorian Foundation for Living Australian Artists', November 2002.
196 Vaughan, interview.
197 Crombie, interview.
198 Roger Leong, interview by the author, August 2010.
199 Dunsmore, interview.
200 Gerard Vaughan, *NGV Annual Report*, 2003–04, pp. 25–6.
201 Corrie Perkin, 'In the spirit of Felton', *Antiques & Art in Victoria*, p. 32.
202 Gerard Vaughan quoted in Jonathan Green, 'The great art robbery', *The Age*, 14 April 2006, p. 1.
203 ibid.
204 ibid.
205 David Walsh quoted in Gabriella Coslovich, 'Change of heart has NGV shouting *The Bar*', *The Age*, 20 March 2009.
206 Gerard Vaughan quoted in ibid.
207 Jean-Pierre Chabrol, interview by the author, August 2010.
208 Gina Panebianco, interview by the author, August 2010.
209 Vaughan, interview.
210 Andrew Grimwade 'Foreword', from Judith Ryan, *Living Water: Contemporary Art of the Far Western Desert*, exh. cat., NGV, 2011, pp. 2–3.
211 Allan Myers, interview by the author, April 2011.
212 Vaughan, interview.
213 ibid.
214 Frances Lindsay, interview.
215 Vaughan, interview.
216 Frances Lindsay, interview.

(p.171 clockwise from top left)

Jeff Wall
Untangling
1994, printed 2006
cibachrome photograph, light box, fluorescent light
207.1 x 241.0 x 26.2 cm
Purchased with the assistance of NGV Contemporary, 2006

Christian Dior, Paris (couture house)
John Galliano (designer)
Dress, hat and boots model no. 39
designed, spring-summer, The tramp collection 2000, made 2003
silk, paint, lacquer, metal, viscose, nylon, water based paint, leather
(a) 224.2 cm (centre back); 35.0 cm (waist, flat) (dress); (b) 123.0 cm (outer circumference); 31.0 cm (height); 58.0 cm (width) (hat); (c-d) 51.8 x 8.2 x 21.2 cm (each) (boots)
Presented through the NGV Foundation by Norma and Stuart Leslie, Governors, 2002

Minton, Stoke-on-Trent, Staffordshire (manufacturer)
Monkey teapot 1874
earthenware (majolica)
(a-b) 15.0 x 22.0 x 10.3 cm (overall)
The Dr Robert Wilson Collection.
Presented through the NGV Foundation by Dr Robert Wilson, Honorary Life Benefactor, 2001

Paris Bordone
Rest on the flight into Egypt with Saint Catherine and angels c.1527–1530
oil on canvas
154.7 x 236.0 cm (image); 156.4 x 237.4 cm (canvas)
Purchased through the NGV Foundation with the assistance of Allan and Maria Myers, Honorary Life Benefactors, 2006

Cornelis de Vos
Mother and child 1624
oil on wood panel
123.4 x 92.8 cm
Purchased with funds donated by Alan and Mavourneen Cowen, two anonymous donors and donors to the Cornelis de Vos Appeal, 2009

Christopher Dresser (designer)
James Dixon & Sons, Sheffield (manufacturer)
Toast rack c.1880
silver electroplate, ebonised wood
9.1 x 25.4 x 9.6 cm
Presented by The National Gallery Women's Association, 2003

Photography credits: Craig Abraham / Fairfax Media p.145; © Josef Albers/VG BILD-KUNST, Bonn. Licensed by VISCOPY, Australia p.97; © The Estate of Howard Arkley, Licensed by Kalli Rolfe Contemporary Art p.121; Bruce Armstrong p.iv; *Australian* magazine p.172; © Francis Bacon/ARS, New York. Licensed by VISCOPY, Australia p.87; © Balthus/ADAGP, Paris. Licensed by VISCOPY, Australia p.86; The Estate of Bruno Benini p.87; © Peter Booth/Licensed by VISCOPY, Australia p.122; © Helen Brack pp. 96, 174; Geoffrey Burke p.130; Sebastian Costanzo / Fairfax Media p.147; Christian Dior p.171; Noel Dunn p.106; Jerry Galea / Fairfax Media p.153; Getty Images / Torsten Blackwood p.174; Gilbert & George pp.108–9; James Gleeson © Courtesy of the artist p.67; Julie Gough p.156; The Estate of Roy Grounds p.101; Keith Haring Estate p. 130; Geoff Hawkshaw p.96; © Bill Henson courtesy Roslyn Oxley9 Gallery, Sydney p.143; Michael Leunig p.38; Estate of Max Meldrum p.54; The Henry Moore Foundation p.99; © Ron Mueck, courtesy Anthony d'Offay, London p.174; © Sidney Nolan Estate. All Rights Reserved 2011 / Bridgeman Art Library p.136; Angus O'Callaghan p.110; © Deborah Paauwe/ Licensed by VISCOPY, Australia p.167; Edwin Pareroultja Licensed by Aboriginal Artists Agency p.78; John Perry p.83; © Pablo Picasso/Sussession Pablo Picasso. Licensed by VISCOPY, Australia p.137; Gerhard Richter p.142; Bridget Riley p.99; © Yinka Shonibare courtesy James Cohan Gallery New York and Shanghai p.164; The Estate of Wolfgang Sievers p.103; State Library of Victoria, Melbourne pp. 4,6,10,13,18,20,23,28,59; Ron Tandberg p.139; Wayne Taylor / Fairfax Media p.147; Eric Thake pp.67, 74, 107; Rover Thomas courtesy Warmun Art Centre p.143; Peter Tyndall p.117; University of Melbourne Archives p. 31; © Jeff Wall, 1994 p.171; Napier Waller © Courtesy of the artist's estate p.60; © Andy Warhol/ARS, New York. Licensed by VISCOPY, Australia p.133; © Estate of Fred Williams p.167; Constanze Zikos © Courtesy of the artist p.149

Published in 2011 by
the Council of Trustees of the
National Gallery of Victoria
180 St Kilda Road
Melbourne, Victoria 3004, Australia
www.ngv.vic.gov.au

National Library of Australia
Cataloguing-in-Publication entry:

Murray, Philippa.
The NGV story/ Philippa Murray.
9780724103393 (pbk.)
Includes bibliographical references.
National Gallery of Victoria—History.
Art museums—Victoria—History.
National Gallery of Victoria.

708.9945

Editor: Eugenie Baulch
Designer: Dirk Hiscock
Publications Coordinator: Megan Patty
Publications Manager: Jasmin Chua
Photography: NGV Photographic Services, unless otherwise indicated
Pre-press: Anne-Marie De Boni, Justine Frost and Philip White
Cover stock: 295gsm Carta Solida
Text stock: 150gsm Revive 50/50 and 150gsm Sovereign Silk
CTP and printing: Adams Print

10 9 8 7 6 5 4 3 2 1

Phip Murray is an independent art writer based in Melbourne. She is also a lecturer in the School of Architecture and Design, RMIT University; the Director of West Space; and a board member of *un Magazine*.

THE NATIONAL GALLERY OF VICTORIA

NGV

ngv
150
YEARS